Henry W. Beecher

American Rebellion

Report of the Speeches of the Rev. Henry Ward Beecher

Henry W. Beecher

American Rebellion
Report of the Speeches of the Rev. Henry Ward Beecher

ISBN/EAN: 9783337210939

Printed in Europe, USA, Canada, Australia, Japan

Cover: Foto ©ninafisch / pixelio.de

More available books at **www.hansebooks.com**

AMERICAN REBELLION.

REPORT OF THE SPEECHES

OF THE

REV. HENRY WARD BEECHER,

DELIVERED

AT PUBLIC MEETINGS

IN

MANCHESTER, GLASGOW, EDINBURGH, LIVERPOOL, AND LONDON;

AND AT THE

FAREWELL BREAKFASTS

IN LONDON, MANCHESTER, AND LIVERPOOL.

UNION AND EMANCIPATION SOCIETY,
51, PICCADILLY, MANCHESTER.

LONDON: SAMPSON LOW & SON.   EDINBURGH: THOMAS NELSON.
GLASGOW: THOS. MURRAY & SONS.   DUBLIN: R. D. WEBB & SON.
BELFAST: JAMES MAGILL.   LIVERPOOL: HENRY YOUNG.

1864.

NOTE.

I HAVE been asked to revise the speeches recently delivered by me in Great Britain, and to allow them to be published together.

In compliance with that request, I have partially revised the speeches delivered in the Free Trade Hall, Manchester, in the City Hall, Glasgow, and in the Free Church Assembly Hall, Edinburgh; the others not at all.

I must leave them with all the imperfections incidental to speeches delivered under circumstances, in several cases, not favourable to literary excellence or reportorial correctness.

To avoid any mistake hereafter, I specify those speeches which, in addition to the above, I permit to be published; and this I deem necessary on account of one of my morning addresses being so inaccurately reported, unintentionally I believe, as to misrepresent what I did say, and attribute to me that which I did not say.

The speech in the Philharmonic Hall, Liverpool, I leave as a curiosity. It may relieve the reading of the others, to follow the course of a speech delivered under difficulties.

The speeches delivered in Exeter Hall, and at the several Breakfast Meetings in London, Manchester, and Liverpool, must remain as they are published in the newspapers, only cautioning the reader that they are not verbatim reports.

H. W. BEECHER.

LIVERPOOL, 30TH OCT., 1863.

MANCHESTER.—OCTOBER 9, 1863.

REPORT OF PROCEEDINGS AT THE MEETING HELD
AT THE FREE TRADE HALL.

ON Friday evening, October 9th, a meeting was held in the Free Trade Hall, according to announcement, "to welcome the Rev. Henry Ward Beecher on his public appearance in this country." The hall was extremely crowded, and there were probably 6,000 persons present. It was supposed, from the paper war of placards for the previous fortnight, that the meeting might be disturbed by partisans of the Confederate cause. Arrangements had, therefore, been made for the prompt suppression of disorder; and notices to that effect were posted about the room. The chair was taken, at half-past six, by Mr. Francis Taylor. At the same time the entrance of Mr. Beecher, accompanied by Mr. Bazley, M.P., and some prominent members of the Union and Emancipation Society, was the signal for enthusiastic and repeated cheering. The following were among the gentlemen present:—Mr. Thomas Bazley, M.P.; Rev. Dr. Parker, Manchester; Rev. J. B. Paton, Sheffield; Mr. Jacob Bright; Mr. W. P. Roberts, Manchester; Mr. Councillor Williams, Salford; Rev. Richard Jones, Manchester; Rev. J. Bertram, Manchester; Mr. Samuel Bennett, Manchester; Mr. W. Heywood, Manchester; Mr. James Galloway, Manchester; Mr. Frederick Cooper, Manchester; Mr. Councillor Clegg, Manchester; Mr. Joseph Spence, Manchester; Rev. P. Prout, Haslingden; Mr. A. Ireland, Mr. Joseph Leese, Mr. Charles Bury, Mr. H. Dunckley; Rev. G. M'Gregor, Farnworth; Mr. R. Cooper, Manchester; Mr. J. R. Cooper, Manchester; Rev. J. Dunckley, Heywood; Rev. W. Duckins, Middlewich; Rev. W. Hanson, Manchester; Rev. J. Turner, Farnworth; Rev. J. M'Pherson, Manchester; Rev. R. Cliff, Bury; Rev. W. Sykes, Rev. W. H. Davidson, Rev. R. Best, Bolton; Rev. J. S. Hill, Pendleton; Rev. J. P. Taylor, Darlington; Rev. G. Robinson, Over Darwen; Rev. G. Pywell, Stockport; Mr. D. Mills, Bowdon; Mr. S. P. Robinson, Manchester; Rev. G. Waldon, Manchester; Rev. J. Morgan, Rev. W. Shuttleworth, Manchester; Rev. J. Taylor, Manchester; Rev. O. B. Beadwell, America; Rev. T. G. Lee, Salford; Professor Newth; Mr. Robert Smith, Manchester; Mr. W. Boyd, Glossop; Mr. T. Roberts, Manchester; Mr. J. B. Whitehead, Rawtenstall;

Mr. J. C. Edwards, Manchester; Mr. T. R. Whitehead, Rawtenstall; Mr. E. O. Greening, Manchester; Mr. S. Watts, jun., Manchester; Mr. J. C. Dyer, Burnage; Mr Councillor T. Warburton, Manchester; Mr. Councillor Butterworth, Mr. Councillor Hampson, Mr. T. H. Barker, Manchester; Mr. J. H. Estcourt, Manchester; and Mr. P. Sinclair, Manchester. Padre Gavazzi was in one of the reserved seats below the platform. The first row was occupied by forty of the students of the Lancashire Independent College.

One of the hon. secretaries (Mr. Greening) stated that the following letter had been addressed to his colleague, Mr. Edwards, and himself, by their president, from Scotland :—

Pitnacre, Dunkeld, October 8, 1863.

Gentlemen,—I regret that I shall not be able to be with you on Friday to join in your welcome to the Rev. Henry Ward Beecher, as I am suffering from the effects of severe influenza. I have firm faith that, purified from the plague spot of slavery, the republic will emerge in its integrity from this war with renewed life and vigour. I desire, however, most earnestly to impress upon the working men of Manchester that the struggle now going on in America is their own battle, for in the maintenance of the great republic in the West depends in a great degree the progress of popular institutions all over the world. This the enemies of freedom well know, and therefore imperial influences abroad, as well as selfish and oligarchical sympathies at home, are brought to bear in favour of the slaveholding conspirators. Mr. Beecher will be able to tell his fellow-countrymen that, whoever else be against them, the hearts of the working men of England, and I believe throughout Europe, beat in unison with those who are fighting the battle of freedom on the other side of the Atlantic.—Yours, &c., (Signed) THOS. BAYLEY POTTER.

The Hon. Secretaries of the Union and Emancipation Society.

(Prolonged applause.) Letters also had been received from Mr. W. E. Forster, M P. for Bradford—(cheers),—and Mr. Bright, M.P.—(prolonged cheering),—regretting their inability to be present. Mr. Bright said : "I am grieved to be away from home when Mr. Beecher is in the neighbourhood." (Loud cheers.)

Mr. TAYLOR having taken the chair, spoke as follows : Ladies and gentlemen.—Your committee has done me the honour to place me in the chair this evening, and by your kind forbearance I shall endeavour to discharge the duties which devolve upon me to the best of my ability. One thing I will promise you : the preliminary proceedings shall be short. We are met together to-night to welcome the Rev. Henry Ward Beecher on his first public appearance in England, and I am glad to witness so large an audience notwithstanding the efforts which have been made, both in public and private, to deter persons from being present on this occasion. A recent number of the *Saturday Review* complains that the friends of the North have restricted the discussion of the American question to the simple issue of slavery. If this were true, the simple issue of slavery is one well worthy the consideration of Englishmen. But who limited the question to the simple issue of slavery? Did not the Southern states in all their Secession ordinances declare that slavery, and slavery alone, was the question at issue? (Applause) Did not the Hon. Alex. Stephens, the vice-president of the Confederacy, boast that they were seeking to found an empire on the "corner-stone of slavery?" The fact is, the South has declared, over and over again, that slavery is the top, and bottom, and middle of the whole question. (Applause.) But we do *not* limit the discussion of the question to the simple issue of slavery, and we are here to-night to declare from this platform to the editor of the *Saturday Review*, and all who think with him, that important as that issue may be, there are others which, in our opinion, are equally important. The South had held the reins of government in its hands for a long series of years, until the election of Mr. Lincoln on the platform of the limitation of the area of slavery turned the scale. That election was the free and unrestricted voice of the people, and against it the South rebelled. It was therefore a rebellion against constitutional government—an armed resistance to a constitutional ruler; and the issues involved in the struggle are the safety of constitutional liberty everywhere—the progress of liberal institutions everywhere— and the development of Anglo-Saxon civilisation everywhere, and therefore it is that we seek to preserve the great Republic from disruption. (Applause.) But, gentlemen, we live in strange times, and in the midst of strange occurrences. During the past week a new society has sprung up amongst us called the "Southern Independence Association," and its birth has been heralded by an earthquake. (Laughter and applause.) Lord Wharncliffe is the president of this association, and he is supported by a number of highly respectable gentlemen as vice-chairmen. Now, I have not a word to say respecting these gentlemen personally, but I will tell you what a facetious friend said to me after comparing the two lists of officers which appeared in the papers the day after the formation of this new society. He said, "Well, one thing is clear, the North has all the '*heads*,' and the South has all the '*tails*.'" But these gentlemen, highly respectable though they be, are the political descendants of the party which has always been opposed to progress. (Hear, hear.) Lord Wharncliffe knows perfectly well, and those who are associated with him know perfectly well, that the issues I have referred to *are* involved in this struggle, and *therefore* they support the South in its attempt to destroy the Republic. Some of us are old enough to remember when Lord Grey's ministry was defeated on the Reform Bill, and proposed to appeal to the country, Lord Wharncliffe—the grandfather of the present lord—rose in his place in the House of Lords, and moved an address to the King, praying His Majesty not to dissolve Parliament, as it would be dangerous to the institutions of the country. This was done in order, if possible, to scotch the Reform Bill. The present Lord Wharncliffe—true to the instincts of his house—proposes to recognise the South, and is even prepared for war with the North, in order, if possible, to scotch the new Reform Bill which he sees looming in the future. (Applause.) Let the question be thus plainly put before the country, and we have no fear of the result. At any rate, having thrown down the gauntlet and appealed to public opinion, we are prepared to abide the issue. I will not detain you longer with any remarks of mine, further than to ask you in case any disturbance should be attempted to leave the management of the meeting entirely to me, but call upon the secretary (Mr. Greening) to read the address to Mr. Beecher, which has been prepared by the society.

Mr. GREENING read the following address :—

Rev. and dear Sir,—As members of the Union and Emancipation Society, we avail ourselves of this, your first public appearance in England, after a tour undertaken for the purpose of relaxation, to welcome you, not only as a citizen of a great and free country, but as one who, for a long series of years, has been a prominent and successful pioneer in the cause of human progress. Though separated from you by the broad Atlantic, we have been earnest spectators of your fearless and persistent advocacy of the personal rights of the coloured race, amidst many perils and dangers, unmoved alike by the blandishments of office, or the threats of opponents ; and also of your consistent adherence to the principles of political and religious liberty. We deeply deplore the dreadful calamity which has come upon your native country ; but, believing as we do, that its sole cause is to be found in that sum of all villanies—human slavery—we recognise in it the hand of retributive justice working out the inevitable punishment of wrong-doing, and overtaking not only the Southern slaveholder, whose hands are imbued with guilt, but our own country, from which you inherited this hideous institution, and the free States of America which have tolerated its existence. Living ourselves under a constitutional government, and having firm faith in representative institutions, we viewed with alarm the outbreak of a rebellion, which its promoters avowed to be an attempt to raise an empire on the "Corner stone of slavery," and which was essentially a rebellion against free constitutional government, and an appeal from the ballot-box to the rifle. The success of such a rebellion would place constitutional liberty in jeopardy everywhere, and we congratulate you and your countrymen on the determined stand you have made to maintain unimpaired the great Republic, which has been handed down to you by your forefathers, and thus to present to the world a noble spectacle of self-denying patriotism. We rejoice that your statesmen, whilst maintaining that the restoration of the Union is a sacred obligation, have been led, step by step, to the recognition of the rights of the negro ; thus vindicating the consistency of those who have laboured in the anti-slavery cause for a quarter of a century, in the midst of obloquy and misrepresentation, supported only by their firm faith in the eternal principles of right and justice ; and establishing for them a claim to the heartfelt gratitude of the lovers of freedom everywhere. In conclusion, we venture to hope that your visit may be the means of correcting some of the misrepresentations as to the position of this country in regard to the American struggle which have been assiduously spread by certain portions of the press, and of cementing the bonds of amity, which ought for ever to bind together in peace the two great representatives of the Anglo-Saxon race—England and America. The cordial alliance of these two powers may not be consistent with the designs of despotism, or be approved by the enemies of liberty here or elsewhere ; but, being one in race, language, religion, and love of freedom, they may thus lead the van of civilisation, and bid defiance to the shocks which jealousy or suspicion might bring upon them. In the firm hope that such a future may be in store for your country and ours, we bid you God speed in the enterprise in which you have been so long engaged and borne such a noble part.—Signed, on behalf of the Union and Emancipation Society, THOS. BAILEY POTTER, President.

Mr. BAZLEY, M.P., on rising was received with loud cheers. He said that not ten months ago the people of Manchester assembled in that spacious hall in overwhelming numbers, as on the present occasion, to express their deep sympathy with constitutional government, with the integrity of empire, and their abhorrence of slavery. (Cheers.) Since then the horrors of civil war had raged in a country that had previously to the breaking out of the present conflict been only known as extensively prosperous, as exceedingly peaceful, and among the nations of the earth pre-eminently successful. But in the pride of the South—[interruption, and cries of "Turn him out." The Chairman: Do not put anyone out, please. If our friends would only be quiet there would be no interruption, as the disorder is all caused by one man]—but in the pride of the South an attempt had been made to build up a nation on the chief corner-stone of slavery, and such an attempt had been alike offensive to the great people of the States of America and to the intelligence of the people of Europe. (Cheers.) The audacity of the South was only equalled by its unfortunate hypocrisy. (A voice: "There has been hypocrisy on both sides.") The South now complained that she could not be let alone and enjoy her assumed independence. Really after having struck the first blow, after having initiated the re bellion which had devastated the country, it was more than temperate reason could sustain to suppose that such a demand could either be maintained by the South or respected by those to whom the appeal had been made. (Cheers.) The South avowed a deep interest in the wellfare of the negro-race. It proclaimed to the world that the negro was better cared for and better taught than if left to his own management and to his native condition in Africa. He knew not that the South had an abstract right to determine what should be the state of a people or nation held in subjection. (Cheers.) If the latter were free, then we might compare facts with assumptions. The inconsistency of the South was clearly shown by its avowing that the negro had equal hope of a future state with the whites. The truths of our common faith were said to be orally taught to the negroes. But see the manifest inconsistency of such doctrine, when the common rights of civilisation and of education were denied to a people whose only doom was incessant labour. (Cheers.) The South having commenced the rebellion, must await the consequences of reclamation ; the North would contend for its territorial right, for the spread of civilisation, of just government, and of equal rights to all; and therefore the time might be coming, he hoped—and soon, too,—when the South, seeing that its attempt had been abortive, would be glad to see itself taken back into the Union. (Applause.) We ought never to forget that in the commencement of the struggle, the South proclaimed cotton to be King and endeavoured to coerce Europe; that rebellion might be respected and the nation, built upon the "corner stone of slavery," might be called into the midst of the nations of the earth. That had been happily prevented ; nothing could be more honest or honourable than the conduct of the labouring classes in the manufacturing districts of England ; their comforts had been diminished, very important interests had been interfered with, and yet in their suffering they had been patient, and they desired not to be fed with the results of the labour of the slave. (Applause.) They wished as free men to have free coadjutors in every part of the globe. On that occasion he hoped he might be excused if he referred to his published opinions, of twelve years ago. He hoped his friends and constituents would not think he was actuated by any impulse to serve the passing moment. (Applause.) Twelve years ago he said,—"There is lamentably a dark spot upon the cultivation of American cotton, which the friends of progress and of humanity would rejoice to see obliterated, not by violence—(applause) —but by rational amelioration—(applause)—and without interfering with the institutions of any country. The sires of the Anglo-Saxon race would well wish their trans-Atlantic descendants to extend the spirit and principles of freedom to the persons, homes, and labours of every colour and of every clime. (Cheers.) Can there be safety in the coercion of labour, and is the cotton planter of the United States secure from the casualties that arbitrary labours engender? (Applause.) May not an epidemic of disease or of revolt destroy the cultivation of the Southern planters of America?" (Hear.) Whilst we recollected the difficulties and troubles of America, let us not forget that our own liberties had been built up out of national trials. Who would have believed in the restoration of our monarchy, when Charles I. paid the tribute of misgovernment, and a Commonwealth ruled in this country, and Cromwell (loud cheers) rendered the name of England alike respected and feared? But the English people were essentially monarchical in their ideas and convictions; and if so great an alteration had taken place with us within a few years at that time, might not in our day the American mind be equally restored, so that before long we should see those who were now misled seeking again the fold of the United States' Government? (Cheers.) No policy, more beneficial, could be pursued by our government than that of non-intervention. Her Majesty's ministers, and Earl Russell in particular, deserved the thanks of their countrymen for having acted upon the wise principle of non-intervention. (Cheers.) His hearty desire was that this country might be just in her dealings, not only at home, but abroad,—(hear, hear)—that in our relations with America we might cling to constitutional government and the rights of freedom,—and he trusted that the alliance would be permanent and solid, with the cordial affections of both people on each side of the Atlantic. (Cheers.) His duty on the present occasion was to move that the address which had been read be presented to the distinguished gentleman who was present. (Applause.) He need not recommend it for adoption, for he felt convinced that it would be carried by overwhelming acclamation. (Loud cheers.) The rev. gentleman was received here as the messenger of peace and of good will (loud cheering and some hissing) to those Anglo-Saxon peoples that were destined, on each side of the Atlantic, to spread civilisation and justice throughout the world. (Loud applause.)

Mr. ESTCOURT seconded the motion. He said he was very anxious that the rev. gentleman should occupy as much time as possible this evening, and his observations therefore would be very few. This great assemblage was convened to welcome the Reverend Henry Ward Beecher, and to witness the presentation to him by the members of the Union and Emancipation Society, of the address which had been read by the honorary secretary, and the adoption of which had been so ably moved by our honourable member, Mr. Bazley. He (Mr. Estcourt) was reminded by the peculiar sounds in different parts of the hall, that other than friends were in attendance, and as the city had been placarded with bills containing an invitation to the citizens to attend this meeting in large numbers and give our esteemed guest a "disgusting reception," he judged that the discordant noises were the acknowledgment of these publicly invited persons that they had responded to the call, and were prepared to shew the refinement of their manners by giving to a stranger to them, but a friend to humanity, the polite but novel reception, characterised by themselves as "disgusting;" he trusted, however, that those gentlemen would see that it would be better to avoid giving that sort of reception. He had hopes that the Southern Independence Association, having now got some respectable names upon its calendar, would maintain for itself that respectability and gentlemanly behaviour that ought to mark the conducting of public affairs. (Laughter, and cheers.) As a member of the Union and Emancipation Society, he, for one, from the commencement of the rebellion till now, had sympathised with the Federal party in America for this reason, that slavery up to that time had only local sanction; but then it claimed to be national; and rather than that it should be national in America, they said "thus far shalt thou go and no further;" and because the South could get no further, the first gun at Sumter was fired. It would have been discreditable alike to the President of the Republic, as well as to the people of that Republic, to have submitted to such an audacious insult to constitutional government. (Loud applause.) And he had no hesitation in saying that those on the other side of the Atlantic who were now fighting for constitutional government, and free speech, and personal, civil, social, political, and religious freedom, ought to have the moral support, and he believed they had, of every intelligent and well informed Englishman. (Loud applause.) He could not say how long it would take to convert and enlighten the unenlightened and uninformed portion of the community, who in establishing the Southern Slaveholding Association, had publicly acknowledged one of their objects to be to obtain "correct information;" but inasmuch as the Union and Emancipation Society was established for the very purpose of supplying such information, he promised to all applicants that which they sought, and hoped they would be diligent in the acquisition of knowledge, and he sincerely trusted that before the year was out this class of the community would be sailing with them in one boat, in an intelligent English career, in favour of a liberty which was the undoubted right of every man. (Loud applause.) He had noticed a peculiarity in Manchester lately which was highly suggestive, at any rate, to intelligent men. A certain party had said that Mr. Beecher was too American, because, forsooth, he did not see things exactly as they saw them. But whereas in 1854 and 1857 that great and noble man, John Bright—(loud applause)—was blamed for being un-English with reference to the Crimean war, now the selfsame party blamed Mr. Beecher for being too American. All good and great men have been misrepresented, and thus it was such men were misunderstood. There were few men in the world who had the moral courage to act out their convictions, and to dare to express broad principles, independent of sect or party; such men possessed an individuality that took them out of the groove wherein the masses of the people are placed. If Mr. Beecher, who had been consistent and persistent in his advocacy of the rights of freedom, had viewed from his standpoint in America certain things in England that to him did not appear to bear that friendship which he thought ought to have been borne, he had a perfect right to express his opinion in a frank and independent manner. (Applause.)

The meeting was not asked to endorse every word Mr. Beecher had said, but to manifest by its welcome, that everything he had done in promoting the extension of the broad principles of liberty, had its hearty approval. (Applause.) The mode of doing this must be left to Mr. Beecher himself, and he (Mr. Estcourt) was quite sure there was not an Englishman in that crowded hall who did not sympathise and wholly approve of a manly, moral, good man, wherever he was found, whether he be an American, an Englishman, or the citizen of any other nation. (Applause.) He therefore, believing Mr. Beecher to be such a man, with the greatest pleasure seconded the adoption of the address.

The CHAIRMAN then put the resolution, and thousands of hands were thrust up high above the heads of the dense audience. After an interval of loud cheers, the chairman put the contrary, and amidst peals of derisive laughter and cheers a few hands were held up.

The CHAIRMAN: I declare the resolution carried by an overwhelming majority. (Enthusiastic cheering.) The chairman, in handing the address to Mr. Beecher, expressed a hope that the rev. gentleman would long live in health and strength to continue his career.

The Rev. Mr. BEECHER then turned to the audience to speak, but for several minutes he was prevented by deafening cheers, followed by a few hisses, which only provoked a renewed outburst of applause.

Mr. BEECHER then said: Mr. Chairman, ladies, and gentlemen, the address which you have kindly presented to me contains matters both personal and national. (Interruption.) My friends, we will have a whole night session but we will be heard. (Loud cheers.) I have not come to England to be surprised that those men whose cause cannot bear the light are afraid of free speech. (Cheers.) I have had practice of more than twenty-five years in the presence of tumultuous assemblies opposing those very men whose representatives now attempt to forestall free speech. (Hear.) Little by little, I doubt not, I shall be permitted to speak to-night. (Hear.) Little by little I have been permitted in my own country to speak, until at last the day has come there, when nothing but the utterance of speech for freedom is popular. (Cheers.) You have been pleased to speak of me as one connected with the great cause of civil and religious liberty. I covet no higher honour than to have my name joined to the list of that great company of noble Englishmen from whom we derived our doctrines of liberty. (Cheers.) For although there is some opposition to what are here called American ideas, what are these American ideas? They are simply English ideas bearing fruit in America. We bring back American sheaves, but the seed-corn we got in England—(hear); and if, on a larger sphere, and under circumstances of unobstruction, we have reared mightier harvests, every sheaf contains the grain that has made Old England rich for a hundred years. (Great cheering.) I am also not a little gratified that my first appearance to speak on secular topics in England is in this goodly town of Manchester, for I had rather have praise from men who understand the quality praised, than from those who speak at hazard and with little knowledge of the thing praised. (Hear.) And where else, more than in these great central portions of England, and in what town more than Manchester have the doctrines of human rights been battled for, and where else have there been gained for them nobler victories than here? (Cheers.) It is not indiscriminate praise therefore: you know what you talk about. You have had practice in these doctrines yourselves, and to be praised by those who are illustrious is praise indeed. (Cheers.) Allusion has been made by one of the gentlemen—a cautionary allusion, a kind of deference evidently paid to some supposed feeling—an allusion has been made to words or deeds of mine that might be supposed to be offensive to Englishmen. (Hear.) I cannot say how that may be. I am sure that I have never thought, in the midst of this mighty struggle at home, which has taxed every power and energy of our people—("Oh," and cheers)—I have never stopped to measure and to think whether my words spoken in truth and with fidelity to duty would be liked in this shape or in that shape by one or another person either in England or America. (Cheers.) I have had one simple, honest purpose, which I have pursued ever since I have been in public life, and that was with all the strength that God has given to me to maintain the cause of the poor and of the weak in my own country. (Cheers.) And if, in the height and heat of conflict, some words have been over sharp, and some positions have been taken heedlessly, are you the men to call one to account? (Hear.) What if some exquisite dancing master, standing on the edge of a battle, where Richard Cœur de Lion swung his axe, criticised him by saying that "his gestures and postures violated the proprieties of polite life." (Laughter.) When dandies fight they think how they look, but when men fight they think only of deeds. (Cheers.) But I am not here either on trial or on defence. (Hear, hear.) It matters not what I have said on other occasions and under different circumstances. Here I am before you, willing to tell you what I think about England, or any person in it. (Cheers.) Let me say one word, however, in regard to this meeting, and the peculiar gratification which I feel in it. The same agencies which have been at work to misrepresent good men in our country to you, have been at work to misrepresent to us good men here; and when I say to my friends in America that I have attended such a meeting as this, received such an address, and beheld such enthusiasm, it will be a renewed pledge of amity. (Cheers.) I have never ceased to feel that war or even unkind feelings between two such great nations, would be one of the most unpardonable and atrocious offences that the world ever beheld—(cheers)—and I have regarded everything therefore, which needlessly led to those feelings out of which war comes, as being in itself wicked. (Cheers.) The same blood is in us. (Cheers.) We are your children, or the children of your fathers and ancestors. You and we hold the same substantial doctrines. We have the same mission amongst the nations of the earth. Never were mother and daughter set forth to do so queenly a thing in the kingdom of God's glory as England and America. (Cheers.) Do you ask why we are so sensitive, and why have we hewn England with our tongue as we have? I will tell you why. There is no man who can offend you so deeply as the one you love most. (Loud cheers.) Men point to France and Napoleon,

and say he has joined England in all that she has done, and why are
the press of America silent against France, and why do they speak as
they do against England? It is because we love England. (Cheers.)
I well remember the bitterness left by the war of our Independence, and
the outbreak of the flame of 1812 from its embers. To hate England was
in my boyhood almost the first lesson of patriotism; but that result of
conflict gradually died away as peace brought forth its proper fruits:
interests, reciprocal visits, the interchanges of Christian sympathy, and
co-operative labours in a common cause lessened and finally removed
ill-feelings. In their place began to arise affection and admiration. For
when we searched our principles, they all ran back to rights wrought
out and established in England; when we looked at those institutions of
which we were most proud, we beheld that the very foundation stones,
were taken from the quarry of your history; when we looked for those
men that had illustrated our own tongue, orators, or eloquent ministers
of the gospel, they were English; we borrowed nothing from France, but
here a fashion and there a gesture or a custom: while what we had to
dignify humanity—that made life worth having—were all brought from
Old England. (Cheers.) And do you suppose that under such circumstances, with this growing love, with this growing pride, with this
gladness to feel that we were being associated in the historic glory of
England, it was with feelings of indifference that we beheld in our midst
the heir-apparent to the British throne? (Cheers.) There is not reigning
on the globe a sovereign who commands our simple, unpretentious, and
unaffected respect, as does your own beloved Queen. (Loud cheers.) I
have heard multitudes of men say that it was their joy and their
pleasure to pay respect to the Prince of Wales, even if he had not won
personal sympathy, that his mother might know that through him the
compliment was meant to her. (Loud cheers.) It was an unarranged and
unexpected spontaneous and universal outbreak of popular enthusiasm;
it began in the colonies of Canada, the fire rolled across the border, all
through New England, all through New York and Ohio, down through
Pennsylvania and the adjacent states; nor was the element quenched
until it came to Richmond. I said, and many said—the past of enmity
and prejudice is now rolled below the horizon of memory: a new era
is come, and we have set our hand and voices as a sacred seal to our
cordial affection and co-operation with England. (Cheers.) Now
(whether we interpreted it aright or not, is not the question) when
we thought England was seeking opportunity to go with the South
against us of the North, it hurt us as no other nation's conduct could
hurt us on the face of the globe; and if we spoke some words of intemperate heat, we spoke them in the mortification of disappointed affection.
(Cheers.) It has been supposed that I have aforetime urged or
threatened war with England. Never. This I have said—and this I repeat now, and here—that the cause of constitutional government and of
universal liberty as associated with it in our country was so dear, so
sacred, that rather than betray it we would give the last child we had—
that we would not relinquish this conflict though other States rose, and
entered into a league with the South—and that, if it were necessary we

would maintain this great doctrine of representative government in America against the armed world—against England and France. (Great cheering, followed by some disturbance, in reference to which the chairman rose and cautioned an individual under the gallery whom he had observed persisting in interruption.) Let me be permitted to say then, that it seems to me the darker days of embroilment between this country and America are past. (Cheers.) The speech of Earl Russell at Blairgowrie, the stopping of those armed ships, and the present attitude of the British government—(renewed cheering)—will go far towards satisfying our people. Understand me; we do not accept Earl Russell's doctrine of belligerent rights nor of neutrality, as applied to the action of the British government and nation at the beginning of our civil war, as right doctrine, but we accept it as an accomplished fact. We have drifted so far away from the time when it was profitable to discuss the questions of neutrality or belligerency, and circumstances with you and with us are so much changed by the progress of the war, that we now only ask of the government strict neutrality and of the liberty-loving people of England moral sympathy. Nothing more! We ask no help, and no hindrance. (Resumed cheers.) If you do not send us a man, we do not ask for a man. If you do not send us another pound of powder, we are able to make our own powder. (Laughter.) If you do not send us another musket nor another cannon, we have cannon that will carry five miles already. (Laughter.) We do not ask for material help. We shall be grateful for moral sympathy—(cheers)—but if you cannot give us moral sympathy we shall still endeavour to do without it. All that we say is, let France keep away, let England keep hands off; if we cannot manage this rebellion by ourselves, then let it be not managed at all. (Cheers.) We do not allow ourselves to doubt the issue of this conflict. It is only a question of time. For such inestimable principles as are at stake,—of self-government, of representative government, of any government at all, of free institutions rejected because they inevitably will bring liberty to slaves unless subverted;—of national honour, and fidelity to solemn national trusts,—for all these war is waged, and if by war these shall be secured, not one drop of blood will be wasted, not one life squandered. The suffering will have purchased a glorious future of inconceivable peace and happiness! Nor do we deem the result doubtful. The population is in the North and West. The wealth is there. The popular intelligence of the country is there. THERE only is there an educated *common people*. (Cheers.) The right doctrines of civil government are with the North. (Cheers, and a voice, "Where's the justice?") It will not be long, before one thing more will be with the North— Victory. (Loud and enthusiastic rounds of cheers.) Men on this side are impatient at the long delay; but if we can bear it, can't you? (Laughter.) You are quite at ease—("not yet"); we are not. You are not materially affected in any such degree as many parts of our own land are. (Cheers.) But if the day shall come in one year, in two years, or in ten years hence, when the old stars and stripes shall float over every state of America,—(loud cheers, and some disturbance from one or two)—oh, let him (the chief disturber) have a chance. (Laughter.)

I was saying, when interrupted by that sound from the other side of the hall, that if the day shall come, in one or five or ten years, in which the old honoured and historic banner shall float again over every state of the South; if the day shall come when that which was the accursed cause of this dire and atrocious war—slavery—shall be done away—(cheers); if the day shall have come, when through all the Gulf States there shall be liberty of speech, as there never has been—(cheers)—when there shall be liberty of the press, as there never has been; when men shall have common schools to send their children to, which they never have had in the South; if the day shall come when the land shall not be parcelled into gigantic plantations, in the hands of a few rich oligarchs—(loud cheers); but shall be divided to honest farmers, every man owning his little—(renewed cheers); in short, if the day shall come when the simple ordinances, the fruition and privileges, of civil liberty, shall prevail in every part of the United States;—it will be worth all the dreadful blood, and tears, and woe. (Loud cheers.) You are impatient; and yet God dwelleth in eternity, and has an infinite leisure to roll forward the affairs of men, not to suit the hot impatience of those who are but children of a day, and cannot wait or linger long, but according to the infinite circle on which He measures time and events! He expedites or retards as it pleases him; and yet if He heard our cries or prayers, not thrice would the months revolve but peace would come. But the strong crying and prayers of millions have not brought peace, but only thickening war. We accept the Providence; the duty is plain. (Cheers and interruption.) I repeat, the duty is plain. (Cheers.) So rooted is this English people in the faith of liberty, that it were an utterly hopeless task for any minion or sympathiser of the South to sway the popular sympathy of England, if this English people believed that this was none other than a conflict between liberty and slavery. It is just that. (Loud cheers.) The conflict may be masked by our institutions. Every people must shape public action through their laws and institutions. We often cannot reach an evil directly, but only circuitously, through the channels of law and custom. It is none the less a contest for liberty and against slavery, because it is primarily a conflict for the Union. It is by that Union, vivid with liberty, that we have to scourge oppression and establish liberty. Union, in the future, means justice, liberty, popular rights. Only slavery has hitherto prevented Union from bearing such fruit. Slavery was introduced into our country at a time, and in a manner, when neither England nor America knew well what were the results of that atrocious system. It was ignorantly received and propagated on our side; little by little it spread through all the thirteen states that then were: for slavery in the beginning was in New England, as really as now it is in the Southern States. But when the great struggle for our independence came on, the study of the doctrines of human rights had made such progress, that the whole public mind began to think it was wrong to wage war to defend our rights, while we were holding men in slavery, depriving them of theirs. It is an historical fact, that all the great and renowned men that flourished at the period of our revolution were abolitionists. Washington was; so was Benjamin Franklin; so was Thomas Jefferson; so was James Munroe; so were the principal Virginian and Southern statesmen, and the first abolition society ever founded in America was founded not in the North, but in the middle and a portion of the Southern States. Before the War of Independence, slavery was decaying in the North, from moral and physical causes combined. It ceased in New England with the adoption of our constitution. It has been unjustly said that they sold their slaves, and preached a cheap emancipation to the South. Slavery ceased in Massachusetts as follows : When suit was brought for the services of a slave, the Chief Justice laid down as law, that our Declaration of Independence, which pronounced all men "equal," and equally entitled to "life, liberty, and the pursuit of happiness," was itself a bill of emancipation, and he refused to yield up that slave for service. At a later period New York passed an Emancipation Act. It has been said that she sold her slaves. No slander was ever greater. The most careful provision was made against sale. No man travelling out of the State of New York after the passing of the Emancipation Act was permitted to have any slave with him, unless he gave bonds for his re-appearance with him. As a matter of fact the slaves were emancipated without compensation on the spot, to take effect gradually class by class. But after a trial of half a score of years the people found this gradual emancipation was intolerable. (Hear, hear.) It was like gradual amputation. They therefore, by another act of legislation, declared immediate emancipation—(hear)—and that took effect; and so slavery perished in the state of New York. (Cheers.) Substantially so it was in New Jersey, and in Pennsylvania ; never was there an example of States that emancipated slaves more purely from moral conviction of the wrong of slavery. I know that it is said that Northern capital and Northern ships were employed in the slave trade. To an extent it was so. But is there any community that lives, in which there are not miscreants who violate the public conscience ? (Cheers.) Then and since, the man who dared to use his capital and his ships in this infamous traffic hid himself, and did by agents what he was ashamed to be known to have done himself. (Hear.) Any man in the North who notoriously had part or lot in a trade so detested, would have been branded with the mark of Cain. (Cheers.) It is true that the port of New York has been employed in this infernal traffic, but it was because it was under the influence either of that "democratic" party that was then unfortunately in alliance with the Southern slavery—(hear, hear)— or because it was under the dark political control of the South itself. For when the South could appoint our marshals,—could, through the national administration, control the appointment of every Federal officer, our collectors, and every customhouse officer,—how could it but be that slavery flourished in our harbours ? For years together New York has been as much controlled by the South in matters relating to slavery, as Mobile or New Orleans ! But, even so, the slave trade was clandestine. It abhorred the light : it crept in and out of the harbour stealthily, despised and hated by the whole community. Is New York to be blamed for demoniac acts done by her limbs while yet under possession of the devil? she is now clothed, and in her right mind. (Cheers.) There was one Judas; is Christianity therefore a hoax? (Hear.) There are hissing men in this audience—are you not respectable? (Cheers and laughter.) The folly of the few is that light which God casts to irradiate the wisdom of the many. (Hear.) And let me say one word here about the constitution of America. It recognises slavery as a *fact;* but it does not recognise the *doctrine* of slavery in any way whatever; it was a fact; it lay before the ship of state, as a rock lies in the channel of the ship as, she goes into harbour; and because a ship steers round a rock, does it follow that that rock is in the ship? (Hear, hear.) And because the constitution of the United States made some circuits to steer round that great fact, does it follow that therefore slavery is recognised in the constitution as a right or a system? (No.) See how carefully that immortal document worded itself. In the slave laws the slave is declared to be— what? expressly, and by the most repetitious phraseology, he is denuded of all the attributes and characteristics of manhood, and is pronounced a "chattel." (Shame.) Now, you have just that same word in your farming language with the *h* left out, "cattle." (Hear, hear.) And the difference between cattle and chattel is the difference between quadruped and biped. (Laughter.) So far as animate property is concerned, and so far as inanimate property is concerned, it is just the difference between locomotive property and stationary property. (Hear, hear.) The laws in all the slave states stand on the radical principle that a slave is not for purposes of law any longer to be ranked in the category of human beings, but that he is a piece of property, and is to be treated to all intents and purposes as a piece of property; and the law did not blush, nor do the judges blush now-a-days who interpret that law. (Hear.) But how does the Constitution of the United States, when it speaks of these same slaves, name them? Does it call them chattels or slaves? Nay, it refused even the softer words *serf* and *servitude*. Conscientiously aware of the dignity of man, and that *service* is not opposed to the grandeur of his nature, it alludes to the slaves barely as, *persons* (not chattels) held to *service* (not servitude). (Hear and cheers.) Go to South Carolina, and ask what she calls slaves, and her laws reply "they are *things:*" but the old capitol at Washington sullenly reverberates, "No, *persons!*" (Cheers.) Go to Mississippi, the State of Jefferson Davis, and her fundamental law pronounces the slave to be only a "thing;" and again, the Federal Constitution sounds back, "Persons." Go to Louisiana and its constitution, and still that doctrine of devils is enunciated—it is "chattel," it is "thing." Looking upon those for whom Christ felt mortal anguish in Gethsemane, and stretched himself out for death on Calvary, their laws call them "things" and "chattels;" and still in tones of thunder the Constitution of the United States says "Persons." The slave states, by a definition, annihilate manhood; the Constitution, by a word, brings back the slave to the human family. (Cheers.) What was it then, when the country had advanced so far towards universal emancipation in the period of our national formation, that stopped this onward tide? Two things, commercial and political.

First, the wonderful demand for cotton throughout the world, precisely when, from the invention of the cotton gin, it became easy to turn it to service. Slaves that before had been worth from 300 to 400 dollars, began to be worth 600 dollars. That knocked away one-third of adherence to the moral law. Then they became worth 700 dollars, and half the law went—(cheers and laughter); then 800 or 900 dollars, and then there was no such thing as moral law—(cheers and laughter); then 1,000 or 1,200 dollars, and slavery became one of the beatitudes. (Cheers and laughter.) The other cause, which checked the progress of emancipation that had already so auspiciously begun, was political. It is very singular, that, in what are called the "compromises" of the constitution, the North, while attempting to prevent advantage to slavery, gave to the slave power the peculiar advantage which it has had ever since. In Congress the question early arose, How should the revenue be raised in the United States? For a long time it was proposed, and there was an endeavour, to raise it by a tax upon all the cultivated land in the different states. When this was found unjust and unequal, the next proposal was, to raise taxes on the "polls," or heads of the voters, in the different states. That was to be the basis of the calculation upon which taxes should be apportioned. Now when that question came up, it was said that it was not right to levy Federal taxes upon the Indians in Georgia, who paid no taxes to the Georgian state exchequer. So the North consented: but in making up the list of men to be taxed, and excluding the Indians, it insisted that the slaves should, nevertheless, be included. That is to say, if Georgia was to pay to the Federal exchequer in proportion to her population, it was the interest of the North that her population should be swelled by counting all her slaves. There was a long debate on this subject; and not to detain you with all the turns on this matter, the two things were coupled together at last—representation and taxation. (Hear.) Their eyes being fixed solely upon the assessment of taxes, it was agreed that five slaves should count as three men, and that it was supposed would give some advantage to the North against slavery. But in a very few years the government ceased to raise taxation by "poll," and raised it by tariff. Thenceforward, as representatives had to be chosen in the same way, and as five slaves counted as three white men, the South has had the advantage; and it has come to this point, that while in the North representatives represent men, in the South the representatives stand for men and property together. I want to drop a word as an egg for you to brood over. It will illustrate the policy of the South. The proposition to make a government undeniably National, as distinct from a mere Confederacy, came from Virginia and South Carolina. The North, having more individuality, was jealous of yielding up the rights of the separate states; but the South, with the love of power characteristic of the Normans, wanted to have a National government in distinction to a Union of several states. In result, when the national government was established, the South came into power; and for fifty years everything that the South said should be done has been done, and whatever she said should not be done, has not been done. The *institutions* of America were shaped by the North; but the *policy* of her government, for half a hundred years, by the South. All the aggression and fillibustering, all the threats to England and tauntings of Europe, all the bluster of war which our government has assumed, have been under the inspiration and under the almost monarchical sway of the Southern oligarchy. (Loud cheering.) And now, since Britain has been snubbed by the Southerners, and threatened by the Southerners, and domineered over by the Southerners—("No")—yet now Great Britain has thrown her arms of love around the Southerners and turns from the Northerners. ("No.") She don't? (Cheers.) I have only to say that she has been caught in very suspicious circumstances. (Laughter.) I so speak, perhaps as much as anything else, for this very sake—to bring out from you this expression—to let *you* know what *we* know, that all the hostility felt in my country towards Great Britain has been sudden, and from supposing that you sided with the South, and sought the breaking up of our country; and I want you to say to me, and through me to my countrymen, that those irritations against the North, and those likings for the South, that have been expressed in your papers, are not the feelings of the great mass of your nation. (Great cheering, the audience rising.) Those cheers already sound in my ears as the coming acclamations of friendly nations—those waving handkerchiefs are the white banners that symbolize peace for all countries. (Cheers.) Join with us then, Britons. (Cheers.) From you we learnt the doctrine of what a man was worth; from you we learnt to detest all oppressions; from you we learnt that it was the noblest thing a man could do TO DIE FOR A RIGHT PRINCIPLE. (Cheers.) And now, when we are set in that very course, and are giving our best blood for the most sacred principles, let the world understand that the common people of Great Britain support us. (Cheers.) You have been pleased to say in this address that I have been one of the "pioneers." No. I am only one of their eldest sons. The Birneys, the Baileys, the Rankins, the Dickeys, the Thoms of the West, the Garrisons, the Quincys, the Slades, the Welds, the Stewarts, the Smiths, the Tappans, the Goodalls of the East, and unnamed hundreds more, these were indeed pioneers. I unloosed the shoe-latchets of the pioneers, and that is all: I was but little more than a boy: I bear witness, that the hardest blows and the most cruel sufferings were endured by men, before I was thrust far enough into public life to take any particular share; and I do not consider myself entitled to rank amongst the pioneers. They were better men than I. Those noble men did resist this downward tendency of the North. They were rejected by society. To be called an abolitionist excluded a man from respectable society in those days. To be called an abolitionist blighted any man's prospects in political life. To be called an abolitionist marked a man's store,—his very customers avoided him as if he had the plague. To be called an abolitionist in those days shut up the doors of confidence from him in the church; where he was regarded as a disturber of the peace. Nevertheless, the witnesses for liberty maintained their testimony. (Loud cheers.) Little by little, they reached the conscience, —they gained the understanding. And as, when old Luther spoke, thundering in the ears of Europe the long buried treasures of the Bible, there were hosts against him, yet the elect few gathered little by little, and became no longer few; just so did many a Luther among ourselves thunder forth a long buried truth from God, the essential right of human liberty; and these were followed for half a score of years, until they began to be numerous enough to be an influential party in the state elections. (Cheers.) In 1848, I think it was, that the Buffalo platform was laid. It was the first endeavour in the Northern States to form a platform that should carry rebuke to the slave-holding ideas in the North. Before this, however, I can say that, under God, the South itself had unintentionally done more than we, to bring on this work of emancipation. (Hear, hear.) First they began to declare, after the days of Mr. Calhoun, that they accepted slavery no longer as a misfortune, but as a divine blessing. Mr. Calhoun advanced the doctrine, which is now the marrow of secession, that it was the duty of the general government not merely to protect the local States from interference but to make slavery equally *national* with liberty! In effect, the government was to see to it, that slavery received equivalents for every loss and disadvantage, which, by the laws of nature, it must sustain in a race against free institutions. (Cheers.) These monstrous doctrines began to be the development of future ambitions. The South, having the control of government, knew from the inherent weakness of their system, that, if it were confined, it was like *huge herds* feeding on small pastures, that soon gnaw the grass to the roots, and must have other pasture or die. (Cheers.) Slavery is of such a nature, that, if you do not give it continual change of feeding ground, it perishes. (Renewed cheering.) And then came one after another from the South assertions of rights never before dreamed of. From them came the Mexican war for territory; from them came the annexation of Texas and its entrance as a slave state; from them came that organised rowdyism in Congress that browbeat every Northern man who had not sworn fealty to slavery; that filled all the courts of Europe with ministers holding slave doctrines; that gave the majority of the seats on the bench to slave-owning judges; and that gave, in fact, all our chief offices of trust either to slave-owners, or to men who licked the feet of slave-owners. (Loud cheers.) Then came that ever-memorable period when, for the very purpose of humbling the North, and making it drink the bitter cup of humiliation, and showing to its people that the South was their natural lord, was passed the Fugitive Slave Bill. (Loud hisses.) There was no need of that. There was already existing just as good an instrument for so infernal a purpose as any fiend could have wished. Against that infamy my soul revolted, and these lips protested, and I defied the government to its face and told them "I will execute none of your unrighteous laws; send to me a fugitive who is fleeing from his master, and I will step between him and his pursuer." (Loud and prolonged cheers.) Not once, nor twice, have my doors been shut between oppression and the oppressed; and the church itself over which I minister has been the unknown refuge of many and many a one. (Cheers.) But whom the devil entices he cheats. Our promised "peace" with the South, which was the thirty pieces of

B

silver paid to us, turned into fire and burnt the hands that took it. For, how long was it after this promised peace that the Missouri compromise was abolished in an infamous disregard of solemn compact? (Loud cheers.) It never ought to have been made; but having been made, it ought never to have been broken by the South. (Cheers.) And with no other pretence than the robber's pretence that might makes right, they did destroy it, that they might carry slavery far North. That sufficed. That alone was needed to arouse the long reluctant patriotism of the North. (Cheers.) In hope that *time* would curb and destroy slavery, that forbearance would lead to like forbearance, the North had suffered insult, wrong, political treachery, and risk to her very institutions of liberty. By the abolition of this compromise another slave state was immediately to have been brought into the Union to balance the ever growing free territories of the North-West. Then arose a majesty of self-sacrifice that had no parallel before. Instead of merely protesting, young men and maidens, labouring men, farmers, mechanics, sped with a sacred desire to rescue free territory from the toils of slavery; and emigrated in thousands, not to better their own condition, but in order that, when this territory should vote, it should vote as a free state. (Loud cheers.) Never was a worse system of cheating practised than the perjury, intimidation, and prostituted use of the United States army, by which the South sought to force a vile institution upon the men who had voted almost unanimously for liberty and against slavery in Kansas. (Hear.) But at last the day of utter darkness had passed, and the gray twilight was on the morning horizon. At length (for the first time, I believe, in the whole conflict between the South and the North), the victory went to the North, and Kansas became a free state. (Cheers.) Now I call you to witness that, in a period of twenty-five or thirty years of constant conflicts with the South, at every single step they gained the political advantage, with the single exception of Kansas. What was the conduct of the North? Did it take any steps for secession? Did it threaten violence? So sure were the men of the North of the ultimate triumph of that which was Right, *provided free speech was left* to combat error and Wrong, that they patiently bided their time. By this time the North was cured alike of love for slavery and of indifference. By this time a new conscience had been formed in the North, and *a vast majority* of all the Northern men at length stood fair and square on anti-slavery doctrine. (Cheers.) We next had to flounder through the quicksands of four infamous years under President Buchanan, in which senators, sworn to the constitution, were plotting to destroy that constitution;—in which the members of the cabinet, who drew their pay month by month, used their official position, by breach of public trust and oath of allegiance, to steal arms, to prepare fortifications, and make ready disruption and war. The most astounding spectacle that the world ever saw was then witnessed—a great people paying men to sit in the places of power and office to betray them. (Hear, hear.) During all those four years what did we? We protested and waited, and said: "God shall give us the victory. It is God's truth that we wield, and in his own good time, He will give us the victory."

(Great cheering.) In all this time we never made an inroad on the rights of the South. (Cheers.) We never asked for retaliatory law. We never taxed their commerce, or touched it with our little finger. We envied them none of their manufactures; but sought to promote them. We did not attempt to abate, by one ounce, their material prosperity; we longed for their prosperity. (Cheers.) Slavery we always hated; the Southern men never. (Cheers.) They were wrong. And in our conflicts with them we have felt as all men in conflict feel. We were jealous, and so were they. We were in the right cause; they in the wrong. We were right, or liberty is a delusion; they were wrong, or slavery is a blessing. (Cheers.) We never envied them their territory; and it was the faith of the whole North, that, in seeking for the abatement of slavery, and its final abolition, we were conferring upon the South itself the greatest boon which one nation—or part of a nation—could confer upon another. That she was to pass through difficulties in her transition to free labour, I had no doubt; but it was not in our heart to humble her, but rather to help and sympathise with her. I defy time and history to point to a more honourable conduct than that of the free North towards the South during all these days. In 1860, Mr. Lincoln was elected. (Cheers.) I ask you to take notice of the conduct of the two sides at this point. For thirty years we had been experiencing sectional defeats at the hands of the Southerners. For thirty years and more we had seen our sons proscribed because loyal to liberty, or worse than proscribed—suborned and made subservient to slavery. (Cheers.) We had seen our judges corrupt, our ministers apostate, our merchants running headlong after gold against principle; but we maintained fealty to the law and to the constitution, and had faith in victory by legitimate means. But when, by the means pointed out in the constitution, and sanctified by the usage of three-quarters of a century, Mr. Lincoln, in fair open field, was elected President of the United States, did the South submit? (Cries of "No," and cheers.) No offence had been committed—none threatened; but the allegation was, that the election of a man known to be pledged against the *extension* of slavery was not compatible with the safety of slavery *as it existed*. On that ground they took steps for secession. Every honest mode to prevent it, all patience on the part of the North, all pusillanimity on the part of Mr. Buchanan, were anxiously employed. Before his successor came into office, he left nothing undone to make matters worse, did nothing to make things better. The North was patient then, the South impatient. Soon came the issue. The question was put to the South, and *with the exception of South Carolina, every State in the South gave a popular vote against secession;* and yet, such was the jugglery of political leaders, that before a few months had passed, they had precipitated every state into secession. That never could have occurred had there been in the Southern States an educated *common people*. But the slave power cheats the poor whites of intelligence, in order to rob the poor blacks. This is important testimony to the nature and tendency of the Union and Government of the United States; and reveals clearly, by the judgment of the very men who of all others best know, that to maintain the Union is, in the end, to destroy slavery. It justifies the North against the slanders of those who declare that she is not fighting for liberty, but only for the Union—as if that were not the very way to destroy slavery and establish freedom! The government of the United States is such that, if it be administered equitably, in the long run it will destroy slavery; and it was the foresight of this which led the South to its precipitate secession. (Cheers.) Against all these facts, it is attempted to make England believe that slavery has had nothing to do with this war. You might as well have attempted to persuade Noah that the clouds had nothing to do with the flood; it is the most monstrous absurdity ever born in the womb of folly. (Cheers.) Nothing to do with slavery? It had to do with nothing else. (Cheers.) Against this withering fact—against this damning allegation—what is their escape? They reply—the North is just as bad as the South. Now we are coming to the marrow of it. If the North is as bad as the South, why did not the South find it out before you did? If the North had been in favour of oppressing the black man, and just as much in favour of slavery as the South, how is it that the South has gone to war against the North because of their belief to the contrary? Gentlemen, I hold in my hand a published report of the speech of the amiable, intelligent, and credulous President, I believe, of the Society for Southern Independence. (Laughter.) There are some curiosities in it. (Laughter.) That you may know that Southerners are not all dead yet, I will read a paragraph:—

> The South had laboured hitherto under the imputation, and it had constantly been thrown in the teeth of all who supported that struggling nation, that they by their proceedings were tending to support the existence of slavery. This was an impression which he thought they ought carefully to endeavour to remove—(cheers and laughter)—because it was one which was injurious to their cause—(cheers)—not only among those who had the feeling of all Englishmen—of a horror of slavery—but, also, because strong religious bodies in this country made a point of it, and felt it very strongly indeed.

(Cheers.) I never like to speak behind a man's back—I like to speak to men's faces what I have to say—and I could wish that the happiness had been accorded to me to-night to have Lord Wharncliffe present, that I might address to him a few simple Christian inquiries. (Cheers.) For there can be no question that there *is* a strong impression that the South has "supported the existence of slavery." (Cheers.) Indeed, on our side of the water there are many persons that affirm it. (Laughter and cheers.) And, as his lordship thinks that it is the peculiar duty of the new association to do away with that sad error, I beg to submit to it, that in the first place it ought to do away with four million slaves in the South; for there are uncharitable men living who think that a nation that has four million slaves, has at least some "tendency" to support slavery. (Cheers.) And when his lordship's association has done that, it might be pertinent to suggest to him, instantly to revise the new "Montgomery" constitution of the South, which is changed from the old Federal constitution in only one or two points. The most essential point is, *that it for the first time introduces and legalises slavery as a national institution,* and *makes it unconstitutional ever to do it away.* Now, I submit, that this wants polishing a little. (Cheers.) Then I would also respectfully lay at his lordship's feet—more beautifully embossed, if I could, than is this address to me—the speech of Vice-President Stephens—(hear, hear)—in which he declares that all nations have been mistaken, and that to trample on the manhood of an inferior race is the only proper way to maintain the liberty of a superior; in which he lays down to Calvary a new lesson; in which he gives the lie to the Saviour himself, who came to teach us, that by as much as a man is stronger than another, he owes himself to that other. (Loud cheers.) Not alone are Christ's blood-drops our salvation, but those word-drops of sacred truth, which cleanse the heart and conscience by precious principles, these also are to us salvation; and if there be in the truths of Christ one more eminent than another, it is, "He that would be chief, let him be the servant of all." But this audacious hierarch of an anti-Christian gospel, Mr. Stephens,—in the face of God, and to the ears of all mankind, in this day of all but universal Christian sentiment, pronounces that, for a nation to have manhood, it must crush out the liberty of an inferior and weaker race. And he declares ostentatiously and boastingly that the foundation of the Southern republic is ON THAT CORNER STONE. (Loud cheers, "No, no," and renewed cheers.) When next Lord Wharncliffe speaks for the edification of this English people—(laughter)—I beg leave to submit that this speech of Mr. Stephens's requires more than a little polishing; in fact, a little scouring, cleansing, and flooding. (Applause.) And if all the other crimson evidences that the South is upholding slavery are to be washed pure by the new association, not Hercules in the Augean stable had such a task before him as they have got. (Loud cheers.) Lord Wharncliffe may bid farewell to the sweets of domestic leisure and to the interests of state. All his amusement hereafter must be derived from the endeavour to purge the Southern cause of the universal conviction that, "by their proceedings, they are tending to support the existence of slavery." (Loud cheers.) But there is another paragraph that I will read :—

> He believed that the strongest supporters of slavery were the merchants of New York and Boston. He always understood, and had never seen the statement contradicted, that the whole of the ships fitted out for the transport of slaves from Africa to Cuba were owned by Northerners.

His lordship, if he will do me the honour to read my speech, shall hear it contradicted in the most explicit terms. There have been enough Northern ships engaged, but not by any means all, nor the most. Baltimore has a pre-eminence in that matter; Charleston, and New Orleans, and Mobile, all of them. And those ships fitted out in New York were just as much despised, and loathed, and hissed by the honourable merchants of that great metropolis, as if they had put up the black flag of piracy. (Loud cheers.) Does it conduce to good feeling between two nations to utter slanders such as these? His lordship goes on to say—

> That in the Northern States the slave is placed in even a worse position than in the South. He spoke from experience, having visited the country twice.

I am most surprised, and yet gratified, to learn that Lord Wharncliffe speaks of the suffering of the slave from experience. (Laughter and cheers.) I never was aware that he had been put in that unhappy situation. Has he toiled on the sugar plantation? Has he taken the night for his friend, avoiding the day? Has he sped through cane brakes, hunted by hounds, suffering hunger, and heat, and cold by turns, until he has made his way to the far Northern States? (Cheers.) Has he had this experience? It is the word *experience* I call attention to. If his lordship says that it is his *observation*, I will accept the correction. I continue :—

In railway carriages and hotels, the negroes were treated as pariahs and outcasts and never looked upon as men and brothers, but rather as dogs. (Cheers.)

In all railway cars where Southerners travel, in all hotels where Southerners' money was the chief support, this is true. But I concede most frankly, that there has been occasion for such a statement: there has been a vicious prejudice in the North against the negro. It has been a part of my duty for the last sixteen years to protest against it. No decently dressed and well-behaved coloured man has ever had molestation or question on entering my church, and taking any seat he pleases; not because I had influence with my people to prevent it, but because God gave me a people whose own good sense and conscience led them aright without me. But from this vantage ground it has been my duty to mark out the unrighteous prejudice from which the coloured people have suffered in the North; and it is a part of the great moral revolution which is going on, that the prejudices have been in a great measure vanquished, and are now well nigh trodden down. In the city of New York there is one street railroad where coloured people cannot ride, but in the others they may, and in all the railroads of New England there is not one in which a coloured man would be questioned. I believe that the coloured man may start from the line of the British dominions in the North and traverse all New England and New York till he touches the waters of the Western lakes and never be molested or questioned, passing on as any decent white man would pass. But let me ask you how came there to be these prejudices? They did not exist before the War of Independence. How did they grow up? As one of the accursed offshoots of slavery. Where you make a race contemptible by oppression, all that belong to that race will participate in the odium, whether they be free or slave. The South itself, by maintaining the oppressive institution, is the guilty cause of whatever insult the free African has had to endure in the North. How next did that prejudice grow strong? It was on account of the multitude of Irishmen who came to the States. (Cheers and interruption.) I declare my admiration for the Irish people, who have illustrated the page of history in every department of society. It is part of the fruit of ignorance, and, as they allege, of the oppression which they have suffered—that it has made them oppressors. I bear witness that there is no class of people in America, who are so bitter against the coloured people, and so eager for slavery, as the ignorant, the poor, uninstructed Irishmen. ("Oh," and "hear," and "Three cheers for old Ireland.") But although there have been wrongs done to them in the North, the condition of the free coloured people in the North is unspeakably better than in the South. They own their wives and children. (Hear, hear.) They have the right to select their place and their kind of labour; their rights of property are protected just as much as ours are. The right of education is accorded to them. There is in the city of New York more than ten million dollars of property owned by free coloured people. (Hear.) They have their own schools; they have their own churches; their own orators, and there is no more gifted man, and no man whose superb eloquence more deserves to be listened to than Frederick Douglass. (Loud cheers.) Further : after the breaking out of this war, the good conduct of the slaves at the South and of the free coloured people at the North, has increased the kind feelings of the whites towards them; and since they have begun to fight for their rights of manhood, a popular enthusiasm for them is arising. (Loud cheers.) I will venture to say, that there is no place on the earth where millions of coloured people stand in a position so auspicious for the future, as the free coloured men of the North and the freed slaves of the South. (Cheers.) I meant to have said a good deal more to you than I have, or than I shall have time to say. ("Go on.") I have endeavoured to place before you some of the facts which show that slavery was the real cause of this war, and that if it had to be legally decided whether North or South were guilty in this matter, there could be no question before any honourable tribunal, any jury, any deliberative body, that the South, from beginning to end, for the sake of slavery, has been aggressive, and the North patient. Since the war broke out, the North has been more and more coming upon the high ground of moral principle, until at length the government has decreed emancipation. It has been said very often in my hearing, and I have read it oftener since I have been in England—the last reading I had of it was from the pen of Lord Brougham—that the North is fighting for the Union, and not for the emancipation of the African. Why are we fighting for the Union, but because we believe that the Union and its government, *administered now by Northern men,* will work out the emancipation of every living being on the continent of America. (Loud cheering.) If it be meant that the North went into this war with the immediate object of the emancipation of the slaves, I answer that it never professed to do it; but it went into war for the Union, with the distinct and expressed conviction *on both sides,* that, if the Union were maintained, slavery could not live long. (Cheers.) Do you suppose that it is wise to separate the interest of the slave from the interest of the other people on the continent, and to inaugurate a policy which takes in him alone ? He must stand or fall with all of us—(hear, hear),—and the only sound policy for the North is that which shall benefit the North, the South, the blacks and the whites. (Cheers.) We hold that the maintenance of the Union as expounded in its fundamental principles by the declaration of independence and the constitution, is the very best way to secure to the African ultimately his rights and his best estate. The North was like a ship carrying passengers, tempest tossed, and while the sailors were labouring, and the captain and officers directing, some grumblers came up from amongst the passengers and said, "You are all the time working to *save the ship,* but you don't care to save the passengers." I should like to know how you would save the passengers so well as by taking care of the ship.

[At this point the Chairman read to the meeting a telegram relative to the seizure of the rams at Liverpool. The effect was startling. The audience rose to their feet, while cheer after cheer was given.]

Allow me to say this of the coloured people, our citizens (for in New York coloured people vote, as they do also in Massachusetts and in several other Northern States;—Lord Wharncliffe notwithstanding):— it is a subject of universal remark, that no men on either side have carried themselves more gallantly, more bravely, than the coloured regiments that have been fighting for their government and their liberty. My own youngest brother is colonel of one of those regiments, and from him I learn many most interesting facts concerning them. The son of one of the most estimable and endeared of my friends in my congregation was the colonel of the regiment which scaled the rampart of Fort Wagner. Colonel Shaw fell at the head of his men—hundreds fell— and when inquest was made for his body, it was reported by the Southern men in the fort that he had been "buried with his niggers;" and on his gravestone yet it shall be written, "The man that dared to lead the poor and the oppressed out of their oppression, died with them and for them, and was buried with them." (Cheers.) On the Mississippi the conduct of the coloured regiments is so good, that, although many of the officers who command them are Southern men, and until recently had the strongest Southern prejudices, those prejudices are almost entirely broken down, and there is no difficulty whatever in finding officers, Northern or Southern, to take command of just as many of these regiments as can be raised. It is an honourable testimony to the good conduct and courage of these long-abused men, whom God is now bringing by the Red Sea of war out of the land of Egypt and into the land of promise. (Cheers.) I have said that it would give me great pleasure to answer any courteous questions that might be proposed to me. If I cannot answer them I will do the next best thing,—tell you so. (Hear.) The length to which this meeting has been protracted, and the very great conviction that I seem to have wrought by my remarks on this Pentecostal occasion in yonder Gentile crowd—(loud laughter)—admonish me that we had better open some kind of "meeting of inquiry." (Renewed laughter.) It will give me great pleasure, as a gentleman, to receive questions from any gentleman— (hear, hear),—and to give such reply as is in my power.

The rev. gentleman remained standing for a few moments, as if to give the opportunity of interrogation, but no one rising to question him, he sat down amidst great cheers. The speech lasted nearly two-and-a-quarter hours.

The CHAIRMAN then declared the business of the meeting to be at an end, and expressed his thanks for the good order which had been maintained, contrary to certain illnatured predictions. (Cheers and laughter.)

The chair having been taken by Mr. Bazley, a vote of thanks to Mr. Taylor for having presided was moved by Mr. BEECHER, seconded by Mr. S. WATTS, jun., and passed by acclamation.

Mr. TAYLOR, in returning thanks, said that it was a subject of congratulation that the enemies to their cause would now be prevented from saying, as they had falsely said before, that the meeting had broken up in confusion. (Loud cheers.)

The National Anthem was then played on the organ, and the audience dispersed, several hundreds previously pressing round Mr. Beecher, to shake hands with him.

GLASGOW.—OCTOBER 13, 1863.

REPORT OF PROCEEDINGS AT THE MEETING HELD AT THE CITY HALL.

THE public meeting announced to be held in the City Hall, to hear an address on "The American Crisis," by the Rev. Henry Ward Beecher, took place last night. The hour appointed for the opening of proceedings was seven o'clock, and long before that time the Hall was filled to excess by a crowd that waited in silence till the entrance of the speaker of the evening on the platform, accompanied by Bailie Govan and a number of clergymen and city councillors.

Bailie GOVAN, on taking the chair, read the advertisement calling the meeting; after which he said—It is not my intention, ladies and gentlemen, to detain you on this occasion by any observations of mine on the tremendous conflict on the other side of the Atlantic. With the convictions which I hold in reference to the origin and nature of the struggle, I dare not, standing here, utter one word in favour of the South. (Cheers, hisses, and renewed applause.) And I am quite willing, on this occasion, to leave the advocacy of the North to our distinguished friend who is this evening to address us. (Cheers.) I have no doubt that he has come here to-night fully prepared to plead the cause of his country with all that eloquence of which he is the master. He comes among us because of the admiration, and respect, and love that he feels for the British nation. (Hear, and applause.) He has not been an abolitionist only since South Carolina voted secession; he has not been an emancipationist only because he felt that emancipation was necessary to carry to success the objects of the Union; but ever since he entered into public life his voice has been raised and his energies have been devoted, in troublous times as in peaceful times, in times of danger to himself as well as in times of security and safety, in behalf of the down-trodden humanity of the South. (Cheers.) I have no doubt that when he rises to address you he will speak out of the fulness of the love that flows within his heart towards the British people, and he would desire to have from you such a reciprocation of that feeling as will make him feel, and make his friends on the other side of the Atlantic feel, that peace and amity between Great Britain and the American Republic must be eternal. (Applause.) I will not longer occupy your time, but beg to introduce to the meeting the Rev. Dr. Anderson.

Dr. ANDERSON, who was received with great applause, said—There are two things which would be exceedingly preposterous were I to attempt to perpetrate them. The first is, were I to attempt to engage your attention for more than five minutes, if even so many. The second is, if I were to execute the commission which friends have, I think very foolishly, entrusted to me, to introduce Mr. Ward Beecher. Introduce him to you! I intend to introduce you to him. (Laughter and applause.) You are all already, to a very great extent, familiar with him. All that you need, friends, to make you more familiar with him is that you should see his countenance and hear his living voice. (Hear, hear.)

The Rev. HENRY WARD BEECHER, who, after the applause with which he was greeted when he rose had subsided, said—Mr. Chairman, ladies, and gentlemen: No one who has been born and reared in Scotland can know the feeling with which, for the first time, such a one as I have visited this land, classic in song and in history. I have been reared in a country whose history is brief. So vast is it, that one might travel night and day for all the week, and yet scarcely touch historic ground. Its history is yet to be written; it is yet to be acted. But I come to this land, which, though small, is as full of memories as the heaven is of stars, and almost as bright. (Applause.) There is not the most insignificant piece of water that does not make my heart thrill with some story of heroism, or some remembered poem; for not only has Scotland had the good fortune to have had men that knew how to make heroic history, but she has reared those bards who have known how to sing her histories. (Applause.) And every steep and every valley, and almost every single league on which my feet have trod, have made me feel as if I was walking in a dream. I never expected to feel my eyes overflow with tears of gladness, that I had been permitted in the prime of life to look upon dear old Scotland. (Applause.) For your historians have taught us history, your poets have been the charm of our firesides, your theologians have enriched our libraries: from your philosophers—Reid, Brown, and Stewart—we have derived the elements of our philosophy, and your scientific researches have greatly stimulated the study of science in our land. I come to Scotland, almost as a pilgrim would go to Jerusalem, to see those scenes whose story had stirred my imagination from my earliest youth; and I can pay no higher compliment than to say that having seen some part of Scotland I am satisfied, and permit me to say that if, when you know me, you are a thousandth part as satisfied with me as I am with you, we shall get along very well together. (Applause.) And yet, although I am not of a yielding mood—(a laugh)—nor easily daunted, I have some embarrassment in speaking to you to-night. I know very well that there are not a few things which prevent me doing a good work among you. I differ greatly from many of you. I respect, although I will not adopt, your opinions. I can only ask as much from you for myself. I am aware that a personal prejudice has been diligently excited against me. There is also the vastness of the subject on which I am about to speak, and the dissimilar institutions of the two countries which stand in my way. There are also those perplexities which arise from conflicting statements made to you. There is also a supposed antagonism between British and American interests. Now I shall not consider any of these points to-night except the first. It is not a pleasant avenue to a speech for a man to walk through himself. (Laughter.) But since every pains is taken to misrepresent me, let me once for all deal with that matter. In my own land I have been the subject of misrepresentation and abuse so long, that when I did not receive it, I felt as though something was wanting in the atmosphere. (Laughter and applause.) I have been the object of misrepresentation at home, simply and only because I have been arrayed ever since I had a voice to speak and a heart to feel—body and soul, I have been arrayed, without regard to consequences and to my own reputation or my own ease, against that which I consider the damning sin of my country and the shame of human nature—slavery. (Great applause.) I thought I had a right, when I came to Great Britain, to expect a different reception; but I found that the insidious correspondence of men in America had poisoned the British mind, and that representations had been made which predisposed men to receive me with dislike. And, principally, the representations were that I had indulged in the most offensive language, and had threatened all sorts of things, against Great Britain. Now allow me to say that, having examined that interesting literature, so far as I have seen it published in British newspapers, I here declare that ninety-nine out of one hundred parts of those things that I am charged with saying I never said and never thought—they are falsehoods wholly, and in particular. (Great applause.) Allow me next to say that I have been accustomed freely, and at all times, at home to speak what I thought to be sober truth both of blame and of praise of Great Britain, and if you do not want to hear a man express his honest sentiments fearlessly, then I do not want to speak to you. (Applause.) If I never spared my own country—(hear, hear)—if I never spared the American church, nor the government, nor my own party, nor my personal friends, did you expect I would treat you better than I did those of my own country? (Applause.) For I have felt from the first that I hold a higher allegiance than any I owe to man—to God, and to that truth which is God's ordinance in human affairs, and for the sake of that higher truth, I have loved my country, but I have loved truth more than my country. (Applause.) I have heard the voice of my Master, saying, "If any man come unto me and hate not father, and mother, and brother, and sister, yea, and his own life also, he is not worthy of me." When therefore the cause of truth and justice is put in the scale against my own country, I would disown country for the sake of truth; and when the cause of truth and justice is put in the scale against Great Britain, I would disown her rather than betray what I understood to be the truth. (Applause.) *We are bound to establish liberty,* regulated Christian liberty, *as the law of the American Continent.* This is our destiny, this is that towards which the education of the rising generation has been more and more assiduously directed as the peculiar glory of America—to destroy slavery, and root it out of our land, and to establish in its place a discreet, intelligent, constitutional, regulated, Christian liberty. We have accepted this destiny and this task: and if in accomplishing this a part of our own people opposes us, we shall go right against our people to that destiny. (Applause.) If France undertakes to interfere, and to say "You shall not," much as we would regret to be at war with any nation on the globe, or with France in particular, who befriended us in our early struggles and trials; still the cause of liberty is dearer to us than any foreign alliance, and we shall certainly say "Stand off, this is our work, and must not be hindered." If they bring war to us, they shall have war. For no foreign nation shall meddle with impunity with our domestic struggle. If Great Britain herself, tied to us by so many interests, endeared by so many historic associations,—to whom we can never pay the debt of love we owe her for those men who wrought out, in fire and blood, those very principles of civil liberty for which we are now contending,—yet, if even Britain shall openly or secretly seek the establishment on our national territory of an Independent slaveholding empire, we will denounce her word and deed;—and, terrible and cruel as will be the necessity, we will, if we must, oppose arms to arms. If Great Britain is for slavery, I am against Great Britain. (Cheers.) If Great Britain is true to her instincts, and the interests of her illustrious history, and to her own documents, laws, and institutions; if she is yet in favour of liberty, as she has always been here and everywhere in the world, I am for Great Britain; and shall be proud of my blood and boast that I have a share in your ancestral glory. My prayer shall be that Great Britain and America, joined in religion and in liberty, may march shoulder to shoulder in the grand enterprise of bearing the blessings of religion and liberty around the globe. (Cheers.) The Slave States may be divided into two classes—the Farming States and the Plantation States. The farming States are Delaware, Maryland, Virginia, Kentucky, Missouri, and parts of Tennessee and North Carolina. The lands there are devoted to a mixed husbandry, such as of corn, or maize, wheat, oats, grass, tobacco, and the grazing of herds of cattle. The farms generally are not large. In those States slave labour is not profitable, and cannot be so. Slave-breeding is profitable, but not the labour of slaves. The plantation States are South Carolina, Georgia, Florida, Alabama, Mississippi, Louisiana, Texas, and Arkansas—eight. These States do not pursue a mixed husbandry. They raise principally cotton, sugar, rice, and tobacco, but chiefly the two great staples—cotton and sugar. They buy the principal part of their food, and almost all manufactured products. The pails they carry their water in are made in New England; their broom handles, their pins, glass, stone, iron, and tinware, and all their household furniture, are the manufacture of the North. There are some local exceptions, but what I state is substantially true of the slave-States of the extreme South. Now, consider some facts. The labour of slaves in the farming States does not pay. Why? Because mixed farming requires much more skill than slaves have. Slave labour must always be applied to the production of rude and raw material. You cannot go much farther than that. Slave labour is rarely ever skilled labour; that would require too much brain, and its development is not consistent with the condition of the slave.

Moreover, slaves are too costly. In the farming States they are better off, and therefore they are more expensive; for a man is expensive just in proportion as he rises in the scale of civilisation, as I shall show you more at length in a moment. The object of slavery therefore in the Northern slave States is not the production of tobacco, or corn, or maize, or wheat, or cattle, or dairy products;—the whole profit of slavery in the Northern slave States is in breeding slaves. (Hear, hear, and sensation.) Virginia has raised as much as $24,000,000 a year for slaves sold South. (Hear, hear.) I will read you the testimony of a gentleman from the slave States. The editor of the *Virginia Times*, in 1836, made a calculation that 120,000 slaves went out of the State during the year, that 80,000 of them went with their owners who removed, leaving 40,000 who were sold, at an average price of $600, amounting to $24,000,000. You can not understand anything about slavery until you are admitted into the secrets of raising slaves as colts and calves are raised for market, and begin to see the inside of this, the most detestable and infernal system that the sun ever shone upon. (Hear, hear, and cheers.) But you may say that this is so only in Virginia. I ask your attention to the words of Henry Clay. In 1829 he said before the Colonization Society, "It is believed that nowhere in the farming portions of the United States would slave labour be generally employed if the proprietors were not tempted to raise slaves by the high prices of the Southern market." That is Mr. Clay's testimony, a Kentuckian, a slaveholder, and certainly he ought to know. Political reasons also help to keep up slavery in these States, and some personal reasons of which I shall not speak. These Northern slave States would emancipate their slaves if it were not that the cotton States give them a market. Gentlemen, you abhor the African slave trade. Let me tell you that the domestic slave trade of America is unspeakably worse. Bred amidst churches, refinements, and comparative civilization, they are capable of a thousand pangs more of suffering at ruthless separations than if they were yet but savages. I call your attention to a few propositions then, in reference to slavery as it exists in the extreme Southern States. And first, the system of slavery requires ignorance in the slave, and not alone intellectual but moral and social ignorance. Anybody who is a slaveholder will find that there are reasons which will compel him to keep slaves in ignorance, if he is going to keep them at all. Not because intelligence is more difficult to govern; for with an intelligent people government is easier. The more you develop a man's intellect, the more you make him capable of self-government; and the more you keep him in ignorance, the more is he the subject of arbitrary government. Virtue and intelligence compel leniency of government; but ignorance and vice compel tyranny in government. (Hear, hear.) These things follow a natural law. The slave would not be less easily governed, if he were educated. If the slaveholder taught him to read and write, if he made him to know what he ought to know as one of God's dear children, the South would not be so much endangered by insurrection as she is now. There is nothing so terrible as explosive ignorance. Men without an idea, striking blindly and passionately, are the men to be feared. Even if the slaves were educated, they would be better slaves. What is the reason then that slaves must be kept in ignorance? The real reason is one of *expense.* In order to make slave labour profitable, you must reduce the cost of the slave; for the difference between the profit and the loss turns upon the halfpenny per pound. If the price of slaves goes up, and cotton goes down a shade in price, in ordinary times the planters lose. The rule is therefore, to reduce the cost of the man; and the slave to be profitable must be simply a working creature. What does a man cost that is a slave? Just a little meal and a little pork, a small measure of the coarsest cloth and leather, that is all he costs. Because that is all he needs — the lowest fare and the scantiest clothing. He is a man with two hands and two feet, and a belly. That is all there is of a profitable slave. But every new development within him which religion shall make—the sense of fatherhood, the wish for a home, the desire to rear his children well, the wish to honour and comfort his wife, every taste, every sentiment, every aspiration, will demand some external thing to satisfy it. His being augments. He demands more time. He strives to organize that little kingdom in which every human being has a right to be king, in which love is crowned,—the family! It is this that makes an educated slave too expensive for profit. Profitable slaveholding requires only so much intelligence as will work well, and only so much religion as will make men patient under suffering and abuse. More than that—more conscience, more ambition, more divine ideas of human nature, of men's dignity, of household virtue, of Christian refinement, only make the slave too costly in his tastes. Not only does the degradation of the slave pass over to his work, but it affects all labour, even when performed by free white men. Throughout the South there is the most marked public disesteem of honest homely industry. It is true that in the mountainous portions of the South-west, North Carolina, Northern Georgian, Eastern Tennessee, and Western Virginia, where slaves are few, and where a hardy people for the most part perform their own agricultural labours, there is *less* discredit attached to homely toil than in the rich alluvial districts where sugar and cotton culture demand exclusive slave labour. But even in the most favoured portions of the South, manual labour is but barely redeemed from the taint of being a slave's business, and nowhere is it honoured as it is in the great and free North. Whereas, in the richer and more influential portions of the South, labour is so degraded that men are ashamed of it. It is a badge of dishonour. The poor and shiftless whites, unable to own slaves, unwilling to work themselves, live in a precarious and wretched manner, but a little removed from barbarism, relying upon the chase for much of their subsistence, and affording a melancholy spectacle of the condition into which the reflex influence of slavery throws the neighbouring poor whites. Having turned their own industry over to slaves, and established the province and duties of a gentleman to consist in indolence and politics, it is not strange that they hold the people of the North in great contempt. The North is a vast hive of universal industry. Idleness there is as disreputable as is labour in the South. The child's earliest lesson is faithful industry. The boy works, the man works. Everywhere through all the North men earn their own living by their own industry and ingenuity. They scorn to be dependent. They revolt at the dishonour of living upon the unrequited labour of others. Honest labour is that highway along which the whole body of the Northern people travel towards wealth and usefulness. From Northern looms the South is clothed. From their anvils come all Southern implements of labour. From their lathes all modern ware. From their lasts Southern shoes. The North is growing rich by its own industry. The small class of slaveholders in the South have precarious wealth, but at the expense of the vast body of poor whites, who live from hand to mouth all their days. No wonder then, that Southerners have been wont to deride the free workmen of the North. Governor Hammond only gave expression to the universal contempt of Southern slaveholders for *work* and workmen, when he called the Northern labourer the "*mudsill of society*," and stigmatized the artizan, as the "greasy mechanic." The North and the South alike live by work; the North by their own work, the South by that of their slaves! Which is the more honourable? I have a right to demand of the workmen of Glasgow that they should refuse their sympathy to the South, and should give their hearty sympathy to those who are, like themselves, seeking to make work honourable, and to give to the workman his true place in society. Disguise it as they will, distract your attention from it as they may, it cannot be concealed, that the American question is the *working man's question*, all over the world! The slave master's doctrine is *that capital should own labour*—that the employers should own the employed. This is Southern doctrine and Southern practice. Northern doctrine and Northern practice is that the labourer should be free, intelligent, clothed with full citizen's rights, with a share of the political duties and honours. The North has from the beginning crowned labour with honour. No where else on earth is it so honourable. The free States of the North and West, in America, are the paradise of labourers. One of the predisposing causes of the present conflict, was the extraordinary contrast of the riches of the North and the unthriftiness of the South, resulting from their respective doctrines of labour and the labourer! It would seem as if Providence had demonstrated the wastefulness and mischiefs of every kind of despotism in church and in state, save one—despotism of work. For a grand and final contrast between the sin and guilt of labour-oppression, and the peace and glory of free-labour, he set apart the Western continent. That the trial might be above all suspicion, to the right he gave the meagre soil, the austere climate, short summers, long and rigorous winters. To the wrong he gave fair skies, abundant soils, valleys of the tropics teeming with almost spontaneous abundance. The Christian doctrine of work has made New England a garden, while Virginia is a wilderness. The free North is abundantly rich, the South bankrupt! Every element of prosperous society abounds in the North, and is lacking in the South. There is more real wealth in the simple little State of Massachusetts than in any ten Southern States. In the free States everything flourishes, in the slave States everything languishes. I point to the North and say, behold the testimony of Providence for free labour! I point to the South, and say, behold the legitimate results of slave labour! Oppression is as accursed in the field as it is upon the throne. It is as odious before God, under the slavedriver's hat, as under the prince's crown, or the priest's mitre. All the world over, slavery is detestable, and bears the curse of God everywhere! The South has complained bitterly of this indisputable superiority of the North in the elements of national wealth and general prosperity. It has been charged to class-legislation, to Yankee shrewdness at the expense of honesty, and to downright advantage taken by Northern commerce. The facts, are, however, that the legislation of the country has been controlled for fifty years by Southern influence. No class-legislation was possible except in her own favour. The North, so far from cheating the South, has itself been obliged largely to make up the wastes and squanderings of the improvident slave system. Southern bankruptcies have every ten years carried home to Northern creditors the penalty of complicity with slave labour. Besides this, the South has contributed less, and received more from the Federal Government, than the North. The peculiar nature of society under such industry and institutions made the functions of Government oppressive and expensive. Yet, with every partiality and favour of Government, and with the North for fifty years almost submissive to her will in public matters, the statesmen of the South beheld with dismay the mighty growth of the free States and the relative weakness of the slave States. To maintain equipollence, new territory must be acquired, and new States brought into the Union, that the fatal weakness resulting from slavery in the older States, might be compensated by the extent of the South, and by the number of votes in the Congress,—controlling legislation in their interest. Out of this radical conflict of free labour and slave labour, have sprung naturally the elements of this war. In the race, slavery has crippled itself. It therefore seeks to escape from institutions and influences that expose its folly, that reveal its degradation and poverty, and would inevitably, in due time, revolutionize and destroy it. Not only is it true that the working men of England have an interest in this conflict, as a political struggle; but, as a conflict between the two grand systems—Slave labour and Free labour—it addresses itself to every labouring man on the globe. If the North succeed and slavery be crushed, labouring men, all the world over, will be benefited. The American conflict is but one form of that contest which is going on in all nations. Men that live by the sweat of their brow are aspiring to more education, to a larger sphere of influence, to some share of political power, to some joint fruition of that wealth which they help to create. They ought to know their fellows. They ought to recognize in every land who are striving for them and who against. It is monstrous that British workmen should help Southern slaveholders to degrade labour. Are there not enough already to crush the poor and helpless labourers of the world, without English working men, too, joining the rebel gang of oppressors? Every word for the South is a blow against the slave!

C

Every stroke aimed at the slave rebounds upon the European labourer! Join the slaveowner in making labour compulsory and dishonourable, and the slaveowner will unite with European extortioners in grinding the poor operatives here! The North is truly fighting the battle of the labourer everywhere. The North honours work. When the labourer is educated, all doors are open to him, and it depends on his own powers and disposition whether he shall be a drudge or an honoured citizen. It will be a burning shame for British workmen to side against their own friends! Consider now, for a moment, what were our respective divisions when this war broke out which has fused all parties into one in the North and one in the South. We are not to expect parties formed methodically to suit any philosophical or ethical theory. Such arrangements never happen in a land so large, so diverse in population, so free in the operation of opinions, and swayed by so many motives. Slavery had long exerted a grave influence upon the condition of the country before it was recognized in politics. Indeed, the first sign of the entrance of this vexed question into active politics was seen in the anxious endeavours of all parties to exclude it. The early anti-slavery men found themselves shut out from all parties, from ecclesiastical bodies, from every organization of society. They gathered adherents outside of all moral and civil institutions. But nothing could long keep out a topic which was forced upon the North by the unwise and arrogant legislation of the South. At length the subject took complete possession of politics, and divided the whole public into parties. But I shall consider the division of *opinions*, rather than of parties, which are seldom homogeneous. There were three degrees of opinion. At the close of the war for independence the term *abolitionist* was applied to such men as Franklin, John Jay, &c., who united in societies for promoting the abolition of slavery. These societies died out, and the name was almost forgotten, till revived about 1830, and applied, then and since, exclusively to Mr. Garrison and his school. They regarded slavery as so established, and the institutions of the country as so controlled by its advocates, that all remedy was hopeless, and they urged an *utter separation from the South*, as the only way of freeing the North from the guilt and contamination of slavery. There was no *political* difference between Mr. Garrison's disunion and Mr. Davis's secession. But the *moral* difference was world wide. The disunionists of the Garrison and Wendell Phillips school were seeking to promote liberty and to weaken slavery. Mr. Davis and his followers are seeking to strengthen slavery and to restrict liberty. But the abolitionists, though a heroic band, sought a right thing by a wrong method. Their party was never large, but their direct and indirect influence was great. Another section was represented by the great body of moral and intelligent men in the North who held that slavery should be *limited* to its present territory: that, since it existed by *State laws* and not by national laws, it should be restricted to those States in which it was found de facto: that congress should leave it where it was, but defend the territories from its incursions; that the government should be put into the hands of men who loved liberty more than slavery; that our courts should be purged of judges appointed to serve Southern interests. It was believed, and I was of this faith myself, that, were slavery rigorously confined to existing bounds, and the institutions of the nation arrayed on the side of liberty, gradually natural laws, with commercial changes, and the exigencies of political economy, would work out a system of emancipation. These views were held by the North both in a latent and an active form, by men who were widely different in politics, and who sought different and even conflicting methods of enforcing them. The third section was represented by that class of men which exists in every land without moral convictions in public affairs, who regard politics as a game, and who look only at *interest* as the end of parties. To such were added vast numbers of ignorant emigrants. With a partial and honourable exception in favour of the Germans, it must be said *that the great body of emigrants flying from foreign hardships and oppression* joined the pro-slavery party in America, and arranged themselves against the negro. This has been the peculiar and chief difficulty of the North in political efforts. We owe to Europe, but chiefly to Great Britain, those hindrances that so long paralyzed political effort, and divided the action of the North. It will be seen by this brief view, that the Northern movement proposed no violence nor any precipitate action. We relied on the inherent superiority of free-labour to develope our embryo territories, and hoped that, with time and patience, moral influences, following the operation of great natural laws, would waste away slavery, without violence or revolution, and with benefit to both the bond and the free. The keynote of Northern policy was NO MORE SLAVE STATES—NO MORE LEGISLATION IN FAVOUR OF SLAVERY. Let it die by its own inherent diseases !— Now let me speak of the South. What have been the divisions of the South ? There have been two tendencies there ; a more moderate and a more extreme party. The former attempted to maintain the South on the basis of slavery; by the multiplication of new States; by the acquisition of territories, and so directing the Government as to fortify slavery till it should stretch across the continent from ocean to ocean. That has been the object of the earlier and main party of the South. The second was the South Carolina party, who date from Mr. Calhoun's time. This party meant to break off from the Union as soon as they were strong enough. Just as long as anything was to be gained by staying, so long they meant to stay ; but as soon as nothing more was to be gained, they meant to go. They included the former plan, but more also. They designed, first, separate national existence as the ultimate aim of the Southern States ; and secondly, the inclusion of the tropics of America in a gigantic cotton-growing slave empire. They meant, ere long, to seize Mexico and central America ; to include the vast central American tropical oceanica, and spread slavery over all. They proudly said—*Cotton is king !* and if we have cotton and the means of raising it, we can control the destiny of the globe ! They meant also to re-open the African slave trade for the purpose of cheapening negroes, who are the most expensive item of labour. In South Carolina this scheme was unblushingly and openly advocated ; and if I had lived in the South and been a slaveholder, I should have been of that party. What! an advocate of the African slave trade? Yes, I should! The day that I make up my mind to keep slaves, I shall have to keep them ignorant; and if I live in the cotton States, I am not likely to pay Virginia, under a home-tariff, a thousand dollars for a slave that I can import from Africa for three hundred dollars. The fact is, the law that makes the foreign slave trade piracy is nothing but a high tariff in favour of the slave breeding States: and the States that do not breed slaves, say,—That tariff must be taken off; if Africa can produce the material cheaper than Virginia, we must have the advantage of it. I declare too, that the inter-State slave trade of America is in many most important respects more cruel than the roughest part of the African slave trade. To bring up men under the gospel; to bring up women with some of the tender susceptibilities of womanhood, and more than half their blood white blood,—to rear them in your household, and then,—if bankruptcy threatens, or exigencies press, to call' out your valuable slaves from a Virginian plantation and sell them to the slave master, to manacle them,—to drive in gangs men reared under the sound of the bell of the Christian Church,—who have acquired something of refinement in their masters' families—to carry them down South in droves of fifties and hundreds, as is done on every great street and road of the middle States,—is I say, more infernal, more wicked, by as much as these northern-bred slaves are more tender, susceptible and intelligent, than the poor half-imbruted African. If God sends one bolt at the ship that brings slaves from Africa, double-shotted thunders are aimed at every gang master that drives them from the Northern slave States to the Southern. (Applause.) It was perfectly natural that South Carolina should include in its project of aggrandizement the opening of the African slave trade ; and every freeman in Great Britain that goes for the South, really goes for the opening of that trade. (Cheers and hisses.) When you put a drunken engineer to drive a train, you may not *mean* to come to any harm, but when you are in that train you cannot help yourselves. It is just the same here. *You* do not mean the slave trade, but *they do ;* and all that they ask of you is—"to be blind." (Laughter and applause.) This Southern plan thus includes the opening of the slave trade for the sake of cheapening negroes, and the secession threw the control of the whole South into the hands of these extremists. You may not be aware that when Secession was proposed, after the election of Lincoln every State by its popular vote, went against secession, except South Carolina. Well, that might have seemed a fatal obstacle. Not at all. The leaders of this extreme party immediately began to work upon the legislatures either to call conventions or to act as conventions, and pass secession acts. The States were carried out of the Union into secession notwithstanding the vote of the people not many months before. How was it that Tennessee was carried out?—how was even such a state as Georgia carried out?—how was Alabama carried out against such a man as Mr. Stephens, the vice-president of the Confederacy—a man who, though on the wrong side, is the best man, I think, in the whole

Southern States of America—(applause)—and—if it were not for the accursed surrounding of slavery—is as true and far sighted a statesman as we have ever had in America. How did they carry out 'these States by their legislatures? They said to the members of the legislatures throughout the South, "the North never stood in a fair stand-up fight. It was always anxious about its mills and stores and its money. They will rouse up at first, but whenever it comes to the last, and we threaten fire and bloodshed, they always knuckle under." Well, I am ashamed to say there was too much truth in this. Commercial interest on one side, and a desire for peace and love of the Union on the other, had always led the North to yield to Southern threats. But that was ended. A new spirit had arisen. The North now for the first time thoroughly believed that the South aimed to nationalize slavery. The North never had believed that it was worth while to agitate the controversy, until the outrageous conduct of the South in Kansas brought the North to its consciousness. Since then it has been true as steel. Well, the South said, "the North will not willingly see us go out of the Union—that is a mere ruse on our part : we will go out by 'secession,' and say, we will come back if you give us new guarantees. Even if they will not do that, there will be no war; for the North will not fight us." With these arguments the legislatures were won, and the secession was accomplished in the greater number of the slave States. The upper classes thought, that secession was only a political trick, through which they were to go back into a reconstructed Union, with guarantees inserted for the nationalization of slavery and for its extension all over the continent. But at this time there happened to be more or less of conference between friends in the North and friends in the South, and it seemed as if the consummation would be prevented. Virginia had refused persistently to pass the secession ordinance. The convention that was by the popular vote elected in Virginia was known to be immensely in favour of remaining in the Union. It was necessary that something should be done to prevent Virginia standing out with the North, and it was done. The gang of slave drivers in Richmond intimidated the members of the convention. When the history shall be written, the fact will appear, that numbers of convention-men were made afraid for their lives. They were told almost in so many words, "You shall never leave Richmond alive, if you fail to vote secession." It was voted, but secretly, and it was not known in Virginia for weeks. I was myself a fellow passenger with one man, who was making a circuitous journey throughout the North to get home alive to his farm in the Western part of Virginia, because he had been true, and refused to vote for secession, even secretly. It was to commit the South, to fire the wavering, and arouse the sectional blood, that orders were sent by telegraph from Washington by the Southern conspirators who were lurking there—"Open your batteries on Fort Sumter." And they fired at that glorious old flag, which had carried the honour of the American name round the globe, in order that they might take Virginia out of the Union, and compel the North to submit either to a degrading compromise, or to

the independence of the South. That is the history of the matter.
(Applause.) Now let me speak of the North. Oh how I wish you could
have seen the North! I have stood on the summit of the noblest mountains in Switzerland : I have seen whatever that country had to show me
of mountain peak, of more than royal mountains of clouds of glaciers :
I have seen the beauties of Northern Italy : I have seen the glories of
the ocean : I have seen whatever Nature has to show of her sublimity
on land and on sea : but the grandeur of the uprising of the Northern
people, when the thunder of the first cannon rolled through their
valleys and over their hills, was something beyond all these ; nor do I
expect, till the judgment day fills me with wondering awe, to see such
a sight again. There had been a secret agreement with a portion of the
democratic leaders in the North, that they were to side with the
South, and paralyze Northern resistance. But with stern unanimity the
public mutterings denounced complicity with the South as a treason
worthy of death. The astounding outburst of patriotic feeling terrified even such men as the two Woods, and they made haste to join
the rolling tide. No rainbow was ever so decked with colour as
was Broadway with flags. Bunting went up in the market. (Laughter.)
High and low, rich and poor, democratic and republican, men that
had been for the South, and men that had been for the North, found
themselves in company. It is said that misery makes one acquainted
with strange bedfellows, but patriotism makes even stranger transformations. I found men that were ready to mob me yesterday for my
anti-slavery agitations, were ready to denounce me to-day because I
was not anti-slavery enough. Propelled by this universal feeling, the
Government of the United States began—to do what ? To defend
the laws and the constitution. If they had failed to do this, if when the
Government and the country was threatened by this rebellion, they
had faltered, not Judas, not the meanest traitor that has ever been
execrated through all time, would have surpassed them in ignominy.
(Cheers.) I have been asked, would it not have been better to
negotiate ? What! with cannon balls firing right into your midst!
(Hear, hear.) The other side was using powder and balls, and you
propose to us wad and paper! The day for talking was gone by for
ever. They had talked too much already. It was then the day for
action. (Cheers.) Men in England, Scotland, or Ireland, ask me, why
did you not consent to let them go, since the whole Southern economy
is so opposed to Northern ? Only on the single matter of *slavery* is there
any antagonism. If that were to be an increasing and perpetual evil,
many men would assent to separation who now do not. But we believe
it to be a removable evil. The nature of our institutions is against it.
The laws of nature are against it. The conscience of the nation, the
public sentiment of Christendom, are against it. The real and general
interest of the South itself is opposed to it. Free labour in place of slave
labour would be the greatest boon that could be conferred upon the
Southern States. Men that profit by slavery are but a handful ; all the
rest suffer from its deadly, wasting nature. If then a limit can be placed
to its growth, and it can be subjected to the unobstructed influences of

natural, moral, and civil laws, it will quickly begin to decay and give place to a healthier system. Already the *tendency* had in many sections been established; and, as it was this fervent hope of a peaceful ending of slavery that disinclined thousands of conscientious men in the North to meddle with it, so now it is the same wish to see slavery ended that leads them to refuse their consent to a separation, which not only dismembers the nation, but gives a new lease of life to slavery, and opens for it a dark empire full of sorrow and tears and blood within, of quarrels and wars without, an empire of belligerent mischiefs to all. When I am asked, Why not let the South go? I return for an answer a question. Be pleased to tell me what part of the British Islands you are willing to let go from under the crown when its inhabitants secede and set up for independence? If you say ten or fifteen States, with twelve millions of inhabitants, are not to be compared to the county of Kent. I say, they *are* to be compared to Kent. For that county bears a greater proportion to the square miles of the British Islands than the rebellious States do to the whole territory of the Union. But the right or wrong of such rebellions are not questions in arithmetic. Numbers do not change civil obligations. Secession was an appeal from the ballot to the bullet. It was not a noble minority defying usurpation or despotism in the assertion of fundamental rights. It was a despotism, which, when put to shame by the will of a free people, expressed through the ballot-box, rushed into rebellion as the means of perpetuating slavery. Northern sentiment, and great natural laws, were preparing the way for the emancipation of four million of slaves: thereupon eight million whites broke allegiance and withdrew from a free government in order to maintain this slave system; and that is praised, in Great Britain, as a heroic struggle for independence! *Whose* independence, the white man's or the black man's? Unreflecting men are deceived by the instances of *colonies* in the past, such as the American colonies, breaking off from the parent Government, and asserting their independence. A remote colony, an outlying and separate territory, whose autonomy is already practically established, and whose connection with the home government is not intimate, territorial, adjacent, but only political,—is not to be compared with home-territory, geographically touching the country along its whole line. This is not cutting off a foot, or a hand. It is cutting across the body right under the heart. The line of fracture proposed by the South, is not a stone's throw from the national capital. France might consent to let Algiers go, but would she let a north and south line be run touching the city of Paris, on the east, and separating all the territory east from her dominions? Great Britain might suffer the Canadas to secede from the crown; but would she suffer an east and west line to be run along the edge of London, and all the territory south of it, to pass into hostile hands? Yet this is the very case of America. Secession accomplished will leave Washington toppling on the edge of the Southern abyss, in whose lurid future loom the elements of quarrel, collision, and terrific war. In asserting the integrity of our territory under the national Government, we shut that door, through which threaten to come just such storms as have for hundreds of years past deluged Europe with blood. Better a single gigantic struggle now than a hundred years of intermittent wars, ending in treacherous truces, and breaking out again at every decade in fierce conflict. I shall now refer to the astonishing pretence that this war has nothing to do with slavery! Never has the South asserted this. The interest of slavery was the very ground alleged for rebellion, and the justification put in for it. Slavery having been adopted as the central principle of Southern political economy,—her politics having for thirty years avowedly and indisputably moved around that centre,—all her quarrels with the North having been about slavery, directly or indirectly,—the issues of the last Presidential election having been issues made upon this very question of slavery,—all her principal statesmen having made interferences with slavery *wrongs* at the hands of the North—wrongs in the past or feared in the future—the very reason of rebellion,—the whole interior history of America for seventy years having been wound up on this spool,—what amazing impudence do they manifest, who, calculating on the ignorance of the British public, dare to affirm, that slavery has *nothing to do with this war!* Slavery has been the very alphabet of the war. Every letter of its history has been taken from the fount of slavery. The whole black literature of the war has been drawn from slavery! To be sure there is a division of opinion in America, whether the five States of the South, or the Abolitionists of the North, are most to blame for making slavery the occasion of the war; but not a sane man on our whole continent can be found denying that slavery is the root of it! You cannot point to a war either in ancient or modern times, that has turned so much upon fundamental principles as this one between the North and the South. There is the South with her gigantic system of slavery, and there is the North with her freedom, her free soil, free labour, free speech, and her free press; and the question is, *which of these two shall govern the American continent?* (Applause.) The North preferred to settle this question by discussion, by moral influence, by legal and constitutional means; but the South threw down the gauntlet, refused a convention, and fired on the old flag; and now her minions are whining and crying in England because the North will make war! If they did not like blows, why did they strike them? I will admit that the South is as gallant a people as ever lived; I will admit that when they shall come back to the Union, as they will—(applause, and cries of "never," and waving of handkerchiefs)—they will come back—(a voice, "never.") —Perhaps *you* will not, but—(laughter)—*they* will. ("Never;" a voice, "they are Anglo-Saxon and will never come back.") Why, if I thought that this thing was to be fought out here, I would say it over and over again till daylight broke; but not your breath denying or mine affirming will alter the issue. The Grants, the Rosecranzes, the Bankses must do that. (Hisses.) But when the South shall come back into the Union— ("never")—we shall honour them more than ever we did for their good management and courage. (Applause.) There are some things that men may pay too much to find out; but if the South, by paying the blood of thrice ten thousand of her sons, finds out that liberty is better than slavery, she will not have paid a drop too much. (Applause.) The triumph of the North in this conflict will be the triumph of free institutions, even if the Northern people and Government could be proved to have been delinquent, in every individual and in every public officer. Large as is our country, independent in opinions, and hitherto divided in sentiment about slavery,—never was any people so sincere, so religiously earnest, as is now the North. But, what if its people were insincere, its president a trickster, his emancipation proclamation a hollow pretence? What if the North were as cruel to coloured people as slavery is? All that would not change the inevitable fact, that the triumph of the North carries with it her free institutions all over the continent! *It is a war of Principles and of Institutions.* The victory will be a victory of Principles and of Institutions. This is avowed by the South as well as by us. If the North prevails, she carries over the continent her pride of honest work, her free public schools, her homestead law, which gives to every man who will occupy it a hundred and sixty acres of land; her free press, her love and habit of free speech, her untiring industry, her thrift, frugality, and morality, and above all her democratic ideas of human rights, and her Old English notions of a commonwealth, transmitted to her from Sydney, Hampden, Vane, Milton; and not least, her free churches with their vast train of charities and beneficences! These results do not depend upon the will of individuals. They go with the society, the civilization, the ineradicable nature of those Northern democratic institutions which are in conflict with Southern despotic institutions. If then any one says, I cannot give my sympathy to the Northern cause, because the people of the North are just as bad as the people of the South, I first utterly deny the fact, but next, for the sake of argument, I for a moment yield it, and reply that the institutions of the North are not so bad as the institutions of the South, even if the people are. This is a war of institutions, not simply of races. It is not necessary to look into the motives of her individual citizens. Look into the spirit and structure of Northern society. Look at her history and see in the vast Western States what is the result of the ascendancy of her ideas. Look into those great natural laws which have generated and controlled her civilization! But I return to the shameless and impudent assertion that the North is not sincere in this conflict. True, the North has her own ways of managing her own affairs. She is guided by the genius of her own institutions, and not by the whims of unsympathizing critics three thousand miles off, ignorant of her ideas, history, institutions, emergencies, and difficulties. But there has never before, since time began, been a spectacle like that in America. A million men have been on foot in the army and navy, *every man a volunteer*, the best blood of the North, her workmen, her farmers and artizans, her educated sons, lawyers, doctors, ministers of the gospel, young men of wealth and refinement, side by side with the modest sons of toil, *and every man a volunteer!* They have come, not like the Goths and Huns from a wandering life or inclement skies, to seek fairer skies and richer soil; but from homes of luxury, from cultivated farms, from busy workshops, from literary labours, from the bar, the pulpit, and the exchange, thronging around the old national flag that had symbolized *liberty* to mankind, all moved by a profound love of country, and firmly, fiercely determined that the mother land shall not be divided, especially not in order that slavery may scoop out for itself a den of refuge from Northern civilization, and an empire to domineer over all the American tropics! It is this sublime patriotism which, on every side, I hear stigmatized as the mad rush of national ambition! Has then the love of country run so low in Great Britain, that the rising of a nation to defend its territory, its government, its flag, and all the institutions over which it has waved, is a theme for cold aversion in the pulpit, and sneers in the pew? Is generosity dead in England, that she will not admire in her children those very qualities which have made the children proud of the memories of their common English ancestors? But, it is asked, since the South is so utterly discordant with the North, why not let them go, and have peace? Go? It is to STAY that they are fighting. If the white population would but go and leave to us and to the negroes a peaceful territory, we might be willing. But it is a rebellious population asking leave to organize political independence on United States territory, for the sake of threatening the peace of the whole future! Our trouble is, that they will stay if we give them leave to go. (Laughter.) No mountains divide the North from the South—they run the other way. No cross rivers divide them—they run the other way. No latitudes or climates divide the one from the other. Don't you know that God has affianced the torrid and the temperate zones in America one to the other, and that they are always running into each other's arms? The Gulf-streams of population are constantly interchanging in such a continent as ours. There is no division-line that you can make, except a merely arbitrary one. There is a line of 1,200 miles, east and west, which you propose in your division to make the fiery line of a slave empire. Do you ask us to such a bequest of peace as that? A Southern boundary of 1,200 miles long, charged with the flames and thunder of war, ready to explode on any occasion? Well, may be—may be—*you* could lie down on a powder magazine, with a thousand tons of powder in it, and a fire raging within an inch of it, but *I* could not! Will so much as one cause of quarrel be taken out of the way? Will there be anything that will stop slaves running across, and the South being irritated because we harbour them? Of course we should harbour them, as you do in Canada. No law could stop it then. (Cheers.) The only thing that ever gave to the fugitive slave-law a shadow, a vestige of power, was that for the sake of peace many in the North consented, somehow or other, to get rid of their consciences. I never did. (Applause.) I hated the law. I trod it underfoot; and I declared, to the face of the magistrates and the government, that I would break it in every way I could. And I did. (Cheers.) Now say, if it were so, when there were motives of patriotism to maintain such an obnoxious law, what would it be when the sections were rent asunder? If separated, would the contrast of free labour and slave labour be less exciting? Would our press be less bold in its proclamation of doctrines of liberty? Would not parties in secret league with

Southern parties torment the border States with new divisions, and make that peace impossible by which we are to be bribed to cease this war? Cruel as the war is, yet to stop it until slavery has its death-wound, would be even more cruel! When the surgeon has cut half the cancer out, is that man the friend of the patient, who, seeing the blood and hearing the groans, should persuade him to leave the operation half performed, and bind up the cancered limb? But, you ask, How long shall we carry violence into the South? I will ask you a question in reply. If in the purlieus of vice in old Glasgow, there should be a ward of which a confederation of burglars and thieves had taken possession, how long would you invade it with your police? (Laughter.) Would Glasgow give up to them or would they have to give up to Glasgow? We may now understand what Southern rebellion means. There seems a need of information on this point in high places. Earl Russell, in replying to Mr. Sumner's arguments upon rebellion, reproached him with inconsistency in such a horror of rebellion, America being the child of two rebellions! Were they rebellious against liberty to more despotism? or against oppression to more freedom? The English rebellion and the American rebellion were both toward greater freedom of all classes of men. This rebellion is for the sake of holding four million slaves with greater security, and less annoyance from free institutions! And now observe! The South, expressly in order to hold fast her four million slaves, makes war against what the Confederate vice-president, Mr. Stephens, in dissuading secession, pronounced to be "the best, freest, justest, most lenient Government that the sun ever shone upon." He declared that the South had no grievances; and since secession, he has glorified the new Confederation, as established with "slavery as its corner-stone." On this is written in lurid letters of infernal light, "The only foundation of our liberty is to own the labourer and to oppress the slave."—When such a body of insurgents comes to ask you to recognize its independence, do you think it just and humane—is it according to the instinct—is it according to the conscience of Great Britain to say "that nation *ought* to have an independence?" And now let me say one word more; for I am emboldened by your courtesy. You now see what it means to give your aid and succour to the South. (Cheers.) Why were you in favour of giving the Hungarians their liberty? Because they said the yoke of Austria is heavier than we can bear, and you sympathized with them because it was a step towards larger liberty. When Greece complained, why did the nations interfere? It was to give her more liberty, not less. When Italy asked help, why did France—then guided by her better genius—give her armies to beat back the Austrians and give Italy her sway in the Northern part of that beautiful peninsula? It was because Italy sighed for the sweets of liberty—that which is the right of every people on the globe. Why to-day does every man wish that the Czar may be baffled, that he may be sent back to the frozen fastnesses of the North, and that Poland may stand erect in her nationality? (Cheers.) Why? It is because Poland is under a despotism and is struggling for independence and liberty. (Applause.)

You know now what I think about sending clothes, arms, powder, ships, and all the muniments of war, or supplies of any kind, to the South. I do not stop to discuss whether it is legal or illegal. I do not discuss this as a question of technical law at all. I lift it up and put it on the ground of moral law. Between two parties, one of whom is labouring for the integrity and sanctity of labour, and the other is for robbery, the degradation of labour, and the integrity of slavery,—I say that the man that gives his aid to the Slave Power is allied to it, and is making his money by building up tyranny. (Hear, and cheers.) Every man that strikes a blow on the iron that is put into those ships for the South, is striking a blow and forging a manacle for the hand of the slave. (Applause and hisses.) Every free labourer in old Glasgow that is labouring to rear up iron ships for the South, is labouring to establish on sea and on land the doctrine that capital has a right to own "labour." (Cheers and hisses.) You are false to your own principles, to your own interests, to mankind, and to the great working classes. You have no right, for the sake of poor pitiful pelf, to go against the great toiling multitudes of Europe that are lifting up their hands for more education and more liberty. You have no right to betray that cause by allying yourselves with despots who, in holding slaves, establish the doctrine that might makes right. (Applause.) It is not in anger that I speak, it is not in pettishness or in vehemence. It is the day-of-judgment view of the matter. O! I would rather than all the crowns and thrones of earth to have the sweet, assuring smile of Jesus when he says, "Come, welcome, inasmuch as ye did it unto the least of these ye did unto me." And I would rather face the thunderbolt than stand before Him when he says on that terrible day, "inasmuch as ye did it not unto the least of these my little ones, ye did it not unto me." Ye strike God in the face when you work for slaveholders. Your money so got and quickly earned will be badly kept, and you will be poor before you can raise your children, and dying you will leave a memory that will rise against you at the day of judgment. By the solemnity of that judgment—by the sanctity of conscience—by the love you bear to humanity—by your old hereditary love of liberty;—in the name of God and of mankind, I charge you to come out from among them, to have nothing to do with the unclean and filthy lucre made by pandering to slavery. One word more. I protest, in the name of all that there is in kindred blood, against Great Britain putting herself in such a position that she cannot be in cordial and ever-during alliance with the free republic in America. (Applause.) I declare to you that it is a monstrous severance of your only natural alliance, for Great Britain to turn aside from free America and seek close relations with despotism! You owe yourselves to us, and we owe ourselves to you. You ought to live at peace with France—you ought to study their reciprocal interest and they yours. But after all, while you should be in Christian peace with France, I tell you it is unnatural for England to be in closer alliance with France than America. (Hear and disapprobation.) Nevertheless, like it or dislike it, so it is! On the other hand, it is truly unnatural for America, when she would go into a foreign alliance to seek her alliance with Russia. (Hear and applause.) Oh, why don't you hiss now? (Laughter.) I declare that America should study the prosperity of Russia, as of every nation of the globe; but when she gives her heart and hand in alliance, she owes it to Great Britain. (Applause.) So! you want to hear that. And when Great Britain turns to find one that she can lean on—can go to with all her heart—one of her own—we are her eldest-born, strongest—to *us* she must come. (Applause.) A war between England and America would be like murder in the family— unnatural—monstrous beyond words to depict. Now, then, if that be so, it is our duty to avoid all cause and occasion of offence. (Hear, hear.) But remember—remember—remember—*we are carrying out our dead.* Our sons, brothers' sons, our sisters' children—they are in this great war of liberty and of principle. We are taxing all our energies : you are at peace, and if in the flounderings of this gigantic conflict we accidentally tread on your feet, are we or you to have most patience ? When the widowed mother sits watching the shortening breath of her child, hovering between life and death,—it may be that the rent has not been paid,—it may be that her fuel has not yet been settled for ; but what would you think of that landlord or of that provision dealer that would send a warrant of distress when the funeral was going out of the door, and arrest her when she was walking to the grave with her firstborn son. Even a brute would say, "Wait—wait!" Yet it was in the hour of our mortal anguish, that when, by an unauthorised act, one of the captains of our navy seized a British ship for which our government instantly offered all reparation, that a British army was hurried to Canada. I do not undertake to teach the law that governs the question : but this I do undertake to say, and I will carry every generous man in this audience with me, when I affirm that if between America, bent double with the anguish of this bloody war, and Great Britain, who sits at peace, there is to be forbearance on either side, it is on your side. (Applause.) Here then I rest my cause to-night, asking everyone of you to unite with me in praying, that God, the arbiter of the fates of nations, would so guide the issue, that those who struggle for liberty shall be victorious ; and that God, who sways the hearts of nations, may so sway the hearts of Great Britain and America, that not to the remotest period of time shall there be dissension, but golden concord between them for their own sakes and for the good of the whole world. (Great cheering.)

Several questions having been put and answered, the Rev. Dr. George Jeffrey moved and Councillor Alexander seconded a resolution expressive of approbation of Mr. Beecher's able and uncompromising advocacy of the rights of the slave to freedom, and thanking him for the very admirable and eloquent address delivered that evening, which was carried amid great and prolonged cheering.

EDINBURGH.—OCTOBER 14, 1863.

GREAT MEETING IN THE FREE CHURCH ASSEMBLY HALL.

LAST night, one of the most crowded meetings that ever took place in this city, was held in the Free Church Assembly Hall, in order to hear the Rev. Henry Ward Beecher. Long before the hour fixed for the meeting, all the entrances to the Hall were besieged by large masses of people; and the rush for places was so great that a few minutes after the opening of the doors every available seat was taken possession of. Crowds of people still continued to pour into the Hall, and the passages became crammed. As the time arrived for the entrance of the chairman and Mr. Beecher, it became a serious question how they were to gain admission to the Hall. All doubt was set at rest on the matter by loud cries arising from the east doorway that Mr. Beecher could not obtain an entrance. A great effort was made to gain a passage for the rev. gentleman, who, after some time, managed to reach the chair, and was received with loud and prolonged cheers. Some of the gentlemen for whom seats had been reserved on the platform also gained admission— some by the passage, and others by climbing to the Moderator's gallery and walking along the ledge—but it was discovered that the chairman, Mr. Duncan M'Laren, was still amissing. After the lapse of a few minutes, however, Mr. M'Laren and four French gentlemen, including M. Garnier Pages, also got in; and the proceedings of the meeting commenced. Amongst those on the platform and that could be noticed in the dense crowd in the Hall, were Professor Rogers, Glasgow University; Revs. W. Arnot, Dr. W. L. Alexander, and G. D. Cullen; Thos. Nelson, Esq., G. H. Stott, Esq., Thos. Ireland, Esq., Dr. Grosvenor, New York; Revs. Dr. Andrew Thomson, Mr. Ogilvie, Mr. Henderson, Mr. Graham, Newhaven, Dr. Liddell, Lochmaben, and John Hutchison, Dunfermline; Hugh Brown, Esq., Stephen Bourne, Esq., David M'Laren, Esq., Professor Anderson, United States, America; Mons. Dasmarest, Mons. Garnier Pages, Henry Martin, Esq., Wm. Duncan, Esq., Jas. Gulland, Esq., Dr. H. Stephenson, D. Williamson, Esq., of Beechwood; J. Carment, S.S.C.; Professor Joseph Henry M'Chesney, M.A., American Consul at Newcastle-on-Tyne; James Robie, Esq., Rev. Dr. Johnston, Rev. Dr. Goold, Mr. Adam, Leith; Mr. George Laing, Rev. W. Pulsford, Wm. Nelson, Esq., R. S. Grieve, Esq., James Balfour, Esq., W.S.; John

M'Laren, Esq., F. W. Brown, Esq., Jas. Robertson, Esq., Wm. Duncan, Esq., W.S., John Pender, Esq., M.P., Totness ; J. H. Raper, Esq., Robt. Heywood, Esq., C. B. Darbyshire, Esq., Thos. Hare, Esq., London; John Smith, Esq., Glasgow ; D. Lewis, Esq., Councillor Mawson, Newcastle ; Jas. Webb, Esq., Dublin ; Jas. Haughton, Esq., Dublin ; Max Kyllman, Esq., Manchester ; L. L. Hyatt, Esq., J. Douglas, Esq.

The CHAIRMAN said—Ladies and Gentlemen,—May I entreat as a great favour that the utmost quietness be preserved, because I have often observed that it is those in a large meeting who, with the best intentions in the world, cry "Peace," that practically make all the noise. (Laughter.) Since I have been made Chairman, every one, I have no doubt, will be quite disposed to give up a little of his personal liberty to my dictation to-night. (Applause.) You know what the meeting is about. The advertisement tells you honestly what the object is in calling you together, and therefore there is no person here present who has any right to take offence at anything that is said within the four quarters of the hall. ("Oh, oh," applause and hisses.) The objects of the meeting are twofold—the first is to hear the Rev. Mr. Henry Ward Beecher. (Loud and prolonged applause.) That means that we are to hear him express his own opinions—(cheers)—and whether or no these opinions may be in unison with your opinions or with mine, that is a matter of which the meeting has, I apprehend, no right to complain. ("Oh, oh," and applause.) We are greatly indebted to him, I think, for responding to the call. He has been toiling night and day, I may say, in Manchester, Liverpool, Glasgow, and other towns ; and he has come here on a very short notice, and your anxiety to hear him has been such that you almost excluded him. The Rev. Dr. Candlish has sent an apology for not being here. There is less cause for regret, because he was the author of the beautiful answer that recently appeared in the newspapers from the ministers of Scotland to the address of the ministers of the United States. As the document met with such universal acceptance, the committee who had charge of making the arrangements for this meeting thought that, in place of originating any resolution of their own, they would just extract a small portion from that admirable paper, convert it into a resolution, and ask you to condemn slavery in the terms in which it is condemned in the address prepared by Dr. Candlish and other distinguished men. That will be the only resolution which will be submitted to you, except the usual formal votes which take place at all meetings. The document to which I have referred has already received the signatures of about a thousand ministers, and they are coming in by scores every day, expressing the opinion of all parts of Scotland. So much for the origin and nature of the meeting. I feel that in this question, which has been so keenly contested in this country, there may be great difference of opinion on the part of the persons who are here present. I entreat that whatever difference of opinion may exist, every one may be heard fairly and courteously—(loud applause)—and if the resolution which is proposed to the meeting be disapproved of, and any gentleman comes forward to the platform to move an amendment, I will do as much to give him a hearing for his speech, if within the scope of the resolution, as I would do to any other gentleman. (Loud cheers.) I am most anxious that everything should be done in such a straightforward manner as will commend itself to all lovers of fair play. (Cheers.) I may just state, in addition, this one fact, that from other circumstances we have been honoured in this city with the presence of many distinguished foreigners, and among these three or four gentlemen who were to have gone by the six o'clock train to-night in order to get to Paris to-morrow morning. They kindly agreed to testify their detestation of slavery by attending at this meeting, in order to say a few words in unison with what I have no doubt will be said by Mr. Beecher. These are M. Garnier Pages—(loud cheers)—M. Desmarest, and M. Henri Martyn, the distinguished historian of France. (Applause.) I have now concluded all that is proper to the business of this meeting. I will, in two sentences, make what is in some respects a personal explanation, but which applies equally to other members here present of the Social Science Association. We who hold anti-slavery opinions have been blamed by many, because, at the meetings which were held, we did not give vent to our opinions in opposition to those that were expressed by our distinguished Chairman; and a paper was prepared and handed about privately for the purpose of entering a protest against the terms in which that distinguished man spoke about the North. I did everything in my power to prevent such a paper being signed, and told the parties to show their opinion by coming here to-night. I have no doubt that, as Chairman of this meeting, I have said things, and will say things, which are distasteful to many here present; but in that respect the Chairman is a privileged person—(laughter)—because he has no liberty of replying. Mr. M'Laren concluded by introducing Mr. Beecher to the meeting.

Mr. BEECHER, on coming forward, was received with loud and prolonged cheers and some hissing. When silence had been restored, he said:—I should regret to have my associations of this, the most picturesque city of the world, disturbed as they would be, if I thought that you needed so much preparatory pleading to persuade you to hear me. (Loud applause and laughter.) I have lived in a very stormy time in my own land, where men who did not believe in my sentiments had pecuniary and political interests in disturbing meetings, but neither in East, nor West, nor in all the Middle States, have I thought it necessary to ask an audience to hear me—not even in America, the country, as we have lately been informed, of mobs! (Loud cheers and laughter.) I am not to-night a partizan seeking for proselytes. I have no other interests to serve but those which are common to all good men—the interests of truth, of justice, of liberty, and of good morals. If I differ with you in the way in which they are to be promoted, what then? Cannot you hear opinions that you do not believe? I am so firm in my convictions that I can bear to hear their opposites. (Cheers.) It is not then so much to persuade you to my views, though I should be glad to do that, as it is to give a full and frank expression of them, supposing that there are many here that would be interested in a statement of affairs, as they are now proceeding on the continent of America, if, for no other reason—at least for the philosophic interest there must be in this passing phenomena. It may be to you but a simple question of national psychology; it may be to some of you a matter of sympathy; but whether it be philosophic interest or whether it be humanitarian and moral interest, it shall be my business to speak, for the most part, of what I know, and so to speak that you shall be in no doubt whatever of my convictions. (Loud cheers and laughter.) America has been going through an extraordinary revolution unconsciously and interiorly, which began when her present national form was assumed, which is now developing itself, but which existed and was in progress just as much before as now that it is seen. The earlier problem was how to establish an absolute *independence* in States from all external control? Next (and this is the peculiar interest of the period which formed our Constitution), how, out of independent States to form a Nation, yet without destroying local sovereignty? The period of germination and growth of the Union of the separate colonies is threefold. The first colonies that planted the American shores were separate, and jealous of their separateness. Sent from the mother country with a strong hatred of oppression, they went with an intense individualism, and sought to set up, each party, its little colony, where they would be free to follow their convictions and the dictates of conscience. (Loud applause.) And nothing is more characteristic of the earlier politics of the colonists than their jealous isolation, for fear that even contact would contaminate. Two or three efforts were made within the first twenty or twenty-five years of their existence to bring them together in Union. Delegates met and parted, met again and parted. Indian wars drove them together. It became by external dangers necessary that there should be a Union of those early colonies, but there was a fear that in going into Union they would lose something of the sovereignty that belonged to them as colonial States. The first real Union that took place was that of 1643, between the colonists of what is now New England. It is a little remarkable, I may say in passing, that the fugitive slave clause of our Constitution is founded almost in so many words on the first Articles of Federation that were made in 1643 between these little New England colonies. This earliest Union was the type and model of later ones. With various alternations of fortune the country grew, but maintained a kind of irregular Union as exigencies pressed upon it. It was not until 1777, a year and a half after the Declaration of Independence, and while the colonies were at full war with the mother country, that what is called the Articles of Federation were adopted; and this was the second period of Union, when the Southern States, the Middle States, and the States of New England came together in Federation, which was declared, in the preamble, to be perpetual. (Cheers.) But about ten years after these articles were framed, they were found to be utterly inadequate for the exigencies of the times; and in 1787 the present Constitution of the United States was adopted by convention, and, at different dates thereafter, ratified by the thirteen States that first constituted the present Union. Now, during all this period of the first Union of 1643, the second Union of 1777, and the third or final

D

Union—the present one—of 1787, there is one thing to be remarked, and that is, the jealousy of State independence. The States were feeling their way towards nationality; and the rule and measure of the wisdom of every step was, how to maintain individuality with nationality. That was their problem. It never had been found out for them. They had some analogies, but these were only analogies. In that wilderness, for the first time, the problem was about to be solved— How can there be absolute independence in local government with perfect nationality ? Slavery was only incidental during all this long period; but in reading from contemporaneous documents and debates that took place in conventions both for Confederation and for final Union, it is remarkable that the difficulties which arose were difficulties of representation, difficulties of taxation, difficulties of tariff and revenue, and, so far as we can find, neither North nor South anticipated in the future any of those dangers which have overspread the continent from the black cloud of slavery. The dangers they most feared, they have suffered least from : the dangers they have suffered most from, they did not at all anticipate, or but little. But the Union was formed. The Constitution, defining the national power conferred by the States on the Federal Government, was adopted. Thenceforward, for fifty years and more, the nation developed itself in wealth and political power, until, from a condition of feeble States exhausted by war, it rose to the dignity of a first-class nation. We now turn our attention to the gradual and unconscious development within this American nation of two systems of policy, antagonistic and irreconcilable. Let us look at the South first. She was undergoing unconscious transmutation. She did not know it. She did not know what ailed her. She felt ill—(laughter)— put her hand on her heart sometimes; on her head sometimes; but had no doctor to tell her what it was, until too late; and when told she would not believe. (Laughter and cheers.) For it is a fact, that when the colonies combined in their final Union, slavery was waning not only in the Middle and Northern States but also in the South itself. When therefore they went into this Union, slavery was perishing, partly by climate in the North, and still more by the convictions of the people, and by the unproductive character of farm-slavery. Slavery is profitable only by breeding and on plantations. In the North it never was very profitable, though somewhat convenient as a household matter; for if you can get a good chambermaid and a good cook, it is worth while to keep them. (Laughter.) There was for the most part in New England only the shadow of slavery—household slavery. *The first period of the South was the wane and weakness of slavery.* Nevertheless it existed. The second period is the increase of slavery, and its apologetic defence; for, with the invention of the cotton gin, an extraordinary demand for cotton sprang up. Slave labour began to be more and more in demand, and the price of slaves rose; but still there was a number of years within my remembrance—and I am not a patriarch—in which men said, "Slavery is among us; we don't know how to get rid of it; we accept it as an evil; we wish we had a better system, but it is a misfortune and not a fault." I remember the apologetic period. Then came the next period, one of revolution of opinion as to the inferior races of the South, a total and entire change in the doctrines of the South on the question of human rights and human nature. It dates from Mr. Calhoun. From the hour that Mr. Calhoun began to teach, there commenced a silent process of moral deterioration. I call it a retrogression in morals—an apostacy. Men no longer apologized for slavery; they learned to defend it; to teach that it was the normal condition of an inferior race; that the seeds and history of it were in the Word of God; that the only condition in which a Republic can be prosperous, is, where an aristocracy *owns the labour* of the community. That was the doctrine of the South, and with that doctrine there began to be ambitious designs, not only for the maintenance but for the propagation of slavery. This era of propagation and aggression constitutes the fourth and last period of the revolution of the South. They had passed through a whole cycle of changes. These changes followed certain great laws. No sooner was the new philosophy set on foot, than the South recognized its legitimacy and accepted it with all its inferences and inevitable tendencies. They gave up wavering and misgivings, adopted the institution—praised it, loved it, defended it, sought to maintain it, burned to spread it. During the last fifteen years, I believe you cannot find a voice, printed or uttered, in the cotton states of the South, which deplored slavery. All believed in and praised it, and found authority for it in God's Word. Politicians admired it, merchants appreciated it, the whole South sang pæans to the new-found truth, that man was born to be owned by man. (Loud cheers.) This change of doctrine made it certain, that the South would be annoyed and irritated by a Constitution which, with all its faults, still carried the God-given principle of human rights, which were not to be taken by man except in punishment for crime. That Constitution, and the policy which went with it at first, began to gnaw at, and irritate, and fret the South, when they had adopted slavery as a doctrine. How could they live in peace under a Constitution, that all the time declared the manhood of men and the dignity of freedom? It became necessary that they should do one of two things, either give up slavery, or appropriate the government to themselves, and in some way or other drain out of the Constitution this venom of liberty, and infuse a policy more in harmony with Southern ideas. They took the latter course. They contrived to possess themselves of the government; and for the last fifty years the policy of the country has been Southern. Was a tariff wanted? It was made a Southern tariff. Was a tariff oppressive? The Southerners overthrew it. Was a tariff wanted again? The Southern policy declared it to be necessary, and it was passed. Was more territory wanted? The South must have its way. Was any man to obtain a place? If the South opposed it, he had no chance whatever. For fifty years most of the men who became judges, who sat in the Presidential chair and in the Courts, had to base their opinions on slavery or on Southern views. All the filibustering, all the intimidations of foreign Powers, all the so-called snubbing of European Powers, happened during the period in which the policy of the country was controlled by the

South. May I be permitted to look on it as a mark of victorious Christianity, that England now loves her worst enemy, and is sitting with arms of sympathy round her neck? (Loud cheers.) There was at the same time a revolution going on in the North unconsciously. The first period of revolution begun in the North was, what might be called the foundation-laying. Material wealth began to be amassed, manufacturing and farm labour flourished, schools were multiplied, colleges were rising. It was a period in which the North was developing and consolidating its power. Then, for many years—and it is a count of about thirty years ago—the North began to be assailed by bold prophets of the truth, and a crusade was commenced against slavery. (Cheers.) I was then a boy, but old enough to be a spectator and a sympathizer. Those men, for the most part, have gone down into their graves—their names not yet honoured as they will be; for the day is coming, when round their names, and the names of all who have been faithful to the sacred cause of liberty, there will be hung garlands, and they shall be clothed with honour; but around the brows of those who have betrayed their country to despotism shall shine lurid light in flame that shall consume. (Cheers.) The man who was an abolitionist when I was twenty-one years of age might bid farewell to any hopes of political advancement; and the merchant who held these opinions was soon robbed of customers. As far as I remember, there was nothing in the world that so ruined a man—not crime itself was so fatal to a man's standing in the country— as to be known to hold abolition-sentiments. The churches sought to keep the question of slavery out; so did the schools and colleges; so did synods and conventions; but still the cause of abolition progressed; and still, as is always the case with everything that is right, though the men who held those sentiments were scoffed at, though such men as Garrison were dragged through the streets with halters round their necks, yet, the more it was spoken of and canvassed, the more the cause prospered, because it was true. (Cheers.) The insanity at last abated; for the command came from on High, saying to the evil spirit concerning the North: "I command thee to come out of her." Then the nation wallowed on the ground, and foamed at the mouth; but the unclean spirit passed out, and she became clean. The more some people wanted to keep down this subject and keep out the air, the more God forced the subject on their minds. If you let a steam-engine, when it is full of steam, only hiss at the rivets, with the scape-valve open, it cannot explode; but if the steam is shut up, and the valve closed, it will be still for a moment, and then, like thunder, it will go off! So it was in regard to this subject. Those who discussed it, became convinced of its truth; but those who would not permit it to be spoken of, and shut it up, exploded. (Laughter and cheers.) About this time the South began to take such steps as more and more brought the North into a rightful frame of mind. The first conflict that arose between the South and the North was in regard to the admission of the new State of Missouri in 1818. (Hear.) The North contended that there should be no more slave States — the doctrine that is now being revived as the Republican doctrine. It was the original doctrine and conviction, that slavery might be tolerated where it was, but that no more States should be admitted. When Missouri knocked at the door, there were those who opposed its admission as a slave State, but by Southern management and intimidation Henry Clay persuaded the North to a compromise. Now, when there is no difference in principle, but only conflicting interests, a compromise is honourable and right, but when antagonistic principles are in question, I believe compromises to be bargains with the devil, who is never cheated. (Loud laughter and cheers.) The North gave up her principles and admitted the Missouri State with slavery as *an exception*, and by the compromise obtained a line of latitude that should limit slavery. Above the latitude of 36° 30' all States, except Missouri, were to be free; south of that line there might be slave States. By this concession they gave up the whole principle, as such compromises always must. Then came the next conflict. The policy of the North and the policy of the South again jarred against each other. The North was striving, according to the spirit of the Constitution and the convictions of the fathers of the country, the founders of the Union, to carry out the doctrines of liberty. The South became ambitious, and having possession of the Government, aimed to enforce their ideas of slavery upon the whole continent. Hence admission of Texas and the war with Mexico for the sake of territory. Next were seized the regions of New Mexico and California. These were added to the Union not by the North, but by the South. Then came the compromise measures of 1850, and the Fugitive Slave Bill, which the North accepted finally, as children take medicine, when the silver spoon is forced into their teeth, and they are almost choked to make them take it. (Laughter.) Then came the only abolition that I ever heard the South were in favour of—the abolition of the Missouri compromise. What that was, I have just been telling you. But now the South suddenly found out, that the compromise was unconstitutional and void. They claimed to abolish the compromise and have slave States north of the line 36° 30'. The North, incensed and indignant, yet held back, from love for the Union of the States, and gave up their own convictions and their proper line of duty. After the abolition of the Missouri Compromise it was declared by the South, that the doctrine of Popular sovereignty should be established—a doctrine to the effect that when the admission of a State was determined on, it should come in a slave State or a free State, according to the vote of the population. The South carried this measure, and the moment they carried it they attempted to get Kansas introduced as a slave state; but the Northern men were too quick for them—(laughter and applause)—for they sent such a superabundant population into Kansas, that they soon lifted the white banner without a black star upon it. (Cheers.) The instant this was done, the South turned round and said, "Popular sovereignty is not constitutional or expedient. (Laughter and applause.) The States applying for admission shall not have the liberty of saying whether they will come in free or slave." This was the work of Mr. Sliddell—(hisses)—now minister for the Southern States in Paris. (Hisses and slight applause). I wish he were in this hall to hear you hissing. (Cheers.) By this time the North was thoroughly roused and indignant. They had at length opened their eyes, and reluctantly began to see that the South meant nothing short of forcing slavery over the whole continent. The North thereupon grew firmer, and in 1856 nominated Fremont, for the purpose of showing that they were no longer to be browbeaten by slavery. He failed; but failed in the noblest way, by the cheats of his opponents. The State that gave us Buchanan to be a burden for four years, was the State in which the cheating took place. Then came the last act of this revolution of feeling in the North—the election of Mr. Lincoln. (Loud and protracted cheering.) The principle that was laid down as a distinct feature of the platform on which Mr. Lincoln was elected, was, that there should be no more slave territories— in other words, the breathing hole was stopped up, and slavery had no air; it was only a question of time how long it would last before it would be suffocated. (Laughter and cheers.) The North respected the doctrine of State rights, when Georgia said, that slavery was municipal and local, and that the government of the United States had no right to touch slavery in Georgia. The North accepted the doctrine. It was true, that they could not touch slavery in the States: yet the North had a right, in connection with the Middle States, to say, "Although in certain States slavery exists beyond our political reach, yet the territory that is free and is *not* beyond our jurisdiction shall not be touched by the foot of a slave. (Loud cheers.) That was the spark which exploded, and this is the war that followed; for the South knew perfectly well,— and there is no place where logic is better understood than in the South,—that if limits were set to the Slave States, if the territory could be no further extended, the prosperity of the slaveholders was at an end. They determined that that doctrine should be broken up, and and they went into the Secession-war for that very purpose. All these were conflicts between the North and the South, about the growth of slavery, and in all but one of them the South had its own way. (Hear.) The States had been charging each other with guilt, and with infidelity to obligations, but it was now collision. It was the attraction of great underlying influences that moved both South and North. The principle which had been operating in the North for many years was the principle of free labour, while the principle which had impregnated all Southern minds was the principle of slave-labour. The result is this. The South is exhausting the whole life of the States in defence of slavery. This is historical now. The great cause of the conflict — the centre of necessity, round which the cannons roar and the bayonets gleam,— is the preservation of slavery. Beyond slavery, there is no difference between North and South. Their interests are identical, with the exception of WORK. The North is for free work—the South is for slave work; and the whole war in the South, though it is for independence, is, nevertheless, expressly in order to have slavery more firmly established by that independence. (Hear, hear, cheers, and some hisses.) On the other hand, the whole policy of the North, now at last regenerated, and made consistent with their documents, their history, and real belief—the whole policy of the North, as well as the whole work of the North, rejoicing at length to be set free from antagonism, bribes, and intimidations,—is for liberty; liberty for every man in the world. (Cheers.) I wish you to consider for a moment what is the result of this state of things in the North. There never was so united a purpose as there is to-day to crush the rebellion. We have had nearly three years of turmoil and disturbance, and it not only has not taken away that determination, but it has increased it. In the beginning of this conflict we were peculiarly English. What do I mean by that? Well, if I have observed aright, England goes into wars to make blunders at first always—(hisses and cheers)—but you must be aware, that in the end it is not England that has blundered. I have noticed, in the course of my study of the Peninsular war under Wellington, that the first whole year was a series of blunders and fraudulent squandering—(cheers);—but, if I recollect aright, at last the same Wellington drove his foes out of the Peninsula. (Cheers.) And so it is with us. We have so much English blood in our veins, that when we began this war we blundered and blundered; but we are doing better and better every step. (Loud cheering.) There has been time enough for mere enthusiasm to have cooled in the North. That has passed away. Enthusiasm is like the vapour, just enough condensed to let the sun striking upon it fill it with gorgeous colours; but when still further it condenses, and falls in drops for the thirsty man to drink, or carries the river to the cataract, then it has become useful and substantial. Enthusiasm, at first, is that airy cloud; but when it has become a principle in the hearts of the people, then it becomes substantial; and such is the case in the North. Enthusiasm has changed its form, and is now based on substantial moral principle. (Cheers.) The loss of our sons in battle has been grievous; but we accept it as God's will, and we are determined that every martyred son shall have a representative in one hundred liberated slaves. (Loud cheers.) Never was such a unity of Christian men in the North as there is to-day. I have in my possession some two hundred resolutions, passed by different Christian churches and denominations in America, saving the Roman Catholics. In every form of language they express themselves alike resolute for the maintenance of the government and the crushing of the rebellion. I may say that there is no seam in the garment that binds us together. We are one. (Cheers.) The Peace-Democrats have tried three times to put a stop to the war, and every time they tried it, it became evident that the only platform in America, on which this subject can be discussed, is this—that the war must be carried on till the Union is re-established. (Loud cheers.) The Americans are a practical people. They know their own business. (Hear, hear.) No one so well able as they are, to judge what they want: and when they have deliberately arrived at a firm resolve, they surely are to be regarded, at least with respect, if not with sympathy. (Cheers.) This much we expect, that when a people twenty millions strong, intelligent, moral, and, as you know, thrifty—when people of this sort, after three years of deliberation, are fixed on one purpose, they at least demand courtesy, if not respect. (Loud cheers.) We are told that we are breaking our constitutional obligations by the measures we have taken; but we were forced to adopt those measures, and the reasons are abundant and plain. How? When a fire first breaks out, the engineer goes down and plays upon the fire, thinking that he will be able to save the furniture and the neighbouring houses; but, as the devouring element increases, and threatens destruction to all around, the engineer says "Bring me powder," and he blows up the neighbouring house, then the next, and then the next, until a sufficient gap is made to prevent the spread of the conflagration (Cheers.) When he began, he did not think that he would require to sacrifice so much: and so it is with us. When this rebellion commenced, we thought to put it down, and to maintain, at the same time, the rights of the States; but, when the war assumed such proportions as seemed to threaten the destruction of the nation and its constitutional Government, it became a question whether the President should put in practice the powers he possessed of saving the Union at all hazards. (Cheers.) Long he paused, I know; for I assisted in bombarding him. (Laughter and cheers.) For months, and months, and months. I both pleaded and inveighed against the dilatory policy at Washington, and at last the President issued a proclamation, declaring that the rebellion had assumed such proportions, that, for the sake of saving the country, he intended to exercise the power he possessed, and to confiscate the total "property" of the South, the whole of the slaves being included, for the sake of saving the Union and the Constitution. (Cheers.) But some men speak to me, and say, "Oh, I am tired of waiting; when is this little quarrel of yours on the other side to be settled?" (Laughter.) A little quarrel—(laughter)—with 1,200 miles of a base line—a little quarrel that commenced only seventy-five years ago. You ask how? The smouldering fire that by some means or other has caught a rafter between the ceilings is not known of at first; but after two or three days it bursts out, and the whole building is consumed. The fire did not begin when it became visible to the eyes; it began some time before. In the same way this war did not begin three years ago. It began when this constitution was adopted—a constitution for liberty with a policy for slavery—(cheers)—and it is as impossible to tell when it will come to a termination as it is to foretell the conclusion of any great matter affecting the welfare of thirty millions of people, contingent partly on great laws and partly on interfering politicians. It might close next year; it might close in three years; it might close in five. We have lost many sons, we have spilled much blood. This is the operation by which the cancer is to be severed from our system; the operation is now far advanced, and woe be to the man who interferes with it before the last bit of the virus is removed. (Cheers.) But, let me say, even a servant who will bear a blow, cannot bear to be beaten and preached at both together. If you insist on groaning over the tediousness of the war, you must not aid to prolong it. Either do not ask us when it will end, or else do not send ships and guns to the rebels in the South. If you want to sympathize with us, do so;

and if you must assist the rebels, do so ; but do not attempt both things at once. ("Hear, hear," and applause.) I thank Earl Russell for his speech at Blairgowrie. It is a speech that has brought comfort and gladness to the hearts of our American friends. (Hear, hear.) A friend of mine in New York has written to me, stating that the whole feeling there has been changed since the intelligence of Earl Russell's speech. We do not want to quarrel ; we do not want animosity between Great Britain and America. No man has spoken of Great Britain words of praise and blame with more honest heart than I have. (Cheers and some hisses.) That man is not your friend who dares not speak of your faults to your face. The man that is your friend tells you when he thinks you are wrong ; and whether I am right or wrong, I assert, that in giving moral sympathy largely to the South, and above all, in allowing the infamous traffic of your ports with the rebels, thus strengthening the hands of the slaveholders,—and that, without public rebuke,—you have done wrong. I have said this, because, dear as your country is to to us, precious as were the legacies given to us of learning and religion, and proud as we have been for years past to think of our ancestry and common relationship to you—yet so much dearer to us than kindred is the cause of God, that, if Great Britain sets herself against us, we shall not hesitate one moment on her account, but shall fulfil our mission ! (Cheers.) Earl Russell was, however, pleased to say that this was a conflict for territory on the one part, and for independence on the other. You know just as well as I, that the North has been adverse to the acquisition of territory. It was the South that brought in Texas, that brought in the whole of the Louisiana tract by purchase ; it was the South that went to war with Mexico, and added New Mexico, and the whole of California ; and it was the South that sent Walker, the filibusterer, to Cuba. The South would have territory. It is not the North that has been avaricious of land, but the South that needed the land for the extension of their slave system. Now, we are striving for the territory that belongs to the Union. (Hear, hear.) Let me see that man who dares to say here that he believes in the kind of patriotism that would let every citizen sit still while their territory was dismembered, and never raise a hand or lift a sword ? If that is your idea of patriotism, it is not mine. I have taught my people, and I have practised the doctrine myself as far as necessary, that it was the duty of every Christian to defend his house, and if any robber broke into his house, that he was bound to resist, and recover any goods that might have been carried off. Now, that which is true of the householder, I declare to be true of the nation. The love of country means this, to defend every part and particle of the country from unjust alienation. (Loud applause.) It amounts then to just this, that we are trying to get back our own ; though Lord John Russell—I beg his pardon, Earl Russell—(laughter)—says that we were ambitious of territory ! Well, here come two men before a Justice of the Peace, the one with the other by the coat. The one says : "I found this man in my house carrying off my wife's silks, finery, and jewels." Suppose the Justice to remonstrate with the complainant, and reprimand him for avarice, and blandly let the thief go without a word!! What would become of a community in which the victim of robbery was scolded and the robber set free? (Applause.) Now, the territory in question was paid for by the money of the Union, and we swore by as solemn an oath as people can swear, to hold it for the good of the nation. Because we are striving to keep our oath, I do not see how that can make us ambitious of territory. (Hear, hear, and applause.) On the other side, Earl Russell says the South are contending for independence. Yes they are, and I would to God that so much gallantry had a better cause. It needs but that, to be illustrious to the end of time. (Cheers.) Ladies and gentlemen, I am proud to say, that we have not in that Western Continent degenerated from your British blood. There is high spirit yet in America just as much as there is here. (Applause.) Yet, Southern *independence*, what is it? When they seceded and went to Montgomery to frame a Constitution, what did they do? They made one or two little alterations in the Constitution. They lengthened the term of the Presidency, and made a few alterations in the forms of procedures in the Congress; but substantially they took the same Constitution as they had just escaped from. (Hear, hear.) The only material clause added was the one that made SLAVERY PERPETUAL, and declared it to be illegal to undertake to abolish it. What then is Southern independence? It is the meteor around the dark body of slavery. King Bomba of Naples wanted to be independent, and his idea of independence was, that he should be let alone whilst he was oppressing his subjects. This very idea of independence has been the same, since the days when Nimrod hunted men. (Laughter and cheers.) This is the only independence the South is fighting for. But it is said, that the North is just as bad as the South in its hatred for the negro. At one time I admit that there was a prejudice against the black man, arising out of the political condition of things: but I can bear witness that this prejudice has almost entirely passed away, in so far as the native population is concerned. (Cheers.) I shall not say who are the bitterest enemies of the black men, because you would hiss me if I did so. (Loud cries of "Speak out," and a voice, "The Irishmen"—another voice, "The Irish Roman Catholics.") There is no doubt that the Irish have a strong prejudice against the negroes, but it arises simply from this, that they have been led to believe by the enemies of the North, that, were the slaves freed, they would dispute the field of labour with them; whereas everybody who knew anything of their disposition could tell, that, were they freed, the Northern negroes would flock to the South, leaving the North for Northern labourers.—The statement has been made that the Americans are seeking to destroy the Anglo-Saxons for the sake of a few millions of negroes. I contend, that, although the freedom of the negroes will no doubt result from this war, yet we are fighting for the good of all mankind—black, white, and yellow —(laughter)—for men of all nations—to save representative government and universal liberty. It is also said, that the proclamation by the President was not sincere—that he had issued it merely as an Official, and that it did not express his personal convictions. All I need to reply, is, that the President, whatever his own feelings, is bound to act as an Official and discharge the duties of his Office. He is bound to administer the Constitution of the country. It was the President and not the man who spoke; and it was the country, and not the President, that was responsible for the proclamation. At the same time I affirm, that the manner in which all these proclamations have been carried out is a sufficient test of their sincerity. The President was very loth to take the steps he did; but, though slow, Abraham Lincoln was sure. A thousand men could not make him plant his foot before he was ready; ten thousand could not move it after he had put it down. This national crisis in my own country is a spectacle worthy of the admiration of the world, and I can only hope that when next the Social Science Congress assembles, this great conflict will have gone so far towards an issue, that it may be found consistent with duty to inaugurate its meeting without sneering at a neighbouring nation. (Great cheering and hisses.) I have a closing word to speak. It is our duty in America, by every means in our power, to avoid all cause of irritation with every foreign nation, and with the English nation most especially. On your side it is your duty to avoid all irritating interference, and all speech that tends to irritate. Brothers should be brothers all the world over, and you are of our blood, and we are of your lineage. May that day be far distant when Great Britain and America shall turn their backs on each other, and seek an alliance with other nations. (Loud cries of "Russia.") The day is coming when the foundations of the earth will be lifted out of their places; and there are two nations that ought to be found shoulder to shoulder and hand in hand for the sake of Christianity and universal liberty, and these nations are Great Britain and America. (Loud and prolonged cheering.)

Dr. ALEXANDER, who was received with loud applause, said—ladies and gentlemen, the resolution which I have had put into my hands is the following :—" That this meeting most earnestly and emphatically protests against American slavery in all its ramifications, as a system which treats immortal and redeemed human beings as goods and chattels, which denies them the rights of marriage and of home, which consigns them to ignorance of the first rudiments of education, and exposes them to the outrages of lust and passion; and that this meeting is therefore of opinion that it should be totally abolished, and, further, that this meeting, rejoicing in the progress which has already been made in America towards this end, desires to encourage, with their cordial sympathy, the earnest abolitionists in that country in the noble efforts they are making." I do not think that it is necessary that I should offer any observations in support of this resolution. After the magnificent oration to which we have just listened, I do not feel myself inclined at all to intrude in the way of speaking upon this question, and I presume the meeting is not all inclined to hear anything I might be disposed to say. I do not think the motion which has been put into my hands requires very much to be said in support of it. I think it is exceedingly moderate, rather more moderate than perhaps I should have expressed it, had it been in my own words. (Applause.) I think it pledges us to nothing but what we may heartily agree to—(loud applause)—from our abhorrence of slavery, our desire to see that feeling acknowledged, and our sympathy with those who are trying to abolish it in America. Some may perhaps think that in the resolution we might directly sympathise with the Federals in their struggle, but that might probably lead to a division in the meeting. I would venture to suggest that our esteemed friend has gone very far to show that the Northeners, as such, are abolitionists. Those who think that he has made out that point might interpret the latter part of this resolution to mean the whole of the Federals as a body; and those who do not think that might restrict it in their own minds to suit their views. (Laughter.)

Dr. GEORGE JOHNSTON then came forward amid loud cheers, and said: It is not necessary that I should say one word in seconding the motion. I am quite satisfied that this meeting is perfectly unanimous in accepting the sentiments expressed in the motion, and why, thereore, should I occupy more time. (Applause.) Just let me say this one word, that I apprehend that the magnificent speech of our friend Mr. Beecher Stowe—(loud laughter)—I mean Mr. Ward Beecher—has removed some prejudices—(hear, hear)—has given some information which, if rightly used, will guide us to the same conclusion to which I long ago came—viz., that the North is banded together to maintain the iberties of mankind. (Loud applause.)

A show of hands was then taken, when only three were held up against the resolution, which were carried amidst loud and prolonged heering.

A gentleman named Wright came forward to the platform to speak, but was ruled to be out of order.

The Rev. DUNCAN OGILVIE said: The motion I have to make is one which will recommend itself to every one, in consequence of what has been manifested as Mr. Beecher has gone on. It has been to every one an immense treat to hear such a speech. (Loud applause.) I felt myself warmed exceedingly by it. (Laughter.) I am quite sure that the sympathies of this large meeting go with Mr. Beecher in a large measure —(applause)—and that you are ready to say Amen to every word almost, if not entirely. (Loud applause and hisses.) I am ready to say Amen to what Dr. Johnston stated, and I think the meeting is ready to do the same. (Loud applause and hisses.) What I now propose is that we give a very hearty vote of thanks to Mr. Beecher for coming, at very much inconvenience, as I know he has done, to address us this evening. (Loud and prolonged applause.)

Mr. NELSON, publisher, rose to second the motion. He said: I have been requested to second this motion of a vote of thanks to Mr. Beecher, and I rise to do it with great diffidence, but at the same time with great pleasure. It is unnecessary, and it would be unbecoming in me, to pay any personal compliment to Henry Ward Beecher. The truth is that, in listening to his address to-night, I forgot Mr. Beecher altogether in the cause of which he is the representative; and I daresay he will think that the best compliment I can pay to his eloquence. In thanking him, perhaps you will allow me, in a single sentence, to bear my humble but willing testimony to what I have seen of the growth of a healthy public opinion in America on the subject of slavery. Ten years ago I happened to visit the United States; and everywhere, from New York to Missouri, I had, like others from the old country, to defend myself as I best could against the defenders of slavery. Conversation on general topics was sure at last to drift into this one great subject; but all is changed now. A few months ago I paid a second visit to the United States, and, except among the Copperheads, I can bear witness that the old hostility to English sentiment against slavery is gone. In the city of New York there is a large and influential association, known as the American Tract Society. This society has for many years been one of the battle-grounds on which the cause of freedom has been fought. Its mutilation of the works of English authors, and its rigid exclusion from its publications of everything against slavery, resulted a few years ago in the formation of a new society pledged to the cause of freedom. When I state that proposals have been made for a re-union of the two societies, because all feel free now to speak out on the subject of slavery, you may receive it as pretty strong evidence that a vast change has taken place. Yes, Mr. Chairman, the tide of public opinion has turned, and you might as well attempt to chain the sea as arrest its progress. In this country we are accustomed to talk of North and South, as if in these two words we expressed the nature of this terrible civil war; but, Mr. Chairman, I beg leave to say that these two words express only one half the truth. There are two Norths and two Souths. There is that North which all along has yielded to the South, and strengthened the hands of the slave power. There is that other North who, for the first time, have the reins of power in their hands, and, amidst tremendous difficulties, are fighting the battle of freedom. It is that party, represented by such men as Mr. Beecher, Charles Sumner, and others, who have a right to appeal to this country for sympathy, and who, I think, are entitled to get it. With the destruction of slavery there will be no South. A distinguished nobleman in this country some time ago set afloat the neat but delusive phrase that this is a war on one side for *empire*, on the other for *independence*. Yes, Mr. Chairman, and so it was. The Southern leaders, at the beginning of the struggle, boasted that they would soon have their flag floating over the Capitol at Washington, and at New York and Boston. Was not that a struggle for empire? On the other side, was it not a struggle for independence when for the first time we saw the North rising up against the domination of the South? Last December, I happened to land in New York soon after the first battle of Fredericksburg, the darkest hour the North has known in this great war; but, Mr Chairman, allow me to say that though the terrible battle of Fredericksburg was a defeat to the North, it was the greatest victory they ever gained. It broke the Democratic party into two—peace Democrats and war Democrats. The Government was stronger after the battle of Fredericksburg than before it; and so has it been with all the other defeats of the North. The Press in this country seemed to rejoice over these defeats and disasters, but they will, I venture to think, find themselves mistaken. They have not weakened the North. These defeats and disasters were all needed to bring round the North to the true position that either slavery must be destroyed or slavery would destroy their country. Every disaster has brought large accessions to that party who have all along been true to the cause of freedom. There is one other point that I would like for a moment to refer to. In this country we attach far too much importance to the newspapers of America, and especially to the vilest of them all—the *New York Herald*. It is a common mistake in this country to suppose that that paper has a larger circulation than any other. In its daily issue among the rowdies of New York it undoubtedly has; but taking its whole issues during the week, it is far outnumbered in circulation by the abolition paper, the *New York Tribune*. We complain against the Americans for writing bitter articles against this country; but allow me to say that the worst of these articles are generally written on the arrival of the English mail, and I confess, from the tone of the Press of this country, I don't wonder at the fierce and bitter replies. In mixing with Americans, I must say that I have found little that was offensive, except a little harmless brag; but remember that this is natural to a young country, and should hardly offend us, as it seems to do. The most offensive things I have read or heard did not come from native-born Americans, but from our own countrymen, and especially from those who were natives of the Green Isle. I believe that among native Americans there is every desire to cultivate the friendship of this country, and that the present bitterness of feeling, having no root in itself, will soon wither away. Mr. Chairman, we must not forget that there are also two Souths. There are blacks as well as whites. Why should we always speak as if the whites alone formed the South; but I feel that I have already detained you too long? Before I sit down I beg to express the belief that, with the destruction of slavery, there will be no South. It is slavery alone that has formed the South. The din and smoke of battle will, ere long, clear away. I believe that the present bitter feelings between North and South will also pass away, and we will see a united country, with the fair form of liberty wielding the sceptre over a free people.

The motion was carried amid loud applause.

The Rev. Mr. CULLEN moved a cordial vote of thanks to the Chairman; and

The Rev. Dr. THOMSON concluded the proceedings with prayer.

LIVERPOOL.—OCTOBER 16, 1863.

GREAT MEETING IN THE PHILHARMONIC HALL.

The Hall was crowded in every part by an audience drawn together by the announcement that the Rev. Henry Ward Beecher, the celebrated American preacher and philanthropist, brother of Mrs. Beecher Stowe, would lecture on the American War and Emancipation. Immediately the doors were opened the hall was filled, and the aspect of the audience showed that the proceedings were anticipated with no little eagerness. Mr. Charles Robertson was the chairman of the evening, and amongst those present on the platform we observed—
Rev. Robert Knox, Fareham; Rev. Josiah Hankinson, Leek; Samuel Mosley, Esq., London; Rev. Dr. Nicholas; Rev. Robert Harley, F.R.S.; Rev. John Jones, Denis Daley, A. Leighton, Robert Trimble; Rev. Henry Tarrant, Derby; William Crossfield, C. E. Macqueen, Rev. Dr. Graham, H. G. Cook, Rev. Thomas Durant, Charles Wilson, E. K. Muspratt, H. C. Long, J. H. Estcourt, E. O. Greening, Peter Sinclair, W. Johnson, J. C. Edwards, R. Goulden, Manchester; George A. Brown, John Innes, Charles E. Rawlins, Rev. C. M. Birrell, Rev. O. B. Bidwell, New York; William Crossfield, junior, Isaac B. Cooke, Rev. Enoch Mellor, M.A., President of the Congregational Union; Rev. Jones Booth, Yorkshire; Rev. Robert Shaw, F. James, Rev. R. Balgarnie, of Scarborough; Rev. J. Gawthorn, Rev. W. Sanders, Maurice Williams, Dr. Hitchcock, Rev. R. J. Milne, the Dean of Dromore; C. R. Hall, John Patterson, Rev. John Lumb, Malvern; Rev. John Jones, Kirkdale; Rev. G. Procter, Isle of Wight; Rev. — Day, Rev. D. G. Smith, Eglish; Rev. Owen Evans, Wrexham; Rev. William Roberts, Rev. James Mahood, Rev. Robert Thomas, Bangor; Rev. William Rees, Rev. E. Evans, Morriston; Rev. William Griffith, Holyhead; Rev. E. T. Davis, Abergele; Rev. Noah Stephens, Rev. John Davis, Cardiff; Rev. J. Stephens, Brecon; Rev. William Edwards, Cardigan; Rev. F. Busby, Southport; Rev. W. P. Davis, Ringmore; Rev. John Thomas, Rev. J. Jenkins, Holywell; Rev. A. Francis, Rhyl; Rev. J. Roberts, Conway; Rev. John Wilde, Nottingham; Rev. Robert Ashton, Secretary of the Congregational Union, London.

On the entrance of Mr. Beecher, preceded by the chairman, a vast shout of mingled welcome and disapprobation was immediately raised.

As is already known, to our readers, placards had been posted throughout the town inciting the people of Liverpool to give the reverend lecturer a hostile reception; and it soon became evident that a small but determined minority of the meeting were present with that intention. The extent to which their exertions, which were sedulously continued throughout, interfered with the proceedings, will be perceived by the report.

CHARLES ROBERTSON, Esq., on rising to introduce the lecturer, was received with loud cheers and hisses. After obtaining silence he said: Ladies and gentlemen, we are met here to-night to hear an address from the Rev. Henry Ward Beecher. (Cheers and hisses.) I hope, gentlemen, this is an assembly of Englishmen—(hear, hear,)—and that everybody will be heard with calmness and impartiality. (Hear, hear.) Well, gentlemen, we are met together this evening to receive such information from Mr. Beecher as he has it in his power to communicate to us respecting the present state of the contest now going on in the United States of America, and its bearing on that most important question which has so powerfully stirred the hearts of Englishmen, the question of the emancipation of the negro race. (Loud applause and hisses.) I need not say to you, gentlemen, it is that aspect of the question which has induced many of us to take a part in this meeting. It is because we believe that this is a contest which has a most important bearing on the emancipation of the negro race, and the introduction, to a larger portion of the population of the Southern States, of those rights and liberties which, as men, they ought to possess—that we have taken a deep interest in this struggle, believing that the success of the Northern States will lead to the emancipation of the slave. ("No, no," hisses and cheers.) The question of emancipation possesses such an immense interest and importance, that we are prepared to give a free expression of our sympathy and support to this movement. We, in common with all our fellow-countrymen, deplore and deprecate the bloodshed and miseries which this war has occasioned. I think there is no man among us who can view with other than feelings of the deepest regret the suffering and the loss which it has occasioned both in the country where the war is being waged and among the European communities. But, while admitting this to the fullest extent, I say, that to establish the great principle of liberty, the sacrifice of all else we hold dear purchases that liberty cheaply. (Hear, hear.) Therefore, while we do regret the misery produced, we do not regret the great issue which we believe will be obtained through that misery. But, gentlemen, we take this side not only in sympathy for the North, but in sympathy for the South. (Cheers.) The great work of negro emancipation is to benefit the inhabitants of these Southern States more than even it will benefit the North. With the North it is a question of humanity; with the South it is a question of progress, liberty, and of all that can contribute to elevate and promote the prosperity of a state. (Hear, hear.) It is with no unfriendly feelings to the South that I say these things. They are our own kinsmen as well as the people of the North. We have admired their courage and unflinching devotedness to what they believe a right cause. (Applause.) But we are equally convinced that their cause is wrong. (Loud cries of "No, no," and " Hear, hear.") If there is a righteous God in Heaven, we believe that cause cannot prosper. (Renewed interruption.) The chairman concluded by asking the respectful attention of the audience to Mr. Beecher's address, adding that that gentleman was perfectly prepared to answer any questions that might be addressed to him after the lecture, provided they were put in writing, with the name of the writer attached, and handed up to him the (chairman). ("Oh, oh.")

The Rev. HENRY WARD BEECHER then rose, and, advancing to the front of the platform, was greeted with mingled cheers, hisses, and groans. A considerable proportion of the audience stood up, waving hats and handkerchiefs, and cheering. A man in the gallery called for "Three cheers for the Southern States," which created much laughter and some uproar. Mr. Beecher proceeded to say—" Ladies and gentlemen," when the uproar again commenced, and efforts were made to eject one noisy individual from the body of the hall.

The CHAIRMAN said: A fair opportunity will be afforded to express approval or dissent at the close of the lecture, but if any one interrupts the meeting by disorderly conduct, I shall be obliged to call in the aid of the police. (Cheers.)

The Rev. Mr. BEECHER then said: For more than twenty-five years I have been made perfectly familiar with popular assemblies in all parts of my country except the extreme South. There has not for the whole of that time been a single day of my life when it would have been safe for me to go South of Mason's and Dixon's line in my own country, and all for one reason; my solemn, earnest, persistent testimony against that which I consider to be the most atrocious thing under the sun— the system of American slavery in a great free republic. (Cheers.) I have passed through that early period, when right of free speech was denied to me. Again and again I have attempted to address audiences that, for no other crime than that of free speech, visited me with all manner of contumelious epithets; and now since I have been in England, although I have met with greater kindness and courtesy on the part of most than I deserved, yet, on the other hand, I perceive that the Southern influence prevails to some extent in England. (Applause and uproar.) It is my old acquaintance; I understand it perfectly—(laughter)—and I have always held it to be an unfailing truth that where a man had a cause that would bear examination he was perfectly willing to have it spoken about. (Applause.) And when in Manchester I saw those huge placards, "Who is Henry Ward Beecher?"—(laughter, cries of "Quite right," and applause)—and when in Liverpool I was told that there were those blood-red placards, purporting to say what Henry Ward Beecher had said, and calling upon Englishmen to suppress free speech—I tell you what I thought. I thought simply this—" I am glad of it." (Laughter.) Why? Because if they had felt perfectly secure, that *you* are the minions of the South and the slaves of slavery, they would have been perfectly still.

(Applause and uproar.) And, therefore, when I saw so much nervous apprehension that, if I were permitted to speak—(hisses and applause)—when I found they were afraid to have me speak—(hisses, laughter, and "No, no")—when I found that they considered my speaking damaging to their cause—(applause)—when I found that they appealed from facts and reasonings to mob law—(applause and uproar)—I said : no man need tell me what the heart and secret counsel of these men are. They tremble, and are afraid. (Applause, laughter, hisses, "No, no," and a voice : "New York mob.") Now, personally, it is a matter of very little consequence to me whether I speak here to-night or not. (Laughter and cheers.) But, one thing is very certain—if you do permit me to speak here to-night you will hear very plain talking. (Applause and hisses.) You will not find a man—(interruption)—you will not find me to be a man that dared to speak about Great Britain 3,000 miles off, and then is afraid to speak to Great Britain when he stands on her shores. (Immense applause and hisses.) And if I do not mistake the tone and the temper of Englishmen, they had rather have a man who opposes them in a manly way—(applause from all parts of the hall)—than a sneak that agrees with them in an unmanly way. (Applause and "Bravo.") Now, if I can carry you with me by sound convictions, I shall be immensely glad—(applause) ; but if I cannot carry you with me by facts and sound arguments, I do not wish you to go with me at all ; and all that I ask is simply FAIR PLAY. (Applause, and a voice: "You shall have it, too.") Those of you who are kind enough to wish to favour my speaking—and you will observe that my voice is slightly husky, from having spoken almost every night in succession for some time past—those who wish to hear me will do me the kindness simply to sit still, and to keep still ; and I and my friends the Secessionists will make all the noise. (Laughter.) There are two dominant races in modern history—the Germanic and the Romanic races. The Germanic races tend to personal liberty, to a sturdy individualism, to civil and to political liberty. The Romanic race tends to absolutism in Government ; it is clanish ; it loves chieftains, it develops a people that crave strong and showy Governments to support and plan for them. The Anglo-Saxon race belongs to the great German family, and is a fair exponent of its peculiarities. The Anglo-Saxon carries self-government and self-development with him wherever he goes. He has popular GOVERNMENT and popular INDUSTRY ; for the effects of a generous civil liberty are not seen a whit more plain in the good order, in the intelligence, and in the virtue of a self-governing people, than in their amazing enterprise and the scope and power of their creative industry. The power to create riches is just as much a part of the Anglo-Saxon virtues as the power to create good order and social safety. The things required for prosperous labour, prosperous manufactures, and prosperous commerce are three. First—liberty ; second, liberty ; third, liberty. (Hear, hear.) Though these are not merely the same liberty as I shall show you. First, there must be liberty to follow those laws of business, which experience has developed, without imposts or restrictions, or governmental intrusions.

Business simply wants to be let alone. (Hear, hear.) Then, secondly, there must be liberty to distribute and exchange products of industry in any market without burdensome tariffs, without imposts, and without vexatious regulations. There must be these two liberties—liberty to create wealth, as the makers of it think best according to the light and experience which business has given them; and then liberty to distribute what they have created without unnecessary vexatious burdens. The comprehensive law of the ideal industrial condition of the world is free manufacture and free-trade. (Hear, hear: a Voice: "The Morrill tariff." Another voice: "Monroe.") I have said there were three elements of liberty. The third is the necessity of an intelligent and free race of customers. There must be freedom among producers; there must be freedom among the distributors; there must be freedom among the customers. It may not have occurred to you that it makes any difference what one's customers are, but it does in all regular and prolonged business. The condition of the customer determines how much he will buy, determines of what sort he will buy. Poor and ignorant people buy little and that of the poorest kind. The richest and the intelligent, having the more means to buy, buy the most, and always buy the best. Here then are the three liberties—liberty of the producer; liberty of the distributor; and liberty of the consumer. The first two need no discussion, they have been long thoroughly and brilliantly illustrated by the political economists of Great Britain, and by her eminent statesmen; but it seems to me that enough attention has not been directed to the third; and, with your patience, I will dwell on that for a moment, before proceeding to other topics. It is a necessity of every manufacturing and commercial people that their customers should be very wealthy and intelligent. Let us put the subject before you in the familiar light of your own local experience. To whom do the tradesmen of Liverpool sell the most goods at the highest profit? To the ignorant and poor, or to the educated and prosperous? (A voice: "To the Southerners." Laughter.) The poor man buys simply for his body; he buys food, he buys clothing, he buys fuel, he buys lodging. His rule is to buy the least and the cheapest that he can. He goes to the store as seldom as he can,—he brings away as little as he can,—and he buys for the least he can. (Much laughter.) Poverty is not a misfortune to the poor only who suffer it, but it is more or less a misfortune to all with whom he deals. On the other hand, a man well off,—how is it with him? He buys in far greater quantity. He can afford to do it; he has the money to pay for it. He buys in far greater variety, because he seeks to gratify not merely physical wants, but also mental wants. He buys for the satisfaction of sentiment and taste, as well as of sense. He buys silk, wool, flax, cotton; he buys all metals—iron, silver, gold, platinum; in short he buys for all necessities and of all substances. But that is not all. He buys a better quality of goods. He buys richer silks, finer cottons, higher grained wools. Now, a rich silk means so much skill and care of somebody's that has been expended upon it to make it finer and richer; and so of cotton, and so of wool. That is, the price of the finer goods runs back to the very beginning, and remunerates the workman as well as the merchant. Now, the whole labouring community is as much interested and profited as the mere merchant, in this buying and selling of the higher grades in the greater varieties and quantities. The law of price is the skill; and the amount of skill expended in the work is as much for the market as are the goods. A man comes to market and says, "I have a pair of hands," and he obtains the lowest wages. Another man comes and says, "I have something more than a pair of hands; I have truth and fidelity;" he gets a higher price. Another man comes and says, "I have something more; I have hands, and strength, and fidelity, and skill." He gets more than either of the others. The next man comes and says, "I have got hands, and strength, and skill, and fidelity; but my hands work more than that. They know how to create things for the fancy, for the affections, for the moral sentiments;" and he gets more than either of the others. The last man comes and says, "I have all these qualities, and have them so highly that it is a peculiar genius;" and genius carries the whole market and gets the highest price. (Loud applause.) So that both the workman and the merchant are profited by having purchasers that demand quality, variety, and quantity. Now, if this be so in the town or the city, it can only be so because it is a law. This is the specific development of a general or universal law, and therefore we should expect to find it as true of a nation as of a city like Liverpool. I know it is so, and you know that it is true of all the world; and it is just as important to have customers educated, intelligent, moral, and rich out of Liverpool as it is in Liverpool. (Applause.) They are able to buy; they want variety, they want the very best; and those are the customers you want. That nation is the best customer that is freest, because freedom works prosperity, industry, and wealth. Great Britain then, aside from moral considerations, has a direct commercial and pecuniary interest in the liberty, civilization, and wealth of every people and every nation on the globe. (Loud applause.) You have also an interest in this, because you are a moral and a religious people. ("Oh, oh," laughter, and applause.) You desire it from the highest motives; and godliness is profitable in all things, having the promise of the life that is, as well as of that which is to come; but if there were no hereafter, and if man had no progress in this life, and if there were no question of civilization at all, it would be worth your while to protect civilization and liberty, merely as a commercial speculation. To evangelize has more than a moral and religious import—it comes back to temporal relations. Wherever a nation that is crushed, cramped, degraded under despotism is struggling to be free, you, Leeds, Sheffield, Manchester, Paisley, all have an interest that that nation should be free. When depressed and backward people demand that they may have a chance to rise—Hungary, Italy, Poland—it is a duty for humanity's sake, it is a duty for the highest moral motives, to sympathize with them; but beside all these there is a material and an interested reason why you should sympathize with them. Pounds and pence join with conscience and with honour in this design. Now,

Great Britain's chief want is—what? They have said that your chief want is cotton. I deny it. Your chief want is consumers. (Applause and hisses.) You have got skill, you have got capital, and you have got machinery enough to manufacture goods for the whole population of the globe. You could turn out four-fold as much as you do, if you only had the market to sell in. It is not so much the want therefore of fabric, though there may be a temporary obstruction of it; but the principal and increasing want—increasing from year to year—is, where shall we find men to buy, what we can manufacture so fast? (Interruption, and a voice, "The Morrill tariff," and applause.) Before the American war broke out, your warehouses were loaded with goods that you could not sell. (Applause and hisses.) You had over-manufactured; what is the meaning of over-manufacturing but this, that you had skill, capital, machinery, to create faster than you had customers to take goods off your hands? And you know, that, rich as Great Britain is, vast as are her manufactures, if she could have four-fold the present demand, she could make four-fold riches to-morrow; and every political economist will tell you that your want is not cotton primarily, but customers. Therefore, the doctrine, how to make customers, is a great deal more important to Great Britain than the doctrine how to raise cotton. It is to that doctrine I ask from you, business men, practical men, men of fact, sagacious Englishmen—to that point I ask a moment's attention. (Shouts of "Oh, oh," hisses, and applause.) There are no more continents to be discovered. (Hear, hear.) The market of the future must be found—how? There is very little hope of any more demand being created by new fields. If you are to have a better market there must be some kind of process invented to make the old fields better. (A voice, "Tell us something new," shouts of "Order," and interruption.) Let us look at it, then. You must civilize the world in order to make a better class of purchasers. (Interruption.) If you were to press Italy down again under the feet of despotism, Italy, discouraged, could draw but very few supplies from you. But give her liberty, kindle schools throughout her valleys, spur her industry, make treaties with her by which she can exchange her wine, and her oil, and her silk for your manufactured goods; and for every effort that you make in that direction there will come back profit to you by increased traffic with her. (Loud applause.) If Hungary asks to be an unshackled nation—if by freedom she will rise in virtue and intelligence, then by freedom she will acquire a more multifarious industry, which she will be willing to exchange for your manufactures. Her liberty is to be found—where? You will find it in the Word of God, you will find it in the code of history; but you will also find it in the Price Current (hear, hear); and every free nation, every civilized people—every people that rises from barbarism to industry and intelligence, becomes a better customer. A savage is a man of one story, and that one story a cellar. When the man begins to be civilized, he raises another story. When you Christianize and civilize the man, you put story upon story, for you develop faculty after faculty; and you have to supply every story with your productions. The savage is a man one story deep; the civilized man is thirty stories deep. (Applause.) Now, if you go to a lodging-house, where there are three or four men, your sales to them may, no doubt, be worth *something*; but if you go to a lodging-house like some of those which I saw in Edinburgh, which seemed to contain about twenty stories—("oh, oh," and interruption)—every story of which is full, and all who occupy buy of you—which is the best customer,—the man who is drawn out, or the man who is pinched up? (Laughter.) Now, there is in this a great and sound principle of political economy. ("Yah! yah!" from the passage outside the hall, and loud laughter.) If the South should be rendered independent—(at this juncture mingled cheering and hisses became immense; half the audience rose to their feet, waving hats and handkerchiefs, and in every part of the hall there was the greatest commotion and uproar.) You have had your turn now; now let me have mine again (Loud applause and laughter.) It is a little inconvenient to talk against the wind; but, after all, if you will just keep good-natured—I am not going to lose my temper; will you watch yours? (Applause.) Besides all that,—it rests me, and gives me a chance, you know, to get my breath. (Applause and hisses.) And I think that the bark of those men is worse than their bite. They do not mean any harm—they don't know any better. (Loud laughter, applause, hisses, and continued uproar.) I was saying, when these responses broke in, that it was worth our while to consider both alternatives. What will be the result if this present struggle shall eventuate in the separation of America, and making the South—(loud applause, hisses, hooting, and cries of "Bravo!")—a slave territory exclusively,—(cries of "No, no," and laughter)—and the North a free territory, what will be the first result? You will lay the foundation for carrying the slave population clear through to the Pacific Ocean. That is the first step. There is not a man that has been a leader of the South any time within these twenty years, that has not had this for a plan. It was for this that Texas was invaded, first by colonists, next by marauders, until it was wrested from Mexico. It was for this that they engaged in the Mexican war itself, by which the vast territory reaching to the Pacific was added to the Union. Never have they for a moment given up the plan of spreading the American institutions, as they call them, straight through towards the West, until the slave, who has washed his feet in the Atlantic, shall be carried to wash them in the Pacific. (Cries of "Question," and uproar.) There! I have got that statement out, and you cannot put it back. (Laughter and applause.) Now, let us consider the prospect. If the South become a slave empire, what relation will it have to you as a customer? (A Voice: "Or any other man." Laughter.) It would be an empire of 12,000,000 of people. Now, of these, 8,000,000 are white and 4,000,000 black. (A Voice: "How many have you got?"—applause and laughter. Another Voice: "Free your own slaves.") Consider that one-third of the whole are the miserably poor, unbuying blacks. (Cries of "No, no," "Yes, yes," and interruption.) You do not manufacture much for them. (Hisses, "Oh!" "No.") You have not got machinery coarse enough. (Laughter, and "No.") Your labour is too skilled by far to manufacture bagging and linsey-woolsey. (A Southerner: "We are going to free them every one.") Then you and I agree exactly. (Laughter.) One other third consists of a poor, unskilled, degraded white population; and the remaining one-third, which is a large allowance, we will say, intelligent and rich. Now here are twelve million of people, and only one-third of them are customers that can afford to buy the kind of goods that you bring to market. (Interruption and uproar.) My friends, I saw a man once, who was a little late at a railway station, chase an express train. He did not catch it. (Laughter.) If you are going to stop this meeting, you have got to stop it before I speak; for after I have got the things out, you may chase as long as you please—you would not catch them. (Laughter and interruption.) But there is luck in leisure; I'm going to take it easy. (Laughter.) Two-thirds of the population of the Southern States to-day are non-purchasers of English goods. (A Voice: "No, they are not;" "No, no," and uproar.) Now you must recollect another fact—namely, that this is going on clear through to the Pacific Ocean; and if by sympathy or help you establish a slave empire, you sagacious Britons—("Oh, oh," and hooting)—if you like it better, then, I will leave the adjective out—(laughter, hear, and applause)—are busy in favouring the establishment of an empire from ocean to ocean that should have fewest customers and the largest non-buying population. (Applause, "No, no." A Voice: "I think it was the happy people that populated fastest.") Now, for instance, just look at this, the difference between free labour and slave labour to produce cultivated land. The State of Virginia has 15,000 more square miles of land than the State of New York; but Virginia has only 15,000 square miles improved, while New York has 20,000 square miles improved. Of unimproved land Virginia has about 23,000 square miles, and New York only about 10,000 square miles. Now, these facts speak volumes as to the capacity of the territory to bear population. The smaller is the quantity of soil uncultivated, the greater is the density of the population—(hear, hear);—and upon that, their value as customers depends. Let us take the States of Maryland and Massachusetts. Maryland has 2,000 more square miles of land than Massachusetts; but Maryland has about 4,000 square miles of land improved, Massachusetts has 3,200 square miles. Maryland has 2,800 unimproved square miles of land, while Massachusetts has but 1,800 square miles unimproved. But these two are little States,—let us take greater States. Pennsylvania and Georgia. The State of Georgia has 12,000 more square miles of land than Pennsylvania. Georgia has only about 9,800 square miles of improved land, Pennsylvania has 13,400 square miles of improved land, or about 2,300,000 acres more than Georgia. Georgia has about 25,600 square miles of unimproved land, and Pennsylvania has only 10,400 square miles, or about 10,000,000 acres less of unimproved land than Georgia. The one is a Slave State and the other is a Free State. I do not want you to forget such statistics as those, having once heard them. (Laughter.) Now, what can England make for the poor white population of such a future empire, and for her slave population?

What carpets, what linens, what cottons can you sell to them? What machines, what looking-glasses, what combs, what leather, what books, what pictures, what engravings? (A Voice: "We'll sell them ships.") You may sell ships to a few, but what ships can you sell to two-thirds of the population of poor whites and blacks? (Applause.) A little bagging and a little linsey-woolsey, a few whips and manacles, are all that you can sell for the slave. (Great applause, and uproar.) This very day, in the Slave States of America there are eight millions out of twelve millions that are not, and cannot be your customers from the very laws of trade. (A Voice: "Then how are they clothed?" and interruption.)

The CHAIRMAN: If gentlemen will only sit down, those who are making the disturbance will be tired out.

Mr. BEECHER resumed: There are some apparent drawbacks that may suggest themselves. The first is that the interests of England consist in drawing from any country its raw material. (A Voice: "We have got over that.") There is an interest, but it is not the interest of England. The interest of England is not merely where to buy her cotton, her ores, her wool, her linens, and her flax. When she has put her brains into the cotton, and into the linen and flax, and it becomes the product of her looms, a far more important question is, "What can be done with it?" England does not want merely to pay prices for that which brute labour produces, but to get a price for that which brain labour produces. (Hear, hear, and applause.) Your interest lies beyond all peradventure; therefore, if you should bring ever so much cotton from the slave empire—("Yah, yah,")—you cannot sell back again to the slave empire. (A Voice: "Go on with your subject; we know all about England.") Excuse me, sir, I am the speaker, not you; and it is for me to determine what to say. (Hear, hear.) Do you suppose I am going to speak about America except to convince Englishmen? I am here to talk to you for the sake of ultimately carrying you with me in judgment and in thinking—("Oh! oh!")—and, as to this logic of cat-calls, it is slavery logic,—I am used to it. (Applause, hisses, and cheers.) Now, it is said that if the South should be allowed to be separate there will be no tariff, and England can trade with her; but if the South remain in the United States, it will be bound by a tariff, and English goods will be excluded from it (interruption). Now, I am not going to shirk any question of that kind. In the first place, let me tell you that the first tariff ever proposed in America was not only supported by Southern interests and votes, but was originated by the peculiar structure of Southern society. The first and chief difficulty—after the Union was formed under our present constitution—the first difficulty that met our fathers was, how to raise taxes to support the government; and the question of representation and taxes went together; and the difficulty was, whether we should tax the North and South alike, man for man *per caput*, counting the slaves with whites. The North having fewer slaves in comparison with the number of its whites; the South, which had a larger number of blacks, said, "We shall be over-taxed if this system be adopted." They therefore proposed that taxes and representation should be on the basis of five black men counting as three white men. In a short time it was found impossible to raise these taxes in the South, and then they cast about for a better way, and the tariff scheme was submitted. The object was to raise the revenue from the ports instead of from the people. The tariff therefore had its origin in Southern weaknesses and necessities, and not in the Northern cities (loud applause). Daniel Webster's first speech was against it; but after that was carried by Southern votes, (which for more than fifty years determined the law of the country,) New England accepted it, and saying, "It is the law of the land," conformed her industry to it; and when she had got her capital embarked in mills and machinery, she became in favour of it. But the South, beginning to feel, as she grew stronger, that it was against her interest to continue the system, sought to have the tariff modified, and brought it down; though Henry Clay, a Southern man himself, was the immortal champion of the tariff. All his life time he was for a high tariff, till such a tariff could no longer stand; and then he was for moderating the tariffs. And there has not been for the whole of the fifty years a single hour when any tariff could be passed without them. The opinion of the whole of America was, tariff, high tariff. I do not mean that there were none that dissented from that opinion, but it was the popular and prevalent cry. I have lived to see the time when, just before the war broke out, it might be said that the thinking men of America were ready for free-trade. There has been a steady progress throughout America for free-trade ideas. How came this Morrill tariff? The Democratic administration, inspired by Southern counsels, left millions of millions of unpaid debt to cramp the incoming of Lincoln; and the Government, betrayed to the Southern States, found itself unable to pay those debts, unable to build a single ship, unable to raise an army; and it was the exigency, the necessity, that forced them to adopt the Morrill tariff, in order to raise the money which they required. It was the South that obliged the North to put the tariff on. (Applause and uproar.) Just as soon as we begin to have peace again, and can get our national debt into a proper shape as you have got yours—(laughter)—the same cause that worked before will begin to work again; and there is nothing more certain in the future than that the American is bound to join with Great Britain in the world-wide doctrine of free-trade. (Applause and interruption.) Here then, so far as *this* argument is concerned, I rest my case, saying that it seems to me that in an argument addressed to a commercial people it was perfectly fair to represent that their commercial and manufacturing interests tallied with their moral sentiments; and as by birth, by blood, by history, by moral feeling, and by everything, Great Britain is connected with the liberty of the world, God has joined interest and conscience, head and heart; so that you ought to be in favour of liberty everywhere. (Great applause.) There! I have got quite a speech out already, if I do not get any more. (Hisses and applause.) Now then, leaving this for a time, let me turn to some other nearly connected topics. It is said that the South is fighting for just that independence of which I have been speaking. (Hear, hear.) The South is divided on that subject. ("No, no.") There are twelve millions in the South. Four millions of them are asking for their liberty. ("No, no," hisses, "Yes," applause, and interruption.) Four millions are asking for their liberty. (Continued interruption, and renewed applause.) Eight millions are banded together to prevent it. ("No, no," hisses, and applause.) That is what they asked the world to recognise as a strike for independence. (Hear, hear, and laughter.) Eight million white men fighting to prevent the liberty of four million black men, challenging the world. (Uproar, hisses, applause, and continued interruption.) You cannot get over the fact. There it is; like iron, you cannot stir it. (Uproar). They went out of the Union because slave property was not recognised in it. There were two ways of reaching slave property in the Union: the one by exerting the direct Federal authority: but they could not do that, for they conceived it to be forbidden. The second was by indirect influence. If you put a candle under a bowl it will burn so long as the fresh air lasts, but it will go out as soon as the oxygen is exhausted; and so, if you put slavery into a State where it cannot get more States, it is only a question of time how long it will live. By limiting slave territory you lay the foundation for the final extinction of slavery. (Applause.) Gardeners say that the reason why crops will not grow in the same ground for a long time together, is that the roots excrete poisoned matter which the plants cannot use, and thus poison the grain. Whether this is true of crops or not, it is certainly true of slavery, for slavery poisons the land on which it grows. Look at the old slave States, Delaware, Maryland, Virginia, Kentucky, Tennessee, and even at the newer State of Missouri. What is the condition of slavery in those States? It is not worth one cent except to breed. It is not worth one cent so far as productive energy goes. They cannot make money by their slaves in those States. The first reason with them for maintaining slavery is, because it gives political power; and the second, because they breed for the Southern market. I do not stand on my own testimony alone. The editor of the *Virginia Times*, in the year 1836, made a calculation that 120,000 slaves were sent out of the State during that year; 80,000 of which went with their owners, and 40,000 were sold at the average price of 600 dollars, amounting to 24,000,000 dollars in one year out of the State of Virginia. Now, what does Henry Clay, himself a slaveowner, say about Kentucky? In a speech before the Colonisation Society, he said: "It is believed that nowhere in the farming portion of the United States would slave labour be generally employed, if the proprietary were not compelled to raise slaves by the high price of the Southern market," and the only profit of slave property in Northern farming slave States is the value they bring. (A voice: "Then if the Northerners breed to supply the South, what's the difference?") So that if you were to limit slavery, and to say, it shall go so far and no further, it would be only a question of time when it should die of its own intrinsic weakness and disease. Now, this was the Northern feeling. The North was true to the doctrine of constitutional rights. The North refused, by any Federal action within the States, to violate the compacts of the constitution, and left local compacts unimpaired; but the North, feeling herself unbound with regard to what we call the territories,—free land which has not yet State rights,—said there should be no more territory cursed with slavery. (Applause.) With unerring instinct the South said, "The Government administered by Northern men on the principle that there shall be no more slave territory, is a Government fatal to slavery," and it was on that account that they seceded—("No, no," "Yes, yes," applause, hisses, and uproar)—and the first step which they took when they assembled at Montgomery, was, to adopt a constitution. What constitution did they adopt? The same form of constitution which they had just abandoned. What changes did they introduce? A trifling change about the Presidential term, making it two years longer; a slight change about some doctrine of legislation, involving no principle whatever, but merely a question of policy. But by the constitution of Montgomery they legalized slavery, and made it the organic law of the land. The very constitution which they said they could not live under when they left the Union they took again immediately afterwards, only altering it in one point, and that was, making the fundamental law of the land to be slavery. (Hear, hear.) Let no man undertake to say in the face of intelligence—let no man undertake to delude an honest community, by saying that slavery had nothing to do with the Secession. Slavery is the framework of the South; it is the root and the branch of this conflict with the South. Take away slavery from the South, and she would not differ from us in any respect. There is not a single antagonistic interest. There is no difference of race, no difference of language, no difference of law, no difference of constitution; the only difference between us is, that free labour is in the North, and slave labour is in the South. (Loud applause.) But I know that you say, you cannot help sympathizing with a gallant people. (Hear, hear.) They are the weaker people, the minority; and you cannot help going with the minority who are struggling for their rights against the majority. Nothing could be more generous, when a weak party stands for its own legitimate rights against imperious pride and power, than to sympathize with the weak. But who ever yet sympathized with a weak thief, because three constables had got hold of him? (Hear, hear.) And yet the one thief in three policemen's hands is the weaker party. I suppose you would sympathize with him. (Hear, hear, laughter, and applause.) Why, when that infamous king of Naples—Bomba, was driven into Gaeta by Garibaldi with his immortal band of patriots, and Cavour sent against him the army of Northern Italy, who was the weaker party then? The tyrant and his minions; and the majority was with the noble Italian patriots, struggling for liberty. I never heard that Old England sent deputations to King Bomba, and yet his troops resisted bravely there. (Laughter and interruption.) To-day the majority of the people of Rome is with Italy. Nothing but French bayonets keeps her from going back to the Kingdom of Italy, to which she belongs. Do you sympathize with the minority in Rome or the majority in Italy? (A voice: "With Italy.") To-day the South is the minority in America, and they are fighting for *independence!* For what? (Uproar. A voice : "Three cheers for independence," and hisses.) I could wish so much bravery had had a better cause, and that so much self-denial had been less deluded; that that poisonous and venomous doctrine of State rights might have been kept aloof; that so many gallant spirits, such as Jackson, might still have lived. (Great applause and loud cheers, again and again renewed.) The force of these facts, historical and incontrovertible, cannot be broken, except by diverting attention by an attack upon the North. It is said that the North is fighting for Union, and not for emancipation. The North is fighting for Union, for that ensures emancipation. (Loud cheers, "Oh, oh," "No, no," and cheers.) A great many men say to ministers of the Gospel—" You pretend to be preaching and working for the love of the people. Why, you are all the time preaching for the sake of the church." What does the minister say ? " It is by means of the church that we help the people," and when men say that we are fighting for the Union, I too say we are fighting for the Union. (Hear, hear, and a voice : "That's right.") But the motive determines the value ; and why are we fighting for the Union ? Because we never shall forget the testimony of our enemies. They have gone off declaring that the Union in the hands of the North was fatal to slavery. (Loud applause.) There is testimony in court for you. (A voice : "See that," and laughter.) We are fighting for the Union, because we believe that preamble which explains the very reason for which the Union was constituted. I will read it. "We"—not the States—"WE, the people of the United States, in order to form a more perfect NATION— (uproar)—I don't wonder you don't want to hear it—(laughter)—" in order to form a more perfect NATION, establish justice, assure domestic tranquillity—(uproar)—provide for the common defence, promote the general welfare, and secure the blessings of LIBERTY—("oh, oh")—to ourselves and our posterity, ordain and establish this constitution of the United States of America." (A Voice : " How many States ?") It is for the sake of that justice, that common welfare, and that liberty for which the National Union was established, that we fight for the Union. (Interruption.) Because the South believed that the Union was against slavery, they left it. (Renewed interruption.) Yes. (Applause, and " No, no.") To-day, however, if the North believed that the Union was against liberty, they would leave it. (" Oh, oh," and great disturbance.) Gentlemen, I have travelled in the West ten or twelve hours at a time in the mud knee-deep. It was hard toiling my way, but I always got through my journey. I feel to-night as though I were travelling over a very muddy road ; but I think I shall get through. (Cheers.) Well, next it is said, that the North treats the negro race worse than the South. (Applause, cries of "Bravo !" and uproar.) Now, you see I don't fear any of these disagreeable arguments. I am going to face everyone of them. In the first place I am ashamed to confess that such was the thoughtlessness—(interruption)—such was the stupor of the North—(renewed interruption)—you will get a word at a time ; to-morrow will let folks see what it is you don't want to hear—that for a period of twenty-five years she went to sleep, and permitted herself to be drugged and poisoned with the Southern prejudice against black men. (Applause and uproar.) The evil was made worse, because, when any object whatever has caused anger between political parties, a political animosity arises against that object, no matter how innocent in itself; no matter what were the original influences which excited the quarrel. Thus the coloured man has been the football between the two parties in the North, and has suffered accordingly. I confess it to my shame. But I am speaking now on my own ground, for I began twenty-five years ago, with a small party, to combat the unjust dislike of the coloured man. (Loud applause, dissension, and uproar. The interruption at this point became so violent that the friends of Mr. Beecher throughout the hall rose to their feet, waving hats and handkerchiefs, and renewing their shouts of applause. The interruption lasted some minutes.) Well, I have lived to see a total revolution in the Northern feeling—I stand here to bear solemn witness of that. It is not my opinion; it is my knowledge. (Great uproar.) Those men who undertook to stand up for the rights of all men—black as well as white—have increased in number; and now what party in the North represents those men that resist the evil prejudices of past years? The Republicans are that party. (Loud applause.) And who are those men in the North that have oppressed the negro? They are *the Peace Democrats; and the prejudice for which in England you are attempting to punish me, is a prejudice raised by the men who have opposed me all my life.* These pro-slavery democrats abused the negro. I defended him, and they mobbed me for doing it. Oh, justice! (Loud laughter, applause, and hisses.) This is as if a man should commit an assault, maim and wound a neighbour, and a surgeon being called in should begin to dress his wounds, and by-and-by a policeman should come and collar the surgeon and haul him off to prison on account of the wounds which he was healing. Now, I told you I would not flinch from anything. I am going to read you some questions that were sent after me from Glasgow, purporting to be from a working man. (Great interruption.) If those pro-slavery interrupters think they will tire me out, they will do more than eight millions in America could. (Applause and renewed interruption.) I was reading a question on your side, too. "Is it not a fact that in most of the Northern States laws exist precluding negroes from equal civil and political rights with the whites? That in the State of New York the negro has to be the possessor of at least two hundred and fifty dollars worth of property to entitle him to the privileges of a white citizen? That in some of the Northern States the coloured man, whether bond or free, is by law excluded altogether, and not suffered to enter the State limits, under severe penalties? and is not Mr. Lincoln's own State one of them; and in view of the fact that the $20,000,000 compensation which was promised to Missouri in aid of emancipation was defeated in the last Congress (the strongest Republican Congress that ever assembled), what has the North done towards emancipation?" Now then, there's a dose for you. (A Voice: "Answer it.") And I will address myself to the answering of it. And first, the bill for emancipation in Missouri, to which this money was denied, was a bill which was drawn by what we call "log rollers," who inserted in it an enormously disproportioned price for the slaves. The Republicans offered to give them $10,000,000 for the slaves in Missouri, and they outvoted it because they could not get $12,000,000. Already half the slave population had been "run" down South, and yet they came up to Congress to get $12,000,000 for what was not worth ten millions, nor even eight millions. Now as to those States that had passed "black" laws, as we call them; they are filled with Southern emigrants. The Southern parts of Ohio, the Southern part of Indiana, where I myself lived for years, and which I knew like a book, the Southern part of Illinois where Mr. Lincoln lives—(great uproar)—these parts are largely settled by emigrants from Kentucky, Tennessee, Georgia, Virginia, and North Carolina, and it was their vote, or the Northern votes pandering for political reasons to theirs, that passed in those States the infamous "black" laws; and the Republicans in these States have a record, clean and white, as having opposed these laws in every instance as "infamous." Now as to the State of New York, it is asked whether a negro is not obliged to have a certain freehold property, or a certain amount of property, before he can vote. It is so still in North Carolina and Rhode Island for *white* folks—it is so in New York State. (Mr. Beecher's voice slightly failed him here, and he was interrupted by a person who tried to imitate him, cries of "Shame" and "Turn him out.") I am not undertaking to say that these faults of the North, which were brought upon them by the bad example and influence of the South, are all cured; but I do say that they are in a *process* of cure which promises, if unimpeded by foreign influence, to make all such odious distinctions vanish. "Is it not a fact that in most of the Northern States laws exist precluding negroes from equal civil and political rights with the whites?" I will tell you. Let us compare the condition of the negro in the North and the South, and that will tell the story. By express law the South takes away from the slave all attributes of manhood, and calls him "chattel," which is another word for "cattle." (Hear, hear, and hisses.) No law in any Northern State calls him anything else but a person. (Applause.) The South denies the right of legal permanent marriage to the slave. There is not a State of the North where the marriage of the slave is not as sacred as that of any free white man. (Immense cheering.) Throughout the South, since the slave is not permitted to live in anything but in concubinage, his wife, so called, is taken from him at the will of his master, and there is neither public sentiment nor law that can hinder most dreadful and cruel separations every year in every county and town. There is not a State, county, or town, or school district in the North where, if any man dare to violate the family of the poorest blackman, 'there would not be an indignation that would overwhelm him. (Loud applause. A Voice: "How about the riots?") Irishmen made that entirely. (Laughter.)*

* A London newspaper disgracefully attacked Mr. Beecher as impudently false, for making this statement; and the paragraph was reprinted in other papers without comment, although Mr. Beecher's statement is notoriously true. Mr. Berkeley, of Bristol, dishonoured himself lately, by adducing the New York riots in proof that the coloured man is treated as ill in the North as in the South, when the riot from beginning to end was Southern.—EDS.

In the South by statutory law it is a penitentiary offence to teach a black man to read and write. In the North not only are hundreds and thousands of dollars expended of State money in teaching coloured people, but they have their own schools, their own academies, their own churches, their own ministers, their own lawyers. (Cheers and hisses.) In the South, black men are bred, exactly as cattle are bred in the North, for the market and for sale. Such dealing is considered horrible beyond expression in the North. In the South the slave can own nothing by law—(interruption)—but in the single city of New York there are ten million dollars of money belonging to free coloured people. (Loud applause.) In the South no coloured man can determine— (uproar)—no coloured man can determine in the South where he will work, nor at what he will work; but in the North—except in the great cities, where we are crowded by foreigners,—in any country part the black man may choose his trade and work at it, and is just as much protected by the laws as any white man in the land. (Applause.) I speak with authority on this point. (Cries of "No.") When I was twelve years old, my father hired Charles Smith, a man as black as lampblack, to work on his farm. I slept with him in the same room. ("Oh, oh.") Ah, that don't suit you. (Uproar.) Now, you see, the South comes out. (Loud laughter.) I ate with him at the same table; I sang with him out of the same hymn-book—("Good");—I cried, when he prayed over me at night; and if I had serious impressions of religion early in life, they were due to the fidelity and example of that poor humble farm-labourer, black Charles Smith. (Tremendous uproar and cheers.) In the South, no matter what injury a coloured man may receive, he is not allowed to appear in court nor to testify against a white man. (A voice: "That's fact.") In every single court of the North a respectable coloured man is as good a witness, as if his face were white as an angel's robe. (Applause and laughter.) I ask any truthful and considerate man whether, in this contrast, it does not appear that, though faults may yet linger in the North uneradicated, the state of the negro in the North is not immeasurably better than anywhere in the South? (Applause.) And now, for the first time in the history of America— (great interruption),—for the first time in the history of the United States a coloured man has received a commission under the broad seal and signature of the President of the United States. (Loud applause.) This day—(renewed interruption)—this day, Frederick Douglas, of whom you all have heard here, is an officer of the United States—(loud applause)—a commissioner sent down to organize coloured regiments on Jefferson Davis's farm in Mississippi. (Uproar and applause, and a Voice, "You put them in the front of the battle too.") There is another fact that I wish to allude to—not for the sake of reproach or blame, but by way of claiming your more lenient consideration—and that is, that slavery was entailed upon us by your action. (Hear, hear.) Against the earnest protests of the colonists the then Government of Great Britain—I will concede not knowing what were the mischiefs— ignorantly, but in point of fact, forced slave traffic on the unwilling colonists. (Great uproar, in the midst of which one individual was lifted up and carried out of the room amidst cheers and hisses.)

The CHAIRMAN: If you would only sit down no disturbance would take place.

The disturbance having subsided,

Mr. BEECHER said: I was going to ask you, suppose a child is born with hereditary disease; suppose this disease was entailed upon him by parents who had contracted it by their own misconduct, would it be fair that those parents, that had brought into the world the diseased child, should rail at that child because it was diseased. ("No, no.") Would not the child have a right to turn round and say, "Father, it was your fault that I had it, and you ought to be pleased to be patient with my deficiencies." (Applause and hisses, and cries of "order;" great interruption and great disturbance here took place on the right of the platform; and the chairman said that if the persons around the unfortunate individual who had caused the disturbance would allow him to speak alone, but not assist him in making the disturbance, it might soon be put an end to. The interruption was continued until another person was carried out of the hall.) Mr. Beecher continued: I do not ask that you should justify slavery in us, because it was wrong in you two hundred years ago; but having ignorantly been the means of fixing it upon us, now that we are struggling with mortal struggles to free ourselves from it, we have a right to your tolerance, your patience, and charitable construction. I am every day asked when this war will end. (Interruption.) I wish I could tell you; but remember slavery is the cause of the war. ("Hear, hear," applause, "yes," "no.") Slavery has been working for more than 100 years, and a chronic evil cannot be suddenly cured; and as war is the remedy, you must be patient to have the conflict long enough to cure the inveterate hereditary sore. (Hisses, loud applause, and a Voice: "We'll stop it.") But of one thing I think I may give you assurance—this war won't end until the cancer of slavery is cut out by the roots. (Loud applause, hisses, and tremendous uproar.) I will read you a word from President Lincoln. (Renewed uproar.) It is a letter from Theodore Tilton. (Hisses, and cheers.) Won't you hear what President Lincoln thinks? ("No, no.") Well you can hear it or not. It will be printed whether you hear it or hear it not. (Hear, and cries of "Read, Read.") Yes, I will read. "A talk with President Lincoln revealed to me a great growth of wisdom. For instance, he said he was not going to press the colonization idea any longer, nor the gradual scheme of emancipation, expressing himself sorry that the Missourians had postponed emancipation for seven years. He said, 'Tell your anti-slavery friends that I am coming out all right.' He is desirous that the Border States shall form free constitutions, recognising the proclamation, and thinks this will be made feasible by calling on loyal men." (A Voice: "What date is that letter?" and interruption.) Ladies and gentlemen, I have finished the exposition of this troubled subject. (Renewed and continued interruption.) No man can unveil the future; no man can tell what revolutions are about to break upon the world; no man can tell what destiny belongs to France, nor to any of the European powers; but one thing is certain, that in the exigencies of the future there will be combinations and re-combinations, and that those nations that are of the same faith, the same blood, and the same substantial interests, ought not to be alienated from each other, but ought to stand together. (Immense cheering and hisses.) I do not say that you ought not to be in the most friendly alliance with France or with Germany; but I do say that your own children, the offspring of England, ought to be nearer to you than any people of strange tongue. (A Voice: "Degenerate sons," applause and hisses; another voice: "What about the *Trent?*") If there had been any feelings of bitterness in America, let me tell you they had been excited, rightly or wrongly, under the impression that Great Britain was going to intervene between us and our own lawful struggle. (A Voice: "No," and applause.) With the evidence that there is no such intention all bitter feelings will pass away. (Applause.) We do not agree with the recent doctrine of neutrality as a question of law. But it is past, and we are not disposed to raise that question. We accept it now as a fact, and we say that the utterance of Lord Russell at Blairgowrie—(Applause, hisses, and a Voice: "What about Lord Brougham?")—together with the declaration of the government in stopping war-steamers here—(great uproar, and applause)—has gone far towards quieting every fear and removing every apprehension from our minds. (Uproar and shouts of applause.) And now in the future it is the work of every good man and patriot not to create divisions, but to do the things that will make for peace. ("Oh, oh," and laughter.) On our part it shall be done. (Applause and hisses, and "No, no.") On your part it ought to be done; and when in any of the convulsions that come upon the world, Great Britain finds herself struggling single-handed against the gigantic powers that spread oppression and darkness—(applause, hisses, and uproar)—there ought to be such cordiality that she can turn and say to her first-born and most illustrious child, "Come!" (Hear, hear, applause, tremendous cheers, and uproar.) I will not say that England cannot again, as hitherto, single handed manage any power—(applause and uproar)—but I will say that England and America together for religion and liberty—(A Voice: "Soap, soap," uproar, and great applause)—are a match for the world. (Applause; a Voice: "They don't want any more soft soap.") Now, gentlemen and ladies—(A Voice: "Sam Slick;" and another Voice: "Ladies and gentlemen, if you please.")—when I came I was asked whether I would answer questions, and I very readily consented to do so, as I had in other places; but I will tell you it was because I expected to have the opportunity of speaking with some sort of ease and quiet. (A Voice: "So you have.") I have for an hour and a half spoken against a storm—(hear, hear)—and you yourselves are witnesses that, by the interruption, I have been obliged to strive with my voice, so that I no longer have the power to control this assembly. (Applause.) And although I am in spirit perfectly willing to answer any question, and more than glad of the chance, yet I am by this very unnecessary opposition to-night incapacitated physically from doing it. (A Voice: "Why did Lincoln delay the proclamation of slavery so long.—Another Voice: "Habeas Corpus." A piece of paper was here

F

handed up to Mr. Beecher.) I am asked a question. I will answer this one. "At the auction of sittings in your church, can the negroes bid on equal terms with the whites?" (Cries of "No, no.") Perhaps you know better than I do. (Hear, hear.) But I declare that they can. (Hear, hear, and applause.) I declare that, at no time for ten years past—without any rule passed by the trustees, and without even a request from me—no decent man or woman has ever found molestation or trouble in walking into my church and sitting where he or she pleased. (Applause.) "Are any of the office-bearers in your church negroes?" No, not to my knowledge. Such has been the practical doctrine of amalgamation in the South that it is very difficult now-a-days to tell who is a negro. (Hear, hear, and "No, no.") Whenever a majority of my people want a negro to be an officer, he will be one; and I am free to say that there are a great many men that I know, who are abundantly capable of honouring any office of trust in the gift of our church. (Applause.) But while there are none in my church there is in Columbia county a little church where a negro man, being the ablest business man, and the wealthiest man in that town, is not only a ruler and elder of the church, but also contributes about two-thirds of all the expenses of it. (Hear, hear, and a Voice : "That is the exception, not the rule.") I am answering these questions, you see, out of gratuitous mercy : I am not bound to do so. It is asked whether Pennsylvania was not carried for Mr. Lincoln on account of his advocacy of the Morrill tariff, and whether the tariff was not one of the planks of the Chicago platform, on which Mr. Lincoln was elected. I had a great deal to do with that election; but I tell you that whatever local—(Here the interruptions became so noisy, that it was found impossible to proceed. The Chairman asked how they could expect Mr. Beecher to answer questions amid such a disturbance. When order had been restored, the lecturer proceeded :)—I am not afraid to leave the treatment I have received at this meeting to the impartial judgment of every fair-playing Englishman. When I am asked questions, gentlemanly courtesy requires that I should be permitted to answer them. (A Voice from the farther end of the room shouted something about the inhabitants of Liverpool.) I know that it was in the placards requested to give Mr. Beecher a reception that should make him understand what the opinion of Liverpool was about him. ("No, no;" and "Yes, yes.") There are two sides to every question, and Mr. Beecher's opinion about the treatment of Liverpool citizens is just as much as your opinion about the treatment of Mr. Beecher. Let me say, that if you wish me to answer questions you must be still; for, if I am interrupted, that is the end of the matter. (Hear, hear, and "Bravo.") I have this to say, that I have no doubt the Morrill tariff, or that which is now called so, did exercise a great deal of influence, not alone in Pennsylvania, but in many other parts of the country; because there are many sections of our country—those especially where the manufacture of iron or wool are the predominating industries—that are yet very much in favour of protective tariffs; but the thinking men and the influential men of both parties are becoming more and more in favour of free-trade. "Can a negro ride in a public vehicle in New York with a white man?" I reply that there are times when politicians stir up the passions of the lower classes of men and the foreigners, and there are times just on the eve of an election when the prejudice against the coloured man is stirred up and excited, in which they will be disturbed in any part of the city; but taking the period of the year throughout, one year after another, there are but one or two of the city horse-railroads in which a respectable coloured man will be molested in riding through the city. It is only on one railroad that this happened, and it is one which I have in the pulpit and the press always held up to severe reproof. At the Fulton Ferry there are two lines of omnibusses, one white and the other blue. I had been accustomed to go in them indifferently; but one day I saw a little paper stuck upon one of them, saying "Coloured people not allowed to ride in this omnibus." I instantly got out. There are men who stand at the door of these two omnibus lines, urging passengers into one or the other. I am very well known to all of them, and the next day, when I came to the place, the gentleman serving asked "Won't you ride, sir?" "No," I said, "I am too much of a negro to ride in that omnibus." (Laughter.) I do not know whether this had any influence, but I do know, that after a fortnight's time I had occasion to look in, and the placard was gone. I called the attention of everyone I met to that fact, and said to them, "Don't ride in that omnibus, which violates your principles, and my principles, and common decency at the same time." I say still further, that in all New England there is not a railway where a coloured man cannot ride as freely as a white man. (Hear, hear.) In the whole city of New York, a coloured man taking a stage of railway will never be inconvenienced or suffer any discourtesy. Ladies and gentlemen, I bid you good evening.—Mr. Beecher's resuming his seat was the signal for another outburst of loud and prolonged cheers, hisses, groans, cat-calls, and every conceivable species of expression of approbation and disapprobation. Three cheers were proposed for the lecturer from the galleries, and enthusiastically given.

The Rev. C. M. BIRRELL then came forward and said it would have been very unlike the fairness of Englishmen if that assembly had not given to a distinguished stranger—(hisses)—a fair and impartial hearing; and it would have been as unlike a free American to demand of Englishmen that they should accept his opinions merely because they were his. But, since Mr. Beecher had given to them, under circumstances of great difficulty, and with marvellous courtesy and patience—(hear, hear,)—an elaborate, temperate, and most eloquent lecture, he called upon them to render him a cordial vote of thanks. (Hear, hear, and renewed hisses.) He expected that that vote would be joined in by all the representatives of the American slaveholders in that assembly, considering that they had had more instruction that night than they had apparently received during all the previous part of their lives. ("Oh, oh," cheers and laughter).

Mr. W. CROSSFIELD, in seconding the resolution, said, as an inhabitant of Liverpool, he had been ashamed at the conduct of that meeting—an assembly of gentlemen, or those who professed to be gentlemen. For himself he most cordially thanked Mr. Beecher for the very interesting lecture they had had.

The vote was carried with loud and prolonged cheering and the waving of hats.

The CHAIRMAN said he was sure Mr. Beecher would be quite satisfied with that unanimous expression of feeling, and the disturbance which had been created was not the expression of the feeling of the meeting, but the work of a few persons in the room who had come for the purpose of opposition. The Chairman then put the negative of the proposition, but the meeting was in a state of confusion. Of those who understood the proceeding there were none to be seen who stood up to negative the vote.

LONDON.—OCTOBER 20, 1863.

GREAT DEMONSTRATION AT EXETER HALL.

LAST night, under the auspices of the Emancipation Society and the London Committee of Correspondence on American Affairs, a meeting was held in Exeter Hall to hear an address from the Rev. Henry Ward Beecher. The distinction which Mr. Beecher has acquired in his own country, and the great public interest which was felt in his subject—"England and America"—left no room for doubt that his audience would only be limited by the capacity of the building. In the first instance it was proposed that only a portion of the hall should be set apart for reserved seats, and that the remaining space should be occupied with free seats; but the demand for tickets far exceeded any possible supply, and long before the day of meeting it became evident that thousands would be disappointed. It is of course quite unnecessary to say that long before the hour of meeting the great hall was densely packed by as many human beings as could find sitting or standing room in any part of the edifice, however inconvenient or perilous the position. They were both patient and good-humoured while waiting for the appearance of Mr. Beecher, who found great difficulty in forcing a way through the enormous mass of people, which, in the Strand and Exeter-street, literally beleaguered the place of meeting. On presenting himself to the audience, accompanied by many of the leading supporters of the Emancipation movement, he was welcomed by long and reiterated plaudits, which were again and again repeated, the audience rising *en masse*. The entire scene brought vividly to mind the great meeting held in the same building ten months ago, although, if possible, the enthusiasm and unanimity were still greater than on that memorable occasion. The friends of Secession had endeavoured to stir up some personal feeling against the lecturer by inflammatory placards, which covered every wall in the metropolis; but the result only exhibited their own weakness and the total absence of any popular sympathy with their cause. There was a small group of Southern sympathizers here and there, but so small as to be utterly unable to do more than give vent to a few hisses, which were always drowned by a torrent of applause. The cheers were now and then relieved by stentorian groans for the *Times*, Mr. Mason, and other unpopular organs of the press and individual Secessionists; and we may remark that this species of honour was very fairly divided between Printing-house-square and the notorious author of the Fugitive Slave Law.

The name of President Lincoln was received, as it always is in an open English audience, with a tempest of applause; and when Mr. Beecher alluded to the retention of the rams, and said that when he returned to America he should have "a different story" to tell of the state of English public opinion from that which had previously obtained credence there, the assembly testified their approbation by a demonstration which has never been surpassed and rarely equalled in the palmiest days of agitation. Dark complexions were not wanting in that vast multitude of upturned faces; and conspicuous in the body of the hall was a venerable negro, who excited some amusement by the vigour with which he acted as fugleman throughout Mr. Beecher's speech. The courage of the malcontents sensibly diminished as the proceedings advanced, and ultimately only three hands were held up against the resolution moved by Professor Newman. Every now and then the cheers of "the outsiders," who extemporised a meeting of their own, echoed through the hall, and helped to swell the plaudits of those who had been fortunate enough to obtain admission. Scarcely anyone left before the meeting was brought to a close, and we venture to say that not one of the assembled thousands will ever forget Mr. Beecher's last public address in England, or the popular enthusiasm which it evoked in his honour and in sympathy with the cause which he represented.

The chair was taken shortly after seven o'clock, by Benjamin Scott, Esq., Chamberlain of London, and the following were among the gentlemen present:—Sir Charles Fox, Professor Newman, Professor Newth, Dr. Halley, President of New College; the Rev. Dr. Hugh Allen, vicar of St. George's, Southwark; the Rev. Dr. Campbell, the Rev. Dr. Jobson, the Revs. W. M. Bunting, W. Dunkerley, L. H. Byrnes, Dr. Waddington, Newman Hall, William Brock, W. Cuthbertson, J. B. French, Geo. Wilkins, H. J. Bevis, E. Davies, Arthur Hall, Sella Martin, A. Hannay, J. C. Galloway, M.A., W. O'Neill, John Curwen, John Howard Hinton, M.A., T. Jones, James Spong, William Tyler, E. Mathews, A. Raleigh, and W. Dorling; Dr. Frederick Tomkins; Messrs. S. Lucas, George Thompson, John Cunnington, G. J. Holyoake, W. R. Spicer, W. Willans, Washington Wilks, John Gorrie, Judge Winter, of Georgia; J. M'Carthy, L. A. Chamerovzow, Dr. D'Aubigné, Passmore Edwards, John Stewart, Edmond Beales, J. R. Taylor, Hugh Williams; M. D. Conway, of Virginia; J. Jewitt, Boston; William Craft, Georgia; W. J. Haynes, John Noble, jun., James Beal, J. B. Langley, R. Moore, J. Lyndall, John Cassell; T. W. Chester, Liberia; J. Kenny; R. Hill, Bedford; John Richardson, C.C.; H. Thompson, J. A. Horner, W. T. Malleson, treasurer, and F. W. Chesson, hon. secretary of the Emancipation Society, &c. Mr. G. Thompson, who was one of the first to appear on the platform, was received with three cheers.

The CHAIRMAN said: Ladies and gentlemen, allow me to inform you that the crowd outside the building is so dense that Mr. Beecher has not been able to force his way punctually. It has been with the greatest difficulty that I and some other members of the committee have found our way here. You will, therefore, I am sure, make all allowance for Mr. Beecher if he should yet be a few minutes behind time. (Cheers.) I will proceed to address a few words pending the arrival of Mr. Beecher. Appearing before you to preside this evening, I regret to say in place of Mr. Bright, whom we had hoped to be present—(cheers)—I must inform you that it is not our object to discuss the great American struggle. There will be and there are presented to us, from day to day, abundant opportunities of discussing that momentous question. Our object to-night is to afford an opportunity to a distinguished stranger—(cheers)—to address us on that absorbing topic—a gentleman who is entitled, whatever opinions we may hold, to our profound respect. (Great cheering.) Whether we regard Henry Ward Beecher as the son of the celebrated Dr. Beecher—(hear)—or as the brother of Mrs. Beecher Stowe— (cheers)—or a stranger visiting our shores—whether we regard him as a gentleman or a Christian minister, and as the uncompromising advocate of human rights—(loud cheers)—he is entitled to our respectful and courteous attention. (Cheers.) I am quite sure that this assembly of Englishmen and English women will support me in securing for him a respectful hearing. It becomes the more incumbent upon us to do so since he states that the rapid and fragmentary reports of speeches delivered in America which were flashed across the Atlantic by the telegraph have been so brief and hurried that they have not conveyed to us his full meaning and sense. He has been very often misunderstood, and, I fear, misrepresented; and, as a stranger about to depart from our shores in a few days, he asks for this opportunity of putting himself right with the London public upon this question. You will hear him and judge of his statements, and I am sure you will accord him a fair hearing. I shall myself abstain advisedly from entering upon the subject of to-night's address. I wish merely to take this opportunity of saying how much I esteem the man personally, and because he has been the uncompromising advocate, for twenty-five years, in times of peace and before the war, of the emancipation of the enslaved and oppressed. He was one of the few thinking men who were the noble pioneers of freedom on the American continent. He was so when it was neither fashionable nor profitable to be so. He took his stand, not on the shifting sands of expediency, but on the immovable rock of principle. (Cheers.) He had put his hand to the plough, and would never turn back. Some people had allowed their ears to be stuffed with cotton—(laughter and cheers)—some were blinded by gold dust, and some had allowed the gag of expediency to be put in their mouths to quiet them. (Cheers.) But Henry Ward Beecher stood before the world of America, and for some time stood almost alone, and called things by their right names. (Cheers.) He had no mealy-mouthed expressions about peculiar institutions, patriarchal institutions, and paternal institutions—("hear, hear," and laughter)— but he called slavery by the old English name of slavery. (Loud cheers.) And he charged to the account of that crime cruelty, lust, murder, rapine, piracy. (Loud cheers.) He minced not his terms or his phrases. He looked right ahead to the course of duty which he had selected; and, regardless of the threats of man or the wrath of man, although the tar-pot was ready for him and the feathers were prepared—although the noose and the halter were ready and almost about his neck—he went straight onward to the object; and now he has converted—as every man who stands alone for the truth and right will eventually convert—a large majority of those who were originally opposed to him. (Cheers.) What the humble draper's assistant, Granville Sharpe, did in this country, Henry Ward Beecher and two or three like-minded men have done on the continent of America. When he heard Christian ministers—God save the mark!—standing in their pulpits with the Book of Truth before them, and stating that the institution of slavery was Christian, he did not mince the matter—he affirmed that it was bred in the bottomless pit. (Loud cheers.) I honour and respect him for his manliness. He is every inch a man. He is a standard by which humanity may well measure itself. (Loud cheers.) Would to God we had a hundred such men. (Cheers.) I will now call upon Mr. Beecher—(great cheering)—but allow me to say that we shall only prolong our meeting in this heated atmosphere by not affording the speakers a fair opportunity of addressing you. (Loud applause.)

Rev. HENRY WARD BEECHER then advanced to the front of the platform amidst the most enthusiastic demonstrations of applause. The whole audience stood up : hats and handkerchiefs were waved, and for some minutes the most exciting manifestations of hearty English good feeling were extended to the American advocate of freedom. As the uproarious greeting subsided, a few hisses rose up from the middle of the room, as if a body of serpents had some how or other found their way into the assembly, and were adding their prolonged tribute to the general display. Mr. Beecher then addressed the audience as follows, speaking distinctly and deliberately : Ladies and gentlemen,—The very kind introduction that I have received requires but a single word from me. I should be guilty if I could take all the credit which has been generously ascribed to me, for I am not old enough to have been a pioneer. And when I think of such names as Weld, Alvin Stewart, Geritt Smith, Joshua Levitt, William Goodell, Arthur and Lewis Tappan, William Lloyd Garrison—(loud applause)—and that most accomplished speaker of the world, Wendell Phillips—(renewed applause)—when I think of multitudes of that peculiar class of Christians called Friends—when I think of the number of men, obscure, without name or fame, who laboured in the earliest days at the foundation of this reformation—and when I remember that I came in afterwards to build on their foundation—I cannot permit in this fair country the honours to be put upon me and wrested from those men that deserve them far more than I do. (Cheers.) All I can say is this, that when I began my public life I fell into the ranks under the appropriate captains, and fought as well as I knew how in the ranks or in command. (Loud cheers.) As this is my last public address upon the American question in England, I may be permitted to glance briefly at my course here. (Hear, hear.) At Manchester I attempted to give a history of the external political movement for fifty years past, so far as it was necessary to illustrate the fact that the present American war was only an overt and warlike form of a contest between liberty and slavery that had been going on politically for half a century. (Hear, hear.) At Glasgow I undertook to show the condition of work or labour necessitated by any profitable system of slavery, demonstrating that it brought labour into contempt, affixing to it the badge of degradation, and that a struggle to extend servile labour across the American continent interests every free working man on the globe. (Cheers.) For my sincere belief is that the Southern cause is the natural enemy of free labour and the free labourer all the world over. (Loud cheers.) In Edinburgh I endeavoured to sketch how, out of separate colonies and States intensely jealous of their individual sovereignty, there grew up and was finally established a NATION, and how in that Nation of United States two distinct and antagonistic systems were developed and strove for the guidance of the national policy, which struggle at length passed and the North gained the control. Thereupon the South abandoned the Union simply and solely because the Government was in future to be administered by men who would give their whole influence to freedom. (Loud cheers.) In Liverpool I laboured, under difficulties—(laughter and cheers)—to show that slavery in the long run was as hostile to commerce and to manufactures all the world over, as it was to free interests in human society—(cheers)—that a slave nation must be a poor customer, buying the fewest and poorest goods, and the least profitable to the producers—(hear hear) —that it was the interest of every manufacturing country to promote freedom, intelligence, and wealth amongst all nations—(cheers)—that this attempt to cover the fairest portion of the earth with a slave population that buys nothing, and a degraded white population that buys next to nothing, should array against it every true political economist and every thoughtful and far-seeing manufacturer, as tending to strike at the vital want of commerce—which is not cotton, but rich customers. (Cheers.) I have endeavoured to enlist against this flagitious wickedness, and the great civil war which it has kindled, the judgment, conscience, and interests of the British people. (Cheers.) I am aware that a popular address before an excited audience more or less affected by party sympathies is not the most favourable method of doing justice to these momentous topics; and there have been some other circumstances which made it yet more difficult to present a careful or evenly balanced statement; but I shall do the best I can to leave no vestige of doubt, that slavery was the cause—the only cause—the whole cause—of this gigantic and cruel war. (Cheers.) I have tried to show that sympathy for the South, however covered by excuses or softened by sophistry, is simply sympathy with an audacious attempt to build up a slave empire pure and simple. (Hear, hear.) I have tried to show that in this contest the North were contending for the preservation of their Government and their own territory, and those popular institutions on which the well-being of the nation depended. (Hear, hear.) So far, I have spoken to the English from an English point of view. To-night I ask you to look to this struggle from an American point of view, and in its moral aspects. (Hear, hear.) That is, I wish you to take our stand-point for a little while—(cheers)—and to look at our actions and motives, not from what the enemy says, but from what we say. (Cheers.) When two men have disagreed, you seldom promote peace between them by attempting to prove that either of them is all right or either of them is all wrong. (Hear, hear.) Now there has been some disagreement of feeling between America and Great Britain. I don't want to argue the question to-night which is right and which is wrong, but if some kind neighbour will persuade two people that are at disagreement to consider each other's position and circumstances, it may not lead either to adopting the other's judgment, but it may lead them to say of each other, "I think he is honest and means well, even if he be mistaken." (Loud cheers.) You may not thus get a settlement of the *difficulty*, but you will get a settlement of the *quarrel*. (Hear, hear.) I merely ask you to put yourselves in our track for one hour, and look at the objects as we look at them—(cheers)—after that, form your judgment as you please. (Cheers.) The first and earliest form in which the conflict took place between North and South was purely moral. It was a conflict simply of opinion and of truths by argument; and by appeal to the moral sense it was sought to persuade the slaveholder to adopt some plan of emancipation. (Hear, hear.) When this seemed to the Southern sensitiveness unjust and insulting, it led many in the North to silence, especially as the South seemed to apologize for slavery rather than defend it against argument. It was said, "The evil is upon us; we cannot help it. We are sullied, but it is a misfortune rather than a fault. (Cheers.) It is not right for the North to meddle with that which is made worse by being meddled with, even by argument or appeal." That was the earlier portion of the conflict. A great many men were deceived by it. I never myself yielded to the fallacy. As a minister of the gospel preaching to sinful men, I thought it my duty not to give in to this doctrine; their sins were on them, and I thought it my duty not to soothe them, but rather to expose them. (Cheers.) The next stage of the conflict was purely political. The South was attempting to extend their slave system into the Territories, and to prevent free States from covering the continent, by bringing into the Union a slave State for every free State. It was also the design and endeavour of the South not simply to hold and employ the enormous power and influence of the Central *Executive*, but also to engraft into the whole Federal Government a slave State *policy*. They meant to fill all offices at home and abroad with men loyal to slavery—to shut up the road to political preferment against men who had aspirations for freedom, and to corrupt the young and ambitious by obliging them to swear fealty to slavery as the condition of success. I am saying what I know. I have seen the progressive corruption of men naturally noble, educated in the doctrine of liberty, who, being bribed by political offices, at last bowed the knee to Moloch. The South pursued a uniform system of bribing and corrupting ambitious men of Northern consciences. A far more dangerous part of its policy was to change the Constitution, not overtly, not by external aggression—worse, to fill the courts with Southern judges—(shame)—until, first by laws of Congress passed through Southern influence, and secondly, by the construction and adjudication of the courts, the Constitution having become more and more tied up to Southern principles, the North would have to submit to slavery, or else to oppose it by violating the law and constitution as construed by servile judges. (Hear, hear.) They were, in short, little by little, injecting the laws, constitution, and policy of the country with the poison and blood of slavery. (Cheers.) I will not let this stand on my own testimony. I am going to read the unconscious corroboration of this by Mr. Stephens, the Vice-President of the present Confederacy—one, to his credit be it said, who at one time was a most sincere and earnest opponent of Secession. It is as follows :—

This step (of Secession) once taken, can never be recalled; and all the baleful and withering consequences that must follow will rest on the convention for all coming time. When we and our posterity shall see our lovely South desolated by the demon of war, which this act of yours will inevitably invite and call forth; when our green fields of waving harvests shall be trodden down by the murderous soldiery and fiery car of war sweeping over our land; our temples of justice laid in ashes; all the horrors and desolation of war upon us ; who but this convention will be held responsible for it ? and who but him who shall have given his vote for this unwise and ill-timed measure, as I honestly think and believe, shall be held to strict account for this suicidal act by the present generation, and probably cursed and execrated by posterity for all coming time, for the wide and desolating ruin that will inevitably follow this act you now propose to perpetrate ? Pause, I entreat you, and consider for a moment what reasons you can give that will even satisfy yourselves in calmer moments—what reasons you can give to your fellow-sufferers in the calamity that it will bring upon us. What reasons can you give to the nations of the earth to justify it? They will be the calm and deliberate judges in the case; and what cause or one overt act can you name or point on which to rest the plea of justification ? *What right has the North assailed ?* What interest of the South has been invaded ? What justice has been denied? and what claim founded in justice and right has been withheld ? Can either of you to-day name one governmental act of wrong, deliberately and purposely done by the Government of Washington, of which the South has a right to complain ? I challenge the answer. While, on the other hand, let me show the facts (and believe me, gentlemen, I am not here the advocate of the North ; but I am here the friend, the firm friend and lover of the South and her institutions, and for this reason I speak thus plainly and faithfully, for your's, mine, and every other man's interest, the words of truth and soberness), of which I wish you to judge, and I will only state facts which are clear and undeniable, and which now stand as records authentic in the history of our country. When we of the South demanded the slave trade, or the importation of Africans for the cultivation of our lands, did they not yield the right for twenty years ? When we asked a three-fifths representation in Congress for our slaves was it not granted? When we asked and demanded the return of any fugitive from justice, or the recovery of those persons owing labour or allegiance, was it not incorporated in the Constitution, and again ratified and strengthened in the Fugitive Slave Law of 1850? But do you reply that in many instances they have violated this compact and have not been faithful to their engagements ? As individual and local communities they may have done so; but not by the sanction of Government; for that has always been true to Southern interests. Again, gentlemen, look at another fact, when we have asked that more territory should be added, that we might spread the institution of slavery, have they not yielded to our demands in giving us Louisiana, Florida, and Texas, out of which four States have been carved, and ample territory for four more may be added in due time if you by this unwise and impolitic act, do not destroy this hope, and perhaps, by it lose all, and have your last slave wrenched from you by stern military rule, as South America and Mexico were, or by the vindictive decree of a universal emancipation, which may reasonably be expected to follow. But, again, gentlemen, what have we to gain by this proposed change of our relation to the general Government? We have always had the control of it, and can yet, if we remain in it and are as united as we have been. We have had a majority of the Presidents chosen from the South; as well as the control and management of most of those chosen from the North. We have had sixty years of Southern Presidents to their twenty-four, thus controlling the executive department. So of the judges of the Supreme Court, we have had eighteen from the South, and but eleven from the North; although nearly four-fifths of the judicial business has arisen in the Free States, yet a majority of the court has always been from the South. This we have required so as to guard against any interpretation of the Constitution unfavourable to us. In like manner we have been equally watchful to guard our interest in the legislative branch of Government. In choosing the presiding Presidents *(pro tem.)* of the Senate, we have had twenty-four to their eleven. Speakers of the house we have had twenty-three, and they twelve. While the majority of the representatives, from their greater population, have always been from the North, yet we have so generally secured the speaker, because he, to a greater extent, shapes and controls the legislation of the country. Nor have we had less control in every other department of the general Government. Attorney-Generals we have had fourteen, while the North have had but five. Foreign ministers we have had eighty-six and they but fifty-four. While three-fourths of the business which demands diplomatic agents abroad is clearly from the Free States, from their greater commercial interests, yet we have had the principal embassies, so as to secure the world's markets for our cotton, tobacco, and sugar on the best possible terms. We have had a vast majority of the higher offices of both army and navy, while a larger proportion of the soldiers and sailors were drawn from the North. Equally so of clerks, auditors, and comptrollers filling the executive department, the records show for the last fifty years that of the three thousand thus employed, we have had more than two-thirds of the same, while we have but one-third of the white population of the Republic. Again, look at another item, and one, be assured, in which we have a great and vital interest; it is that of revenue, or means of supporting Government. From official documents we learn that a fraction over three-fourths of the revenue collected for the support of Government has uniformly been raised from the North. Pause now, while you can, gentlemen, and contemplate carefully and candidly these important items. Leaving out of view, for the present, the countless millions of dollars you must expend in a war with the North; with tens of thousands of your sons and brothers slain in battle, and offered up as sacrifices upon the altar of your ambition—and for what? we ask again. Is it for the overthrow of the American Government, established by our common ancestry, cemented and built up by their sweat and blood, and founded on the broad principles of right, justice, and humanity? And, as such, I must declare here, as I have often done before, and which has been repeated by the greatest and wisest of statesmen and patriots in this and other lands, that *it is the best and freest Government—the most equal in its rights, the most just in its decisions, the most lenient in its measures, and the most inspiring in its principles to elevate the race of men, that the sun of heaven ever shone upon.* Now, for you to attempt to overthrow such a Government as this, under which we have lived for more than three-quarters of a century—in which we have gained our wealth, our standing as a nation, our domestic safety while the elements of peril are around us, with peace and tranquillity accompanied with unbounded prosperity and rights unassailed—is the height of *madness, folly,* and *wickedness,* to which I can neither lend my sanction nor my vote.

Was there ever such an indictment unconsciously laid against any people? (Cheers.) Here Mr. Stephens, talking to people in Georgia, quite unconscious that his speech would be reported, that it would appear in the Northern press, and be read in Exeter Hall to an English audience—tells you what has been the plan and what have been the effects of Southern domination on the national policy, on the Government, and on the courts during the last fifty years. The object of Southern policy, early commenced and steadily pursued, was to control the Government and to establish a slave influence throughout North America. Now, take notice first, that the North, hating slavery, having rid itself of it at its own cost, and longing for its extinction throughout America, was unable until this war to touch slavery directly. The North could only contend against slave *policy*— not directly against slavery. Why? Because slavery was not the creature of national law, and therefore not subject to national jurisdiction, but of State law, and subject only to State jurisdiction. A direct act on the part of the North to abolish slavery would have been revolutionary. (A Voice: "We do not understand you.") You will understand me before I have done with you to-night. (Cheers.) Such an attack would have been a violation of a fundamental principle of State independence. This peculiar structure of our Government is not so unintelligible to Englishmen as you may think. It is only taking an English idea on a larger scale. We have borrowed it from you. A great many do not understand how it is that there should be State independence under a national Government. Now I am not closely acquainted with your affairs, but the Chamberlain can tell you if I am wrong, when I say, that there belong to the old city of London certain private rights that Parliament cannot meddle with. Yet there are elements in which Parliament—that is, the will of the nation—is as supreme over London as over any town or city of the realm. Now, if there are some things which London has kept for her own judgment and will, and yet others which she has given up to the national will, you have herein the principle of the American Government—(cheers)—by which certain local matters belong exclusively to the local jurisdiction, and certain general matters to the national Government. I will give you another illustration that will bring it home to you. There is not a street in London, but, as soon as a man is inside his house, he may say, his house is his castle. There is no law in the realm which can lay down to that man how many members shall compose his family—how he shall dress his children—when they shall get up and when they shall go to bed—how many meals he shall have a day, and of what those meals shall be constituted. The interior economy of the house belongs to the members of the house, yet there are many respects in which every householder is held in check by common rights. They have their own interior and domestic economy, yet they share in other things which are national and governmental. It may be very wrong to give children opium, but all the doctors in London cannot say to a man that he shall not drug his child. It is his business, and if it is wrong it cannot be interfered with. I will give you another illustration. Five men form a partnership of business. Now, that partnership represents the national Government of the United States; but it has relation only to certain great commercial interests common to them all. But each of these five men has another sphere—his family—and in that sphere the man may be a drunkard, a gambler, a lecherous and indecent man, but the firm cannot meddle with his morals. It cannot touch anything but business interests that belong to the firm. Now, our States came together on this doctrine—that each State, in respect to those rights and institutions that were local and peculiar to it, was to have undivided sovereignty over its own affairs; but that all those powers, such as taxes, wars, treaties of peace, which belong to one State, and which are common to all States, went into the general Government. The general Government never had the power—the power was never delegated to it—to meddle with the interior and domestic economy of the States, and it never could be done. You will ask what are we doing it for now. I will tell you in due time. Have I made that point plain? (Cheers.) It was only that part of slavery which escaped from the State jurisdiction, and which entered into the national sphere, which formed the subject of controversy. We could not justly touch the Constitution of the States, but only the policy of the national Government, that came out beyond the State and appeared in Congress and in the territories. (Cheers.) We are bound to abide by our fundamental law. Honour, fidelity, integrity, as well as patriotism, required us to abide by that law. The great conflict between the South and North, until this war began, was, which should control the Federal or central Government and what we call the *Territories;* that is, lands which are the property of the Union, and have not yet received *State* rights. (Cheers.) That was the conflict. It was not "Emancipation" or "No Emancipation;" Government had no business with that question. Before the war, the only thing on which politically the free people of the North and South took their respective sides was, "Shall the *National* policy be free or slave?" And I call you to witness that forbearance, though not a showy virtue—fidelity, though not a shining quality—are fundamental to manly integrity. (Cheers.) During a period of eighty years, the North, whose wrongs I have just read out to you, not from her own lips, but from the lips of her enemy, has stood faithfully to her word. With scrupulous honour she has respected legal rights, even when they were merely civil and not moral rights. The fidelity of the North to the great doctrine of State rights, which was born of her—her forbearance under wrong, insult, and provocation—her conscientious and honourable refusal to meddle with the evil which she hated, and which she saw to be aiming at the life of Government, and at her own life—her determination to hold fast pact and constitution, and to gain her victories by giving the people a new *National* policy—will yet be deemed worthy of something better than a contemptuous sneer, or the allegation of an "enormous national vanity." (Cheers.) The Northern forbearance is one of those themes of which we may be justly proud—("Oh," and cheers)—a product of virtue, a fruit of liberty, an inspiration of that Christian faith, which is the mother at once of truth and of liberty. (Cheers.) I am proud to think that there is such a record of national fidelity as that which the North has written for herself by the pen of her worst enemies. Now that is the reason why the North did not at first go to war to enforce emancipation. She went to war to save the National institutions;—(cheers)—to save the Territories; to sustain those laws, which would first circumscribe, then suffocate, and finally destroy slavery. (Cheers.) That is the reason why that most true, honest, just, and conscientious magistrate, Mr. Lincoln—(The announcement of Mr. Lincoln's name was received with loud and continued cheering. The whole audience rose and cheered for some time, and it was a few minutes before Mr. Beecher could proceed.) From having spoken much at tumultuous assemblies I had at times a fear that when I came here this evening my voice would fail from too much speaking. But that fear is now changed to one that *your* voices will fail from too much cheering. (Laughter.) How then did the North pass from a conflict with the South and a slave policy, to a direct attack upon the institutions of slavery itself? Because, according to the foreshadowing of that wisest man of the South, Mr. Stephens, they beleaguered the national Government and the national life with the institution of slavery—obliged a sworn President, who was put under oath not to invade that institution—to take his choice between the safety and life of the Government itself, or the slavery by which it was beleaguered. (Cheers.) If any man lays an obstruction on the street, and blocks up the street, it is not the fault of the people if they walk over it. As the fundamental right of individual self-defence cannot be withdrawn without immorality—so the first element of national life is to defend life. As no man attacked on the highway violates law, but obeys the law of self-defence—a law inside of the laws—by knocking down his assailant; so, when a nation is assaulted, it is a right and duty, in the exercise of self-defence, to destroy the enemy, by which otherwise it will be destroyed. (Hear.) As long as the South allowed it to be a moral and political conflict of policy, we were content to meet the issue as one of policy. But when they threw down the gauntlet of war, and said that by it slavery was to be adjudicated, we could do nothing else than take up the challenge. (Loud cheers.) The police have no right to enter your house as long as you keep within the law, but when you defy the laws and endanger the peace and safety of the neighbourhood they have a right to enter. So in constitutional Governments; it has no power to touch slavery while slavery remains a State institution. But when it lifts itself up out of its State humility and becomes banded to attack the nation, it becomes a national enemy, and has no longer exemption. (Cheers.) But it is said, "The President issued his proclamation after all for political effect, not for humanity." (Cries of "Hear, hear.") Of course the right of issuing a proclamation of emancipation was political, but the disposition to do it was personal. (Loud cheers.) Mr. Lincoln is an officer of the State, and in the Presidential chair has no more right than your judge on the bench to follow his private feelings. (Applause.) He is bound to ask "What is the law?"—not "What is my sympathy?" (Hear, hear.) And when a judge sees that a rigid execution or interpretation of the law goes along with primitive justice, with humanity, and with pity, he is all the more glad because his private feelings go with his public office. (Cheers.) Perhaps in the next house to a kind and benevolent surgeon is a boy who fills the night with groans, because he has a cancerous and diseased leg. The surgeon would fain go in and amputate that limb and save that life; but he is not called in, and therefore he has no business to go in, though he ever so much wish it. (Hear, hear.) But at last the father says to him, "In the name of God, come in and save my child;" and he goes in *professionally* and cuts off his leg and saves his life, to the infinite disgust of a neighbour over the way, that says, "Oh, he would not go in from *neighbourly* feeling and cut his leg off." (Loud applause.) I should like to know how any man has a right to cut your leg or mine off except professionally — (laughter and cheers)—and so a man must often wait for official leave to perform the noblest offices of justice and humanity. Here then is the great stone of stumbling. At first the President could not touch slavery, because in time of peace it was a legal institution. How then can he do it now? Because in time of war it has stept beyond its former sphere, and is no longer a local institution, but a national and public enemy. (Applause.) Now I promised to make that clear; have I done it? ("Hear, hear,". and applause.) It is said, "Why not let the South go?" ("Hear, hear," and cheers.) "Since they won't be at peace with you, why do you not let them separate from you?" *Because they would be still less peaceable when separated.* (Hear, hear.) Oh, if the Southerners only would go! (Laughter.) They are determined to stay—that is the trouble. (Hear, hear.) We would furnish free passage to all of them if they would go. (Laughter.) But we say, "The land is ours." (Cheers) Let them go, and leave to the nation its land, and they will have our unanimous consent. (Renewed cheers.) But I wish to discuss this more carefully. It is the very marrow of the matter. I ask you to stand in our place for a little time, and see this question as we see it, afterwards make up your judgment. (Hear, hear.) And first, this war began by the act of the South—firing at the old flag that had covered both sections with glory and protection. (Applause.) The attack made upon us was under circumstances which inflicted immediate severe humiliation and threatened us with final subjugation. The Southerners held all the keys of the country. They had robbed our arsenals. They had made our treasury bankrupt. They had possession of the most important offices in the army and navy. They had the vantage of having long anticipated and prepared for the conflict. (Hear, hear.) We knew not whom to trust. One man failed, and another man failed. Men, pensioned by the Government, lived on the salary of the Government only to have better opportunity to stab and betray it. There was not merely one Judas, there were a thousand in our country. ("Hear, hear," and hisses.) And for the North to have lain down like a spaniel—to have given up the land that every child in America is taught, as every child in Britain is taught, to regard as his sacred right and his trust—to have given up the mouths of our own rivers and our mountain citadel without a blow, would have marked the North in all future history as craven and mean. (Loud cheers and some hisses.) Secondly, the honour and safety of that grand experiment, self-government by free institutions, demanded that so flagitious a violation of the first principles of legality should not carry off impunity and reward, thereafter enabling the minority in every party conflict to turn and say to the majority, "If you don't give us our way we will make war." Oh, Englishmen, would you let a minority dictate in such a way to you? (Loud cries of "No, no, never!" and cheers.) Three thousand miles off don't make any difference, then? ("No. no.",

The principle thus introduced would literally have no end—would carry the nation back to its original elements of isolated States. Nor is there any reason why it should stop with States. If every treaty may be overthrown by which States have been settled into a Nation, what form of political union may not on like grounds be severed? There is the same force in the doctrine of Secession in the application to counties as in the application to States, and if it be right for a State or a county to secede, it is equally right for a town and a city. (Cheers.) This doctrine of Secession is a huge revolving millstone that grinds the national life to powder. (Cheers.) It is anarchy in velvet, and national destruction clothed in soft phrases and periphrastic expressions. (Cheers.) But we have fought with that devil "Slavery," and understand him better than you do. (Loud cheers.) No people with patriotism and honour will give up territory without a struggle for it. (Cheers.) Would you give it up? (Loud cries of "No.") It is said that the States are owners of their territory! It is theirs to use, not theirs to run away with. We have equal right with them to enter it. Let me inform you when those States first sat in convention to form a Union, a resolution was introduced by the delegates from South Carolina and Virginia, "That we now proceed to form a *National* Government." The delegate from Connecticut objected. The New Englanders were State-right men, and the South, in the first instance, seemed altogether for a National Government. Connecticut objected, and a debate took place whether it should be a Constitution for a mere Confederacy of States, or for a nation formed out of those States. (A Voice: "When was that?") It was in the Convention of 1787. He wants to help me. (Laughter.) I like such interruptions. I am here a friend amongst friends. (Cheers.) Nothing will please me better than any question asked in courtesy and in earnest to elucidate this subject. I am not afraid of being interrupted by questions which are to the point. (Cheers.) At this convention the resolution of the New England delegates that they should form a Confederacy instead of a Nation was voted down, and never came up again. (Cheers.) The first draft of the preamble contained these words, "We, the people of the United States, for the purpose of forming a Nation;" but as there was a good deal of feeling amongst the North and South on the subject, when the draft came to the committee for revision, and they had simply to put in the proper phraseology, they put it "for the purpose of forming a Union." But when the question whether the States were to hold their autocracy came up in South Carolina—which was called the Carolina heresy—it was put down, and never lifted its head up again until this Secession, when it was galvanised to justify that which has no other pretence to justice. (Cheers.) I would like to ask those English gentlemen who hold that it is right for a State to secede when it pleases, how they would like it, if the county of Kent would try the experiment. (Hear, hear.) The men who cry out for Secession of the Southern States in America would say, "Kent seceding? Ah, circumstances alter cases." (Cheers and laughter.) The Mississippi, which is our Southern door and hall to come in and to go out, runs right through the territory which they tried to rend from us. The South magnanimously offered to let us use it; but what would you say if, on going home, you found a squad of gipsies seated in your hall, who refused to be ejected, saying, "But look here, we will let you go in and out on equitable and easy terms." (Cheers and laughter.) But there was another question involved—the question of national honour. If you take up and look at the map that delineates the mountainous features of that continent, you will find the peculiar structure of the Alleghany ridge, beginning in New Hampshire, running across the New England States, through Pennsylvania and West Virginia, stopping in the Northern part of Georgia. (Hear, hear.) Now, all the world over, men that live in mountainous regions have been men for liberty—(cheers)—and from the first hour to this hour the majority of the population of Western Virginia, which is in this mountainous region, the majority of the population of Eastern Tennessee, of Western Carolina, and of North Georgia, have been true to the Union, and were urgent not to go out. They called to the National Government, "We claim that, in fulfilment of the compact of the constitution, you defend our rights, and retain us in the Union." (Cheers.) We would not suffer a line of fire to be established one thousand five hundred miles along our Southern border out of which, in a coming hour, there might shoot out wars and disturbances, with such a people as the South, that never kept faith in the Union, and would never keep faith out of it. They have disturbed the land as old Ahab of accursed memory did— (cheers and hisses)—and when Elijah found this Ahab in the way, Ahab said, "It is Elijah that has disturbed Israel." (A laugh.) Now we know the nature of this people. We know that if we entered into a truce with them they would renew their plots and violences, and take possession of the continent in the name of THE DEVIL AND SLAVERY. (Cheers.) One more reason why we will not let this people go is because we do not want to become a military people. A great many say America is becoming too strong; she is dangerous to the peace of the world. But if you permit or favour this division, the South becomes a military nation, and the North is compelled to become a military nation. Along a line of 1,500 miles she must have forts and men to garrison them. These 250,000 soldiers will constitute the national standing army of the North. Now any nation that has a large standing army is in great danger of losing its liberties. ("No, no.") Before this war the legal size of the national army was 25,000. That was all; the actual number was 18,000, and those were all the soldiers we wanted. The *Tribune* and other papers repeatedly said that these men were useless in our nation. But if the country were divided, then we should have two great military nations taking its place, and instead of a paltry 18,000 soldiers, there would be 250,000 on one side and 100,000 or 200,000 on the other. And if America, by this ill-advised disruption, is forced to have a standing army, like a boy with a knife she will always want to whittle with it. (Laughter and cheers.) It is the interest, then, of the world, that the nation should be united, and that it should be under the control of that part of America that has always been for peace—(cheers, and cries of "No, no")—that it should be wrested from the control and policy of that part of the nation that has always been for more territory, for fillibustering, for insulting foreign nations. (Cheers.) But that is not all. The religious-minded among our people feel that in the territory committed to us there is a high and solemn trust—a national trust. We are taught that in some sense the world itself is a field, and every Christian nation acknowledges a certain responsibility for the moral condition of the globe. But how much nearer does it come when it is one's own country! And the Church of America is coming to feel more and more that God gave us this country, not merely for material aggrandisement, but for a glorious triumph of the Church of Christ. (Cheers.) Therefore we undertook to rid the territory of slavery. Since slavery has divested itself of its municipal protection, and has become a declared public enemy, it is our duty to strike down the slavery which would blight this far Western territory. When I stand and look out upon that immense territory as a man, as a citizen, as a Christian minister, I feel myself asked, "Will you permit that vast country to be over-clouded by this curse? Will you permit the cries of bondmen to issue from that fair territory, and do nothing for their liberty?" What are we doing? Sending our ships round the globe, carrying missionaries to the Sandwich Islands, to the islands of the Pacific, to Asia, to all Africa. And yet, when this work of redeeming our continent from the heathendom of slavery lies before us, there are men who counsel us to give it up to the devil, and not try to do anything with it.—Ah! independent of pounds and pence, independent of national honour, independent of all merely material considerations, there is pressing on every conscientious Northerner's mind this highest of all considerations—our duty to God to save that continent from the blast and blight of slavery. (Cheers.) Yet how many are there who up, down, and over all England are saying, "Let slavery go—let slavery go?" It is recorded, I think, in the biography of one of the most noble of your own countrymen, Sir T. Fowell Buxton—(cheers)—that on one occasion a huge favourite dog was seized with hydrophobia. With wonderful courage he seized the creature by the neck and collar, and against the animal's mightiest efforts, dashing hither and thither against wall and fence, held him until help could be got. If there had been Englishmen there of the stripe of the *Times*, they would have said to Fowell Buxton, "Let him go;" but is there one here who does not feel the moral nobleness of that man, who rather than let the mad animal go down the street biting children and women and men, risked his life and prevented the dog from doing evil? Shall we allow that hell hound of slavery, mad, mad as it is, to go biting millions in the future? (Cheers.) We will peril life and limb and all we have first. These truths are not exaggerated—they are diminished rather than magnified in my statement; and you cannot tell how powerfully they are influencing us unless you were standing in our midst in America; you cannot understand how firm that national feeling is which God has bred in the North on this subject. It is deeper than the sea; it is firmer than the hills; it is serene as the sky over our head, where God dwells. (Cheers.) But it is said, "What a ruthless business this war of extermination is?" I have heard it stated that a fellow from America, purporting to be a minister of the gospel of peace, had come over to England, and that that fellow had said he was in favour of a war of extermination. Well, if he said so he will stick to it;—(cheers)—but not in the way in which enemies put these words. Listen to the way in which I put them, for if I am to bear the responsibility it is only fair that I should state them in my own way. We believe that the war is a test of our institutions; that it is a life-and-death struggle between the two principles of liberty and slavery —cheers—that it is the cause of the common people all the world over. (Renewed cheers.) We believe that every struggling nationality on the globe will be stronger if we conquer this odious oligarchy of slavery, and that every oppressed people in the world will be weaker if we fail. (Cheers.) The sober American regards the war as part of that awful yet glorious struggle which has been going on for hundreds of years in every nation between right and wrong, between virtue and vice, between liberty and despotism, between freedom and bondage. It carries with it the whole future condition of our vast continent—its laws, its policy, its fate. And standing in view of these tremendous realities we have consecrated all that we have—our children, our wealth, our national strength —and we lay them all on the altar and say "It is better that they should all perish than that the North should falter and betray this trust of God, this hope of the oppressed, this Western civilisation." (Cheers.) If we say this of ourselves, shall we say less of the slaveholders? If we are willing to do these things, shall we say "Stop the war for their sakes?" If we say this of ourselves, shall we have more pity for the rebellious, for slavery seeking to blacken a continent with its awful evil, desecrating the social phrase "National Independence" by seeking only an independence that shall enable them to treat four millions of human beings as *chattels?* (Cheers.) Shall we be tenderer over them than over ourselves? Standing by my cradle, standing by my hearth, standing by the altar of the church, standing by all the places that mark the name and memory of heroic men, who poured out their blood and lives for principle, I declare that in ten or twenty years of war we will sacrifice everything we have for principle. (Cheers.) If the love of popular liberty is dead in Great Britain you will not understand us; but if the love of liberty lives as it once lived, and has worthy successors of those renowned men that were our ancestors as much as yours, and whose example and principles we inherit as so much seed corn in a new and fertile land—then you will understand our firm, invincible determination—to fight this war through at all hazards and at every cost. (Immense cheering, accompanied with a few hisses.) I am obliged for this little diversion; it rests me. Against this statement of facts and principles no public man and no party could stand up for one moment in England if it were permitted to rest upon its own merits. It is therefore sought to darken the light of these truths and to falsify facts. I will not mention names, but I will say this, that there have been important organs in Great Britain that have deliberately and knowingly spoken what is not the truth. (Applause, and loud cries of "*The Times!*" "Three groans for the *Times!*") It is declared that the North has no sincerity. It is declared that the North treats the blacks worse than the South does. (Hear, hear.) A monstrous lie from beginning to end. It is declared that emancipation is a mere political trick—not a moral sentiment. It is declared that this is the cruel unphilanthropic squabble of men gone mad with national vanity. (Cheers and hisses.) Oh, what a pity that a man should "fall nine times the space that measures day and night" to make an apostasy which dishonours his closing days, and to wipe out the testimony for liberty that he gave in his youth! But even if all this monstrous lie about the North—this needless slander—were true, still it would not alter the fact that Northern success will carry liberty—Southern success, slavery. (Cheers.) For when society dashes against society, the results are not what the *individual* motives of the members of society would make them—the results are what the *institutions* of society make them. When your army stood at Waterloo, they did not know what were the vast moral consequences that depended on that battle. It was not what the individual soldiers meant nor thought, but what the British empire— the national life behind, and the genius of that renowned kingdom which sent that army to victory—meant and thought. (Hear, hear.) And even if the President were false—if every Northern man were a juggling hypocrite—that does not change the Constitution; and it does not change the fact that if the North prevails, she carries Northern ideas and Northern institutions with her. (Cheers.) But I hear a loud protest against war. (Hear, hear.) Ladies and gentlemen, Mr. Chairman,—there is a small band in our country and in yours—I wish their number were quadrupled—who have borne a solemn and painful testimony against all wars, under all circumstances; and although I differ with them on the subject of defensive warfare, yet when men that rebuked their own land, and all lands, now rebuke us, though I cannot accept their judgment, I bow with profound respect to their consistency. ("Hear, hear," and cheers.) But excepting them, I regard this British horror of the American war as something wonderful. (Renewed cheers and laughter.) Why, it is a phenomenon in itself! On what shore has not the prow of your ships dashed? (Hear, hear.) What land is there with a name and a people, where your banner has not led your soldiers? (Hear, hear.) And when the great resurrection réveille shall sound, it will muster British soldiers from every clime and people under the whole heaven. (Cheers.) Ah! but it is said this is a war against your own blood. (Hear, hear.) How long is it since you poured soldiers into Canada, and let all your yards work night and day to avenge the taking of two men out of the *Trent*? (Loud applause.) Old England shocked at a war of principle! She gained her glories in such wars. (Cheers.) Old England ashamed of a war of principle! Her national ensign symbolises her history—the cross in a field of blood. (Cheers.) And will you tell us—who inherit your blood, your ideas, and your high spirits—(cheers)—that we must not fight? (Cheers.) The child must heed the parents, until the parents get old and tell the child not to do the thing that in early life they whipped him for not doing. And then the child says, father and mother are getting too old; they had better be taken away from their present home and come to live with us. (Cheers and hisses.) Perhaps you think that the old island will do a little longer. (Hisses.) Perhaps you think there is coal enough. Perhaps you think the stock is not quite run out yet; but whenever England comes to that state that she does not go to war for principle, she had better emigrate and we will give her room. (Laughter.) I have been very much perplexed what to think about the attitude of Great Britain in respect to the South. I must, I suppose, look to the opinion of the majority of the English people. I don't believe in the *Times*. (Groans for the *Times;* groans for the *Telegraph*.) You cut my poor sentence in two, and all the blood runs out of it. (Laughter.) I was just going to say that like most of you I don't believe in the *Times*, but I always read it. (Laughter.) Every Englishman tells me that the *Times* is no exponent of English opinion, and yet I have taken notice that when they talk of men, somehow or other their last argument is the last thing that was in the *Times*. (Laughter.) I think it was the *Times* or *Post* that said, that America was sore, because she had not the moral sympathy of Great Britain, and that the moral sympathy of Great Britain had gone for the South. ("No, no.") Well, let me tell you, that those who are represented in the newspapers as favourable to the South are like men who have arrows and bows strong enough to send the shafts 3,000 miles; and those who feel sympathy for the North are like men who have shafts, but have no bows that could shoot them far enough. (Hear.) The English sentiment that has made itself felt on our shores is the part that slandered the North and took part with the South; and if you think we are unduly sensitive, you must take into account that the part of English sentiment carried over is the part that gives its aid to slavery and against liberty. (Hear, hear.) I shall have a different story to tell when I get back. (The assembly rose, and for a few moments hats and handkerchiefs were waved enthusiastically amidst loud cheering. A Voice : "What about the Russians?" Hear, hear.) A gentleman asks me to say a word about the Russians in New York harbour. As this is a little private confidential meeting—(laughter)—I will tell you the fact about them. (Laughter.) The fact is this—it is a little piece of coquetry. (Laughter.) Don't you know that when a woman thinks her suitor is not quite attentive enough, she takes another beau, and flirts with him in the face of the old one? (Laughter.) New York is flirting with Russia, but she has got her eye on England. (Cheers.) Well I hear men say this is a piece of national folly that is not becoming on the part of people reputed wise, and in such solemn and important circumstances. It is said that when Russia is now engaged in suppressing the liberty of Poland it is an indecent thing for America to flirt with her. I think so too. (Loud cheers.) Now you know what we felt when you were flirting with Mr. Mason at your Lord Mayor's banquet. (Cheers.) Ladies and gentlemen, it did not do us any hurt to have you Englishmen tell us our faults I hope it don't do you Britishers any hurt to have us tell you some of yours. (A laugh.) Let me tell you my honest sentiments. England, because she is a Christian nation, because she has the guardianship of the dearest principles of civil and religious liberty, ought to be friendly with every nation and with every tongue. But when England looks out for an ally she ought to seek for her own blood, her own language, her own children. (Cheers.) And I stand here to declare that America is the proper and natural ally of Great Britain. (Cheers.) I declare that all sorts of alliances with Continental nations as against America monstrous, and that all flirtations of America with pandoured and whiskered foreigners are monstrous, and that in the great conflicts of the future, when civilization is to be extended, when commerce is to be free round the globe, and to carry with it religion and civilization, then two flags should be flying from every man-of-war and every ship, and they should be the flag with the cross of St. George and the flag with the stars of promise and of hope. (Cheers.) Now, ladies and gentlemen, when anybody tells you that Mr. Beecher is in favour of war you may ask, "In what way is he in favour of war?" And if any man says he seeks to sow discord between father and son and mother and daughter you will be able to say, "Show us how he is sowing discord." If I had anything grievous to say of England I would sooner say it before her face than behind her back. I would denounce Englishmen, if they were maintainers of the monstrous policy of the South. However, since I have come over to this country you have told me the truth, and I shall be able to bear back an assurance to our people of the enthusiasm you feel for the cause of the North. And then there is the very significant act of your Government — the seizure of the rams in Liverpool. (Loud cheers.) Then there are the weighty words spoken by Lord Russell at Glasgow, and the words spoken by the Attorney-General. (Cheers.) These acts and declarations of policy, coupled with all that I have seen, and the feeling of enthusiasm of this English people, will warm the heart of the Americans in the North. If we are one in civilization, one in religion, one substantially in faith, let us be one in national policy, one in every enterprize for the furtherance of the gospel and for the happiness of mankind. (Cheers.) I thank you for your long patience with me. ("Go on!") Ah! when I was a boy they used to tell me never to eat enough, but always to get up being yet a little hungry. I would rather you go away wishing I had spoken longer than go away saying, "What a tedious fellow he was!" (A laugh.) And therefore if you will not permit me to close and go, I beg you to recollect that this is the fifth speech of more than two hours' length that I have spoken, on some occasions *under difficulties*, within seven or eight days, and I am so exhausted that I ask you to permit me to stop. (Great cheering.)

Professor NEWMAN then rose and moved the following resolution: "Resolved,—That this meeting presents its most cordial thanks to the Rev. Henry Ward Beecher for the admirable address which he has delivered this evening, and expresses its hearty sympathy with his reprobation of the slaveholders' rebellion, his vindication of the rights of a free Government, and his aspirations for peace and friendship between the English people and their American brethren; and as this meeting recognises in Mr. Beecher one of the early pioneers of negro emancipation, as well as one of the most eloquent and successful of the champions of that great cause, it rejoices in this opportunity of congratulating him on the triumph with which the labours of himself and his associates have been crowned in the anti-slavery policy of President Lincoln and his cabinet." (Cheers.) He said that in the present state of this controversy it was necessary that the English people should see whether their sentiments on slavery were still the same. The people he remembered in his boyhood were in great majority anti-slavery; and it was but recently that half a million British ladies of all classes sent addresses to the women of America deploring this terrible curse. America wanted to see whether they were changed since then. It was but lately that Lord Brougham publicly insulted the American ambassador, Mr. Dallas, from his *excessive* zeal against the Southern domestic institution: the wonderful contrast of that noble lord's recent conduct led many people, and pre-eminently their Northern brethren, to suppose that there had been a great change among them. The writings of such men as Mr. Carlyle, the articles in the *Times* and of a large portion of the metropolitan press, had tended to induce the same feeling; but it was for them to show that they still adhered to their old anti-slavery views. The only way to do that was never to read those papers; or at any rate never to pay for reading them. (Cheers.)

Rev. NEWMAN HALL seconded the resolution. He said: Last evening I was visited by a fugitive slave. Her intelligent countenance, her modest demeanour, her clear, calm, refined voice at once interested me. I soon learnt her history. Her owner, as I at once guessed, was both her father and her master. (Shame.) While she was yet a child she so felt the cruelties of slavery that she escaped. She was pursued, tracked by bloodhounds, brought back, and subjected to the fearful torments which are generally inflicted upon a captured slave. She was made to marry early, and became a mother. Then she was employed as wet nurse to her father's children—that is, she suckled her own brothers and sisters. (Sensation.) But the grief that she felt most was the selling of her own little girl at the age of ten years. Then, as child after child was born, she wished that child after child might die rather than endure the cruelties which she had suffered. With all the tender instincts of a mother she yet rejoiced to see her babe in the cradle of death. She had been taught to believe at first that her owner was her God, and for a time she did believe that her master was God Almighty. But when she afterwards learned that there was a God in heaven she looked to Him for help, and resolved at any risk to get away. She fled to the woods, and was soon pursued, and her master was so near her at one time that she heard him, when hiding in the hollow of a tree, saying that if he caught her she would never put a step on the ground again. "Surely," I said, "he would not have maimed you?" "No," she said, he would have tarred, feathered, and burnt me alive"—a fate which many a captured fugitive has undergone as an example to others. For ten days she wandered in the woods, feeding, or rather starving, upon roots and leaves, till she was found under a hedge, exhausted, by a good Samaritan, a minister of the Gospel, who assisted her, and got her shipped in a vessel that was going to New York, and thence to Calcutta, from whence she has come to England. On her right ankle there is the mark of the red-hot branding-iron put there by her father, and on her left shoulder is the mark of the red-hot branding-iron put there also by her father! (Shame.) On her wrists you will see the scars made by the links of the chains by which she was bound by her father, and where the iron gnawed into her flesh! (Sensation.) She bears the mark of a terrible blow struck by her father with a heavy iron on her side, which has made her crooked and incapacitated her for hard work. It is for the purpose of maintaining and extending the liberty to exercise such abominations as these over four millions of their fellow-creatures that the Southerners are in arms. (Cheers.) It is for the purpose of maintaining a Government and the carrying out of laws which will put a stop to these abominations—it is now actually and avowedly, whatever it may have once been, for the purpose of sweeping the American continent of such atrocities as these—that the North is fighting. (Cheers.) Can there be a moment's hesitation on which side—if there is to be a quarrel—the sympathies of Christian and free England shall be placed? (Cries of "No.") There may be and there are differences of political opinions among us, but there is no difference worth mentioning with reference to the abomination of the slave system. There are many of our countrymen—I would have Mr. Beecher take note of it—and there may be some in this meeting, who think that it would have been as well that the South should have been let go at first, or that the war having commenced and gone on so long it should now cease. I give them credit for being as ardent haters of slavery as I am. (Hear, hear.) There are on the other hand those who consider that if the war were now to be brought to a premature close the cause of emancipation would be lost, and that more bloodshed and war would ensue than if now the battle were fought out. (Hear, hear.) And if I give those other gentlemen credit for being haters of slavery, I demand that on our part we shall have credit for being haters of war. (Cheers.) But whatever differences of political opinion there may be amongst us, there is no difference worthy of mentioning with reference to our abhorrence of the system of slavery; there is no difference of opinion in this hall as to the honour we would pay to one of the noblest and boldest champions of freedom in the world. (Loud applause.) And though we are not bound by our principles to agree with every word and sentiment uttered to-night, we do all agree in heartily thanking the lecturer for his eloquent oration and the assistance he has thus given us to understand this great question. (Renewed applause.) We may also say that we agree in wishing him hearty farewell as a true friend to Great Britain. (Hear, hear.) We may have misunderstood America—we shall henceforth understand her better. Mr. Beecher may have misunderstood us—he will understand us better. He is going back to his country to bear this testimony, that whatever difference of political opinions there may be here, the heart of Old England beats true to freedom—that in spite of caricatures and leading articles, the heart of Great Britain beats true to America. He will go back to his own country to do there what we pledge ourselves to do here—everything that will promote harmony between the two great nations. (Loud applause.) He will go home to do what we pledge ourselves to do—discourage every word and act calculated to excite international irritation and discord. He will go to teach his countrymen, as we teach ours, that the true alliances for the free to make are with free peoples, and not with despotic emperors or czars. (Renewed cheering.) We will both of us—they on that side and we on this—do all we can to promote true and brotherly love between these two great peoples—do all we can to discourage every act or word that may tend to beget disunion between two nations that are, as we have heard, one in blood, one in speech, one in literature, one in freedom, one in faith—two nations over whose disunion I could fancy hell from beneath would be moved with exultation, while all the tyrannies on the earth would clap their hands—(loud and prolonged cheering)—two nations over whose indissoluble alliance the heaven-born spirits of freedom, civilisation, and religion will sing rapturous anthems of praise to God, beckoning us onwards, as sworn brothers in the van of human progress, to share together the toil and to reap together the divine honour of the final victory of truth, righteousness, and love. (Immense applause.)

G. THOMPSON, Esq.: Mr. Chairman, ladies, and gentlemen,—I promise you that my words shall be exceedingly few. Two "new men" have set you and me the example of brevity, and I an old man, will not violate the example they have furnished. I may, however, be permitted to say that it is with more than ordinary interest I attend such a meeting as this, when I recollect that more than nine-and-twenty years ago I was labouring with a handful of faithful men and women in the city of Boston, in the State of Massachusetts, amid much obloquy and frequent danger, in disseminating those very truths which are now convulsing and converting America—regenerating and establishing America—and which will through many future ages, and I trust centuries, cement together the several parts of America, and in no long period from this moment exhibit to the world a continent in which there neither domineers a tyrant nor crawls a slave. (Loud cheers.) I can, from the study and observation of thirty years, during which I have paid two visits to America, and held familiar intercourse with many of the wisest—certainly of the best—in that country, and have enjoyed uninterrupted intercourse with them by correspondence and the reception of newspapers through the whole time,—I can bear my humble testimony to the truth of all that, in substance at least, Mr. Beecher has said tonight. (Hear, hear.) Let Mr. Beecher know that the heart of England would have beaten in all its pulses but for—whatever may have been the motives—the perversities of the truth which have been steadily kept before the public. Let Mr. Beecher know that the men throughout this country who have manifested a decided leaning towards the South are men who belong to two classes, and two classes only—either the unteachable, and therefore the ignorant, or the informed, and therefore the wilful. (Cheers.) I have heard in this meeting occasional cries of "No." Now I have had an opportunity, in almost every part of

England, of taking the amount of information possessed by those who at public meetings like this shout, "No, no." If the provincial papers had not to a great extent followed the example of some members of the London press, Mr. Beecher need not have come to this country to know what the opinions of the honest and uncorrupted millions of Englishmen on this subject have ever been. (Cheers.) Had the North been disposed to pay the price which the South has paid, the venal pens that have slandered the North would have been as ready to magnify and exalt the North. (Hear, hear.) It comes within my knowledge that in the city of Manchester, where there is a feeble imitator of a great public instructor of this metropolis—(A Voice : The *Manchester Guardian*)—in that city many public meetings have been held, in all of which, by immense majorities, and frequently with perfect unanimity, resolutions have been passed in favour of the North, and approving and supporting the anti-slavery policy of President Lincoln, and in all the great surrounding towns similar meetings have been held and resolutions passed, and yet that newspaper has given no publicity whatever to the occurrence of such meetings—(shame)—while it has blazoned forth every little and insignificant meeting held by little knots of Secessionists, whose names until recently we could not by all diligence obtain. (Hear, hear.) Let Mr. Beecher see that while this hall has been crowded, and while thousands have been gathered in the hall below, and in the Strand and neighbouring streets, and while in all the various districts of London and its suburbs there have been multitudinous meetings, always with the same results, and almost unanimous in their support of the North, only two meetings have been held in London—or, at least, meetings only in two places—in support of the South : one, a meeting called to hear a lecture from some redoubtable Colonel Fuller, who volunteered to tell us all about the question, and the other a meeting held up a pair of stairs in Devonshire-street, Portland-place. (Laughter and cheers.) And yet the *Times* and the *Manchester Guardian* ignore the occurrence of meetings like this ! But what for ? It serves their masters for the time ; it pleases their patrons for the time ; and it manages the market for the time. But it will come to pass on this question, as it came to pass with regard to other questions discussed on this platform, that the "brayings" of Exeter Hall will become the utterance of the feelings of the English people. (Cheers.) You are asked to commend the address of Mr. Beecher because in it he has rightly reprobated the slaveholders' rebellion. (Hear, hear.) There are a few Copperheads in this assembly. (Laughter.) I don't know whether you all are aware what they are, and Mr. Beecher could tell you better than I can. South Carolina is called the Palmetto State, but besides having the palmetto for its ensign it has also the rattlesnake. (Hear, hear,) The rattlesnake loses its skin every year and gets a new one—and I hope that South Carolina, will also lose its skin and get a new one—but while the process is going on the rattlesnake becomes blind, and the copperhead snake brings it the food it requires. Therefore the people in the North who sympathise with the South have got the name of Copperheads. (Laughter.) Now if, on leaving this hall, you should hear any gentleman finding fault with Mr. Beecher, I do not say call him a Copperhead—(laughter)—but you may at any rate suspect that he is very nearly one. (Great laughter.) Mr. Beecher has said that this is a slaveholders' rebellion. Slaveholders conceived it, and developed, and formed all that is vital and influential in the Southern Confederacy. Their President is a slaveholder, and if not he was one until the advance of the Federal troops set his slaves at liberty. (Hear, hear.) The simple object of the South is to raise an empire by the subjugation of a weaker race. But I believe that the South will not succeed in her criminal designs, and that notwithstanding temporary checks and reverses, the Federals, who have been compelled to draw the sword, will in the end achieve the victory. (Cheers.) And I earnestly pray that when the smoke of battle shall have passed away, and the tears have been wiped from the eye of every mourner, and when the grass has begun to grow upon the graves of those who have fallen, universal liberty will prevail, and the whole of America be made hallowed ground. (Protracted applause.)

The motion was then carried amidst loud cheers, only three hands being held up against it.

The Rev. H. W. BEECHER briefly acknowledged the vote of thanks.

The Rev. W. M. BUNTING moved, and Sir CHARLES FOX seconded, a vote of thanks to the Chairman, which was unanimously passed, and the proceedings then terminated.

OUTSIDE THE HALL.

The scene outside Exeter Hall last evening was one of a most extraordinary description. The lecture of the Rev. Mr. Beecher had been advertised to commence at seven o'clock, and it was announced that the hall doors would be opened at half-past six. The crowd, however, began to assemble as early as five o'clock, and before six o'clock it became so dense and numerous as completely to block up, not only the footway, but the carriage way of the Strand; and the committee of management wisely determined at once to throw open the doors. The rush that took place was of the most tremendous character, and the hall, in every available part, became filled to overflowing in a few minutes. No perceptible diminution, however, was made in the crowd, and at half-past six there were literally thousands of well-dressed persons struggling to gain admission, despite of the placards exhibited announcing the hall to be "quite full." The policemen and hall-keepers were powerless to contend against this immense crowd, who ultimately filled the spacious corridors and staircases leading to the hall, still leaving an immense crowd both in the Strand and Burleigh-street. At ten minutes before seven o'clock Mr. B. Scott, the City Chamberlain, and the chairman of the meeting, accompanied by a large body of the committee of the Emancipation Society, arrived, but were unable to make their way through the crowd, and a messenger was despatched to the Bow-street Police-station for an extra body of police. About thirty of the reserve men were immediately sent, and those aided by the men already on duty at last succeeded in forcing a passage for the chairman and his friends. Mr. Beecher at this time arrived, but was himself unable to gain admittance to the hall until a quarter of hour after the time appointed for the commencement of his address. The rev. gentlemen bore his detention in the crowd with great good humour, and was rewarded with a perfect ovation, the crowd pressing forward in all directions to shake hands with him. He was at last fairly carried into the hall on the shoulders of the policemen, and the doors of the hall were at once closed, and guarded by a body of police, who distinctly announced that no more persons would be admitted whether holding tickets or not. This had the effect of thinning to some extent the crowd outside ; but some two thousand or more people still remained eager to seize on any chance of admission that might arise. At a quarter-past seven a tremendous burst of cheers from within the building announced that Mr. Beecher had made his appearance on the platform. The cheering was taken up by the outsiders, and re-echoed again gand again. The bulk of the crowd had now congregated in Burleigh-street, which was completely filled, and loud cries were raised for som member of the Emancipation Committee to address them. The call was not, however, responded to. Several impromptu speakers, however, mounted upon the shoulders of some working-men, addressed the people in favour of the policy of the North, and their remarks were received with loud cheering from the large majority ot those present. One or two speakers raised their voices in sympathy with the South, but these were speedily dislodged from their positions by the crowd, whose Northern sympathies were thus unmistakably exhibited. Every burst of cheers that resounded from within the hall was taken up and as heartily responded to by those outside. Indeed, they could not have been more enthusiastic had they been listening to the eloquent lecturer himself. This scene continued without intermission until the close of the meeting. When Mr. Beecher and his friends issued from the building they were again received with loud cheers. A call for a cheer for Abraham Lincoln was responded to in a manner that only an English crowd can exhibit. A strong body of police were stationed in the Strand and Burleigh-street, but no breach of the peace occurred calling for their interference, During the evening a large number of placards denouncing in strong language the President, the North, and its advocates were posted in the neighbourhood of the hall.

LONDON.—OCTOBER 23, 1863.

FAREWELL TO THE REV. H. W. BEECHER.

YESTERDAY morning, at Radley's Hotel, between 200 and 300 gentlemen, chiefly ministers of various denominations, met the Rev. Henry Ward Beecher at breakfast, upon the invitation of the Committee of Correspondence on American Affairs, for the purpose of wishing him farewell prior to his departure to the United States. The chair was occupied by the Hon. and Rev. B. W. Noel. Among the gentlemen present were:—Messrs. B. Scott, Chamberlain, S. Lucas, Joshua Wilson, E. Fisher, W. B. Underhill, George Thompson, L. A. Chamerovzow, John Cassell, S. H. Skeats, James Grant, W. Wilks, H. Wharton, F. W. Chesson, D. Pratt, Thomas Walker, M. D. Conway, of Virginia; Edmond Beales, Victor Schœlcher, E. Dicey, F. Evans, T. C. Turberville, Capt. T. W. Chester, of Massachusetts Coloured Regiment; the Revs. Dr. Waddington, Dr. Campbell, Dr. Davis, Dr. Angus, Dr. Burns, Dr. Tomkins, W. M. Bunting, Newman Hall, C. Stovel, J. Curwen, F. Soden, John Graham, J. H. Hinton, F. Tucker, C. Gilbert, Kilsby Jones, Thos. Jones, G. Rogers, W. Ballantyne, J. Pillans, E. White, J. Miall, J. C. Galloway, J. Corbin, T. W. Aveling, W. Tarbottom, J. Spong, J. V. Mummery, T. Lessey, A. Hannay, W. Dorling, J. Bevis, H. B. Bowen, F. Neller, R. Fletcher, J. H. Hitchens, John Hall, Ebenezer Davies, E. Matthews, J. P. Lyon, J. W. Richardson, W. M. Statham, H. J. Gamble, R. Ashton, H. B. Ingram, W. Owen, A. M. Mackennell, J. Viney, R. W. Betts, R. Macbeth, A. M. Henderson, J. Northrop, J. Bramall, S. March, G. Wilkins, W. O'Neill, J. Russell, Rev. Sella Martin, of Virginia; Mr. W. Craft, of Georgia; Mr. Gerard Ralston, Consul-General of Liberia, &c.

The CHAIRMAN said that they were met to express their sympathy with the country of which their guest was a citizen, with the Government which he upheld, and with the great movement of which he was an ardent supporter. Mr. Beecher had been for many years a brave advocate of the oppressed, a manly patriot, and he had shown during his stay in England a boldness not easily daunted, and a good temper that no provocation could disturb. (Applause.)

Dr. F. TOMKINS, the secretary of the Committee of Correspondence, read several letters from gentlemen who were unable to be present, but who wished to express their sympathy with the objects of the meeting.

The Rev. Dr. WADDINGTON read the following address:

To the Christian Church under the pastoral care of the Rev. Henry Ward Beecher.

DEAR BRETHREN,

At a very numerous assembly of ministers and other Christian gentlemen, held this morning, to bid your beloved pastor an affectionate farewell, it was desired by an unanimous vote of the meeting that we should forward to you the subjoined copy of an address given on the occasion.

We willingly comply with this request, and in doing so congratulate you most sincerely on the honour God has put on your faithful minister in his absence from you by strengthening him to bear the testimony which we are well assured will produce the best effect in this country. Your prayers have been answered on his behalf, and not many days hence we trust you will see him once more in Plymouth Church, and hear from himself how many mercies have been multiplied to him during his temporary sojourn in Europe. Continue your prayers for him, and you will yet see greater things. The following is the address adopted at the meeting:—

" Sir,—I am requested by the Committee of Correspondence on American Affairs, to give a brief but full expression of the sentiments of fraternal regard we cherish toward our distinguished guest, the Rev. Henry Ward Beecher, and to the deep sympathy we feel for his countrymen, now suffering the innumerable calamities of civil war.

" In our opinion, it would have been a matter for the most profound and lasting humiliation, if Mr. Beecher had been denied a fair and fitting opportunity to state, from observation and experience, the facts so important for all to understand and to weigh at this momentous crisis, as well as to give the freest utterance of his own strong convictions. Partisans in any sense we are not—we desire for all parties a candid and impartial hearing; but as between truth and error, right and wrong, liberty and slavery, Christ and Belial, we affect no neutrality, the very thought of it is to our minds perfectly abhorred.

" With the history before us of the great moral conflict which has continued in various forms from the days of the Stuarts, we cannot look on with indifference at the American conflict.

" We have welcomed our beloved and honoured brother to our shores—to the land of Milton, of Hampden, of Sydney, of Cromwell, and of Russell, and we are glad that he has not found in Old England a mere asylum for the dumb.

" It will ever be a source of satisfaction to us, that in London Mr. Beecher met an audience worthy of the occasion, and of the speaker, and that the cordial and unbought sympathies of the people awakened in his own breast sympathies that will thrill the hearts of millions on both sides of the Atlantic; there can be no doubt but that the people are in this struggle on the side of the North.

" For the past thirty years we have not had a public meeting so united and so earnest in the manifestations of the spirit of freedom.

" We tender to Mr. Beecher our warmest acknowledgments for the service he has rendered to the cause of truth—of right and of liberty by his manliness, high moral courage, admirable temper, clear intelligence, sound argument, and, above all, by the kindliness of his spirit.

" It is known to us that even those who are opposed to war under all circumstances, frankly acknowledge that the tendency of Mr. Beecher's public speeches in Manchester, in Glasgow, in Edinburgh, in Liverpool, and pre-eminently in London, has been to produce in the highest degree international good will.

" He has sought not to irritate but to convince. He has administered rebuke with mingled fidelity and affection. He has been courteous without servility. He has met passion with patience, prejudice with reason, and blind hostility with glowing charity. He has cast the seed of truth amidst the howling tempest with a clear eye and a steady hand—the effect will, we doubt not, be seen after many days.

" We respond most sincerely to the sentiment so eloquently enforced by Mr.

Beecher, that every human being on the face of the globe has an interest in the speedy abolition of slavery in America, and that the establishment of a slave empire would send its withering blight through all nations.

"Our sympathies are with the four millions of American sable bondsmen, but our interest in this momentous struggle arises, to a great extent, from the desire we cherish for the advancement of the sacred cause of freedom in England.

"The precious heritage left to us by our common ancestry, we hold in trust for all mankind. We are placed, therefore, under the most solemn obligation to stand firmly by all right-hearted men who contend for the full and practical recognition of the rights of humanity, irrespective of colour, clime, or social condition.

"In this cause we recognise in Mr. Beecher a faithful witness and a true soldier. From the time that he stood up as a youth to plead in Indianapolis for the liberation of those who are in worse than Egyptian bondage, until he confronted his opponents in Liverpool, he has evinced the sternest fidelity, the most unfaltering courage, with the most consummate skill. Our estimate of the services he has rendered, is enhanced by the remembrance of his forbearance and moderation at many a critical juncture. He urged the claim of the negro years ago against the selfishness of those who would exclude him from the labour market in New York—and no man has spoken in more conciliatory terms of the misguided men of the South, so long as the attempt at reconciliation, without the sacrifice of principle, seemed to be possible. If the energy of Mr. Beecher is terrible in the hour of conflict, no one knows better than himself that "calmness hath great advantage."

"In the openness of the rebukes uttered by Mr. Beecher in this country, we have the guarantee that he will at home stand to his testimony as to what is sound in the heart of Old England.

"We part with our friend with sincere regret—for we find on better mutual acquaintance, we cherish for him deeper and stronger affection. But we are willing that he should now go speedily to tell his countrymen, that we are not indifferent, as some have supposed, to their long national agony. We pray that by the interposition of the unseen arm of Omnipotence, the conflict may cease with the removal of the only cause of alienation and hostility. We trust the day will soon come when the multitudinous armies of the North and South can be safely disbanded—and the march of Christian civilisation will be continued without interruption from the Atlantic to the Pacific.

"For Mr. Beecher we desire every personal, domestic, and ministerial blessing— a safe and prosperous voyage, and that when his family and his church sing "Home again from a foreign shore," he will not think dear Old England quite so foreign as some other lands. We know that when the telegraph signals his arrival in American waters thousands will go out to bid him welcome, and in their joyful salutations they will not regard our testimony as impertinent when we say, that no man could have served the cause we love better, and that he has said nothing we could wish him to retract. We adopt in conclusion his own words on the memorable 20th of October:—"Let there be one alliance—if not in form—yet of heart, sympathy, and love between parent and child—for civil liberty—for Christian civilisation—for the welfare of the world which yet groans and travails in pain, but whose redemption draweth nigh."

"With sentiments of fraternal sympathy and the most affectionate Christian regard,

"We are, dear Brethren, faithfully yours,
"In the name and on behalf of the Meeting,

"BAPTIST W. NOEL, M.A., Chairman.
"BENJAMIN SCOTT, F.R.A.S., Chamberlain of London, Treasurer.
"FREDK. TOMKINS, M.A., D.C.L., Secretary.
"JOHN WADDINGTON, D.D., Mover of the Address

"Radley's Hotel, London.
Oct. 23rd, 1863."

The address was carried by acclamation, the company standing.

The Rev. H. WARD BEECHER, whose rising was the signal for protracted and enthusiastic cheering, replied to the address as follows:

Mr. Chairman and gentlemen,—I propose this morning to say a good many things on a good many subjects, and I am influenced in the direction in which I shall begin by the request of the esteemed brother who has been pleased to honour me this morning, and to confer a favour upon me which I shall never forget. (Cheers.) In conversation with our chairman I made some statements which he said would have weight with you, and I therefore consented to make them again. That, gentlemen, is my introduction. (Cheers.) Now I wish it to be understood as a matter of fact that this Secession is rebellion, even judged according to the principles and professions of the South hitherto. Let me then go back and state generally that the South as a whole never has believed in Secession. On the contrary, it has been condemned again and again in all the Southern States but one, and has been only held by a small section throughout the country. Until this rebellion, in fact, it has never been held that the Constitution gives the right to a State to secede. When the Convention of 1787 came together to amend the Articles of the Constitution, the first thing they had to do was to ascertain what their own power was, and what was the province of their action, and the question arose whether they could proceed to institute a national Government. That, I believe, was almost the first question brought before them. After a good deal of debate it was determined, almost unanimously, that they should proceed to make a national Government as distinguished from a perpetual Confederation. And what is remarkable is this, that the proposition for a National as distinguished from a Confederated Government was made by the delegates from Virginia and South Carolina, and it was opposed by Connecticut and some others—I forget which—of the Northern States. It was debated thoroughly, and the Northern proposition that we should continue a mere Confederation in perpetuity was voted down by an immense majority, and it was voted in express terms—though it does not appear so verbally in our Constitution—that they should proceed to form a National Government in distinction to a Confederated Government. After the resolution was passed it was put—like all the other resolutions—into the hands of what was called the revising committee, and they, as a kind of verbal compromise, introduced the present phraseology, putting the words "Union" and "United States" in the place of "Nation." The change was unfortunate, but it was purely the work of the committee of revision, whereas the Convention themselves had voted for the word "Nation." And there never was any change in that until Mr. Calhoun's day; but Mr. Calhoun's doctrine was repudiated in Virginia and Georgia, and, if I do not mistake, in every one of the South-Western States it was in a minority. It was also repudiated by our courts, and by the national Government themselves it was judged that nullification was itself a nullity. (Cheers.) Therefore, the South in going into rebellion has not been following out a doctrine held by it from the first, but has suddenly reversed its own principles, gone against the records of its own parties, and dragged in this alleged right of a State to secede, as a mere excuse, against its own records and creeds, and against the spirit of the Constitution of the

II

United States. (Hear, hear.) I have a right therefore to say to you as ministers of the Gospel, as men who believe in the powers that be, and in the legitimacy of unoppressive governments, that this is nothing more or less than a rebellion. So much for that. (Cheers.) And now, my Christian brethren, I feel I have freedom here. (Renewed cheers.) There are some things, you know, that one can say in a lecture-room that one cannot say in the pulpit, and there are things which a man can say in a social festival meeting of this kind that he cannot say on a platform before a mingled audience, where he is liable to have a sentiment cut in two by a hoot or a hiss. (Laughter.) Now, I want to introduce some matters here that would not well suit a public meeting. I wish to acknowledge the many kind providences which have attended me at every step since I have been in England. I go home, not for the first time believing in a special Providence, but to be once more a witness to my people to the preciousness and truth of the doctrine "God present with us." In ways unexpected, and as if the very voice of God had sounded in my ears, I have been frequently assisted during my sojourn in this country. When I returned from the continent I had not spoken in public during the previous twenty weeks. I began my course by addressing about 6,000 people in Manchester. I then went to Glasgow, Edinburgh, and Liverpool. The reception I met with at the latter town, was very different from the "Welcomes" of the other centres of commerce. I did not feel the slightest animosity towards the people of Liverpool. I saw that those who opposed me were merely partisans. (Cheers.) I knew that the people of Liverpool were on the right side. I remember that in the midst of the wild uproar at the Liverpool meeting I felt almost as if a door had been thrown open, and a wind had swept by me. I never prayed more heartily in my life than I prayed for my opponents in the midst of that hurricane of interruption. But it so affected my voice that a reaction came upon me on Saturday and Sunday, and I was almost speechless on Monday. I felt all day on Monday that I was coming to London to speak to a public audience, but my voice was gone; and I felt as though about to be made a derision to my enemies—to stand up before a multitude, and be unable to say a word. It would have been a mortification to anybody's natural pride. I asked God to restore me my voice, as a child would ask its father to grant it a favour. But I hoped that God would grant me His grace, to enable me, if it were necessary for the cause, that I should be put to open shame, to stand up as a fool before the audience. When I got up on Tuesday morning, I spoke to myself to try whether I could speak and my voice was quite clear. (Cheers.) Many might say this was because I slept in a wet jacket, but I prefer to feel that I had a direct interposition in my favour. (Cheers.) Last night I was saying to myself, "I am going among Christian ministers, and I should wish to represent to them the state of things in New York," when my servant brought to me a letter from America, from the superintendent of my Sabbath-school—my dear friend Mr. Bell, of Scotland, by-the-by—(laughter)—but he is a good man notwithstanding. (Laughter.) He said, "It may be that you will have occasion to refer to the report of the committee who inquired into the case of the coloured people who suffered from the riots," and so he forwarded their report to me. *A gentleman who has been my opponent* for the last sixteen years—a gentleman who, because he thought I was opposed to the best interests of America, hated me with Christian fervour—(laughter)—was appointed on the committee. The testimony that *he gave* to the committee as to that riot was that, with the exception of a few leaders, it was the work of *Irishmen*. The papers, for prudential reasons, did not put that forward in New York. It was no more an American riot than if it had taken place in Cork or Dublin. Therefore, when misinformed persons in England say this riot is a specimen of what Americans can do, I say it is a specimen of what can be done by foreigners, and by ignorance and misrepresentation. Some of the most eminent names in New York are on the committee—many of them *devoted Democrats strongly opposed* to the Republican movement. They collected upwards of $47,000 for the *immediate relief* of these poor blacks. The men, women, and children who were relieved amounted to some 12,000. A committee was appointed at once among the lawyers of New York, who gratuitously offered their services to make out the claims of all property of the blacks that was destroyed. There were 2,000 claimants who appeared, and their case was put into legal train without any expense to themselves. (Cheers.) The aggregate of their claims in the city of New York was 145,000 dollars. The committee's report contains the following account of the martyrdom of a poor black child during the riots :—

Early in the month of May a boy of some seven summers presented himself for admission to the Sunday School of the Church of the Mediator in this city. From the first Sunday he was the object of special interest on the part of both his pastor and teacher. Always punctual in his attendance, tidy in appearance, and eager to learn, he soon won the affection of all his fellows in the infant-class to which he belonged. But though comely, he was black. The prejudice which his colour excited amongst those of meaner mould he quickly disarmed by his quiet, respectful, Christian manner. He was a child-Christian. What more lovely is there on earth! What more highly esteemed is there in heaven! Little did those who thus casually met him from Sunday to Sunday imagine the witness of suffering God had purposed to perfect in him! At the time of the late riot he was living with an aged grandmother and widowed mother at No.—, East 28th-street. On Wednesday morning of that fearful week a crowd of ruffians gathered in the neighbourhood, determined on a work of plunder and death. They stole everything they could carry with them, and, after threatening and affrighting the inmates, set fire to the house. The coloured people, who had the sole occupancy of the building, were forced in confusion into the midst of the gathering crowd. And then the child was separated from his guardians. He was alone among lions. But ordinary humanity, common decency, had exempted a child so young anywhere from brutality. But no. No sooner did they see his unprotected, defenceless condition than a company of fiendish men surrounded him. They seized him in their fury, and beat him with sticks, and bruised him with heavy cobble-stones. But one, ten-fold more the servant of Satan than the rest, rushed at the child, and with the stock of a pistol struck him on the temple and felled him to the ground. A noble young fireman— God bless the firemen for their manly deeds—a noble young fireman by the name of M'Govern instantly came to the rescue, and single-handed held the crowd at bay. Taking the wounded and unconscious boy in his arms, he went to the house of an American citizen close by and asked to have him received. But on her knees the woman begged him not to leave the dying sufferer with her, "lest the mob should tear her to pieces." It was a suffering Saviour in the person of His humblest child.

Naked and wounded, and a stranger, they took him not in. But a kind-hearted German woman made him a sharer of her poverty. With more than a mother's care did she nurse the forsaken one. A physician was called, and both night and day she faithfully watched over the bed of him outcast from his brethren. Our hearts bless her for her goodness to our child. By name she is as yet unknown, but by her deeds well known and well beloved. His distracted mother found her cherished boy in these kind hands. And when she saw him in the earnest simplicity of her spirit she kneeled in prayer to thank God for the fulfilment of His promise. "God hath taken him up." The lad lingered until Thursday evening, when the Saviour released him from his sufferings; and "the child was caught up to God and the throne." This is the pastor's memorial to little Joseph Reed, a martyr by the brutality and inhumanity of men to the cause of law, and order, and right. A tablet to his memory shall be placed on the walls of the Sunday-school room to which he loved to come. Those who were kind to him we count as benefactors to us. May the God of all grace richly reward them with the blessings of His love. Buried on earth without prayer, but with praises welcomed in Heaven, the chosen loved child of the family "Joseph is not."

The coloured people sent in their thanks to the committee. There are blacks who can write as beautiful English as the white people of America, and amongst the blacks there are men as high-minded as any to be found among white men. Some people have said that blacks are the connecting link between monkeys and white men. Well, if monkeys have endowments such as I have seen in black men, all I can say is, that it is time to begin preaching the Gospel to monkeys. (Laughter.) Take as an example of their intelligence the following address :—

Gentlemen,—We have learned that you have decided this day to bring to a close the general distribution of the funds so liberally contributed by the merchants of New York and others for the relief of the coloured sufferers of the late riots, which have recently disgraced our city. We cannot in justice to our feelings permit your benevolent labours to terminate, even partially, without offering some expression of our sincere gratitude to the Universal Father for inspiring your hearts with that spirit of kindness of which we have been the recipients during the severe trials and persecutions through which we have passed. When in the pursuit of our peaceful and humble occupations we had fallen among thieves, who stripped us of our raiment and had wounded us, leaving many of us half dead, you had compassion on us. You bound up our wounds, and poured in the oil and wine of Christian kindness, and took care of us. You hastened to express your sympathy for those whose fathers, husbands, sons, and brothers had been tortured and murdered. You also comforted the aching hearts of our widowed sisters, and soothed the sorrows of orphan children. We were hungry and you fed us. We were thirsty and you gave us drink. We were made as strangers in our own homes and you kindly took us in. We were naked and you clothed us. We were sick and you visited us. We were in prison and you came unto us. Gentlemen,—this generation of our people will not, cannot forget the dreadful scenes to which we allude, nor will they forget the noble and spontaneous exhibition of charity which they excited. The former will be referred to as one of the dark chapters of our history in the Empire State, and the latter will be remembered as a bright and glorious page in the records of the past. In the light of public opinion we feel ourselves to be among the least in this our native land, and we therefore earnestly pray that in the last great day the King may say to you and to all who have befriended us, "Inasmuch as you have done it to one of the least of these my brethren you have done it unto me; come ye, blessed of my father, inherit the kingdom prepared for you from the foundation of the world." But as great as have been the benefits that we have received from your friendly and unlooked for charity, they yet form but the smaller portion of the ground of our gratitude and pleasure. We have learned by your treatment of us in these days of our mental and physical affliction that you cherished for us a kindly and humane feeling of which we had no knowledge. You did not hesitate to come forward to our relief amid the threatened destruction of your own lives and property. You obeyed the noblest dictates of the human heart, and by your generous moral courage you rolled back the tide of violence that had well-nigh swept us away. This ever memorable and magnanimous exhibition of heroism has had the effect to enlarge in our bosoms the sentiment of undying regard and esteem for you and yours. In time of war or peace, in prosperity or in adversity, you and our great State and our beloved conntry may count us among your faithful friends, and the proffer of our labours and our lives shall be our pleasure and our pride. If in your temporary labours of Christian philanthropy, you have been induced to look forward to our future destiny in this our native land, and to ask what is the best thing we can do for the coloured people—this is our answer. Protect us in our endeavours to obtain an honest living. Suffer no one to hinder us in any department of well-directed industry, give us a fair and open field, and let us work out our own destiny, and we ask no more. We cannot conclude without expressing our gratification at the manner in which the arduous and perplexing duties of your office have been conducted; we shall never forget the Christian and gentlemanly bearing of your esteemed secretary, Mr. Vincent Colyer, who on all occasions impressed even the humblest with the belief that he knew and felt he was dealing with a crushed and heart-broken people. We also acknowledge the uniform kindness and courtesy that has characterised the conduct of all the gentlemen in the office in the discharge of their duties. We desire likewise to acknowledge the valuable services contributed by the gentlemen of the legal profession, who have daily been in attendance at the office to make out the claims of the sufferers free of charge. In the name of the people we return thanks to all. In conclusion, permit us to assure you that we will never cease to pray to God for your prosperity, and that of every donor to the Relief Fund. Also for the permanent peace of our country, based upon liberty, and the enjoyment of man's inalienable rights, for the preservation of the American Union, and for the reign of that righteousness in the hearts of the people that saves from reproach and exalteth the nation.

Let this document be an answer to the harsh things that some people have said of the coloured people in New York. I regard my reception of this document last night as Providential, because it reached me just in time to read to this meeting. (Cheers.) I should have wished, had the time permitted, to make a statement respecting what is doing for coloured people in South Carolina, and in and about Norfolk. I have a son in the army, who has had an opportunity of seeing something in that respect. In schools, attended by thousands of coloured people, adult and young, education is given without fee or reward by highly educated and pious men and women. My son has narrated to me many beautiful testimonies of the piety of the old coloured people who attend these schools, and the great interest they take in the education of the young coloured people. One old coloured saint with white hair made some remarks to him wh ch struck me very much. He said, "We shall never get any good by this education, massa; we expect to suffer as long as we live; but our children will get the benefit of this education." Now, think of this old saint having passed his life in slavery, and being in a position in which, had his master lived, he would have had a refuge for his old age. Think of him now thrown out in his old age, in a state of liberty, it is true, but with powers ill qualified to use it, saying, "We have been praying for this all our lives, and now our children are going to get it." (Cheers.) I cannot go into details respecting the state of the freedmen along the valley of the Mississippi; but I may say this comprehensively, that the churches of the North are taking up their burden and awakening to their duty. They understand what is required of them, and are determined not to let the men come out of slavery and feel that they are worse off than when they were in it. I don't pretend to say that our people have not made mistakes and blunders; but, judging by the ordinary manner in which persons in difficult circumstances conduct themselves, I do say that the Christian churches in America of all denominations are stirred up by the spirit of their Master to do their duty to the coloured men of the North and South. (Cheers.) I now proceed to another topic that is very pleasant to me. I want you to see how American Christians and ministers have felt during the whole of this war. I have here an immense amount of matter—(spreading out a number of printed sheets and cuttings from newspapers on the table)—and if you don't believe me, I will read it all to you. (Laughter.) I shall first read extracts from the reports of various ecclesiastical bodies in America in 1861, the first year of the war. I have not packed or garbled them—indeed, they have not been put together by me, but by a friend in Manchester. I may read perhaps those which are least to the point; but I want you to see what has been the feeling of our Christian churches. I also want to show you another thing. Many of you are opposed to war. (Hear, hear.) Now I must say that for any Englishmen to be opposed on principle to war is a greater mark of sincerity and frankness than anything I know of. (Laughter) You Englishmen are always fighting. Why, you have two wars on hand now, and I hardly know the time when you have not had one. The testimony therefore of those of you who are opposed to war is worthy of double attention. ("Hear," and laughter.) But really you talk to us in America about war as though it were about as pleasant to us as a campaign by the sea-side; as though it were nothing to us to have our sons killed, or brought home wounded or maimed, or to have a widow coming home to her father's house with her helpless children. Some people seem to think that the North is in such a savage fury, that nothing tickles them more than to hear of the slaughter of 3,000 or 4,000 men. Oh, gentlemen, war is more terrible by far than anything which comes home to you. (Hear, hear.) You who send your armies to China to fight, or to the Continent, do not see what war is. Let war ravage your own island,—let it come upon London, and penetrate into your own homes, while the wounded and maimed are lying around you on every side, or brought into your houses,—then you will realize what war is. Do you suppose, brethren, that we love the war for itself? Do you suppose that anything but the very strongest principle could lead us to submit to it? (Hear, hear.) I do not wish you to accept these statements on my testimony, but will read to you a few extracts which will show you how these matters were talked about in 1861. The following is from the report adopted by Ripley Presbytery :—

More than two hundred years have passed away since the buying and selling of human beings as property commenced in this country, and the slave trade was allowed to be continued twenty years after the formation of the National Constitution. What a system of murder! What multitudes have been murdered in procuring slaves in Africa! How vast the number that died in the passage to this country! How much death has been occasioned by change of climate, by excessive labour, by starvation, and by direct violence and cruel scourging! Have not millions of human beings suffered death in the most horrible forms, under the operation of the system of slavery in this country during the last 200 years? Does not the blood of millions lie upon this nation?

The report goes on to make an attack on the Fugitive Slave Law, and to enunciate the OBLIGATION of the Government TO PROTECT the four millions or more of coloured people, and to SECURE THEIR RIGHTS in accordance with the spirit of the Constitution. It then says :—

We now enter our solemn *protest against all compromises with the monstrous system of oppression existing in the slaveholding States*, and the enforcement of the barbarous Fugitive Slave Law, and the giving of aid in *any form to the system of slavery*.

The following is from the report of the Maine Conference in May, 1861 (after Mr. Lincoln's call for armed support) :—

Resolved—That we will not cease to pray that Divine wisdom may guide our rulers—that the Lord God of Sabbaoth may give success to our arms and establish the right—that our sons and brothers who have so nobly responded to the call of their country in this hour of peril, may be under His peculiar care—that we will supplicate God to interpose, to overrule, that these trying events may speedily result in permanent peace—*the liberation of the enslaved*, and the " opening of the prison to them that are bound."

I turn now to the session of the General Association held in Indianopolis, my old home. I will give only one resolution :—

Resolved—That as Christian men, having a living faith in the superintending providence of Almighty God, we recommend the churches to be more instant in prayer for the maintenance of the Government, the integrity of the Union, the *perpetuity of those principles of liberty* upon which it is founded, not forgetting those in bonds as bound with them, and especially for the preservation and spiritual welfare of those who have volunteered in defence of their country.

Now I turn to the General Association of Congregational churches of Illinois :—

Resolved—That as the war is but *the ripe and bitter fruit of slavery*, we trust the American people will demand that it shall result in relieving our country entirely and for ever of that sin and curse, that the future of our nation may never again be darkened by a similar night of treason.

Then follows a resolution urging the churches to attend to the spiritual wants of the army. Here is a resolution from the Welsh Congregational Churches :—

Resolved—That we hope and pray that God in His wise and beneficent providence may overrule the present disturbances in our country *to hasten the overthrow of slavery*, which disgraces our land and threatens the existence of our Government.

One from Pennsylvania :—

Resolved—That we regard the war in which our country is now engaged as a *conflict between freedom and slavery*, and the advocates of slavery have tendered the issue, and it is the duty of the friends of liberty both in the Church and in the State, to accept the issue directly, and give it the prominence before God and the world that rightfully belongs to it.

These resolutions, you will mark, *were all passed before the proclamation of emancipation.* The following is from the General Association of Congregational Churches in New York :—

Whereas, the *immediate occasion* of this rebellion and its fomenting spirit was the *determination of its leaders to secure and perpetuate the system of slavery*; and, whereas, there can be no guarantee of peace and prosperity in the Union while slavery exists,—therefore, Resolved, **That we rejoice in every act and declaration** of the Government that brings freedom to any of the enslaved, and earnestly hope for some definite and reliable measure *for the abolition of slavery* as the conclusion of this great conflict for the support of the Government and the Union. Whereas in His good providence God has opened the way for the emancipation of the enslaved in this land, either by the instructions of the Government to military commanders to enfranchise all slaves within their several districts, or by general proclamation of the President, or by Act of Congress under the state of war—therefore,—Resolved, That it is our duty as Christian patriots in all proper ways to urge this measure upon the attention of the Government, and to pray for its consummation, lest the condemnation of those who knew their duty to the poor and oppressed, and did it not, should be visited upon the nation.

I read that to show you that while, on the one hand, they were conscious of their obligations to the Government and nation, they had also their convictions of humanity towards the oppressed. (Hear, hear.) In 1862 these deliverances became stronger and clearer throughout the length and breadth of the land. Then we come to 1863, and first I will refer to the report of the Dutch reformed Church—the most immovable church in the world. They come out, however, in a most unmistakeable manner. The Methodist Church has covered itself with perpetual honour—thanks be to God for their fidelity. Page after page of their reports is made up of resolutions on the subject full of clear instructions as to Christian duty. Here is the testimony of the American Baptist Missionary Union :—

Resolved—That the developments of the year since elapsed, in connection with this attempt to destroy the best government on earth, have tended only to deepen our conviction of the truth of the sentiments which we then expressed, and which we now and here solemnly reiterate and re-affirm.

Resolved—That the *authors, aiders,* and *abettors,* of this slaveholder's rebellion, in their desperate efforts to *nationalise* the *institution of slavery,* and to extend its despotic sway throughout the land, have themselves inflicted on that institution a series of most terrible and fatal and suicidal blows, from which, we believe, it can never recover, and they have themselves thus fixed its destiny and hastened its doom ; and that, for thus overruling what appeared at first to be a terrible national calamity, to the production of results so unexpected and glorious, our gratitude and adoration are due to that wonder-working God, who still "maketh the wrath of man to praise him, while the remainder of that wrath he restrains."—Psalm 76, verse 10.

And there is much more to the same purpose. Then I have one from Vermont, and one from Maine, which is scarcely cold yet. (Hear, hear.) It is a most honourable utterance, drawn up I think by Dr. Dwight, of Portland, a descendant of the honoured and well-known Dr. Dwight. But I will not read all these documents, which are, however, quite at your service, if you wish to inspect them. I have not counted them, but it seems to me that there are two hundred of them, and if you read them all you would say there were a thousand. (Laughter and cheers.) I seek by this not so much to make an argument as, what is better a great deal, to produce in you the moral conviction that the American churches, under great difficulties, having been long involved in a trying crisis, have come to the conclusion, through their representatives, that this rebellion ought to be crushed, and that slavery should be destroyed with the rebellion. I have not seen Dr. Massie, but I know that now he has been to America, and seen there things with his own eyes, he is prepared to come to the same conclusion. I know that he is an honest man, and I am sure that an honest man could come to no other. (Hear.) And now it is not a question with us whether this war should stop. We are not going to stop this war whatever you do. You have not—let me say—stood up for us so strongly for the last two or three years that you can influence us now to stop the war. ("Hear," and laughter.) I don't pretend to say that, considering your own difficulties, you have not taken the right path. (Hear, hear.) I see a great many things in your internal affairs here in England that I was not aware of before. We thought that you were all well-informed on this question, and that you sat in your ease and arrogance—allow me to say what I would say in the States —and that having thus settled your principles you refused to make an application of them to the States which needed them more than any other country in the world. (Cheers.) Now, I find that you are far from well-informed, and it is a great comfort to me to know that your conduct has not all arisen from depravity. I shall go back and say, "You must not think that England simply refused to bear witness to her own principles. She is yet in the battle herself about this question, not as to slavery, but as to her own institutions, and if she had borne witness, as some of her people would have done, it would have created a party movement." I shall not discuss whether there was not higher ground to take than this, and whether England should not have risen in the providence of God and occupied it, but you are men, and we are men, and we are glad to find a reason for not being angry with you. (Cheers.) This has been our feeling in the past, and it has been unlike a common national feeling. Generally speaking, the uneducated and passionate men have their prejudices and bitternesses, while the intelligent classes have their better opinions and judgments. But it has been the reverse with us. Those that have felt the most grief and indignation with England have been just the educated and Christian public, who have felt, with scarcely an exception, that England has been selfishly cold and cruel. I don't intend to say whether that *has* been your state or not. I am not here to make a case against you. I am a Christian amongst Christians. I am for doing what will unite us, if we have not been united before—(cheers)—and what will keep our countries together in Christian fellowship. (Renewed cheers.) But somebody ought to tell you this—a great many would think it, and would not have grace to say it plainly to you. (Hear.) But God has strengthened me to speak my mind to you, dear Christian brethren, and to tell you, that, so far as your influence has gone hitherto, it has all been against liberty and for slavery. I do not mean that that is what you meant, but I do say that was the effect of your conduct in America. From one cause or another, unfortunately, the moral influence of Christians in England, with individual exceptions which I live to remember, has been on the side of slavery and against those who were struggling to put it down. Now I know that in such an hour as this, and in the presence of Christ, who is in our midst, you will receive such a statement from me in the same spirit as I make it. (Cheers.) I know that you will give this subject your consideration,—

that you will revise your opinions, if needs be, and not allow yourselves to be influenced by a commercial bias, nor by unscrupulous papers. (Hear, hear.) I wish you to understand how much harm has been done on our side, too, by "the coppersmith." (Hear, hear.) I beg of you to examine this question of duty to God's people—of duty to God. Yea, I will humble myself for Christ's sake, and for the fellowship of the body of Christ, and beg of you for your sakes to examine this fairly. We wish not to be separated from the English people. (Loud cheers.) We want to see the old links rubbed brighter. (Renewed cheers.) Let me tell you, however, we *cannot* stop this war—not if you were to line our shores with fleets, which I know you will not do ; not if you were to fill Canada with your armies, which I know you will not; not if you remain still indifferent or adverse. That would make no difference : but is there not to be unity between the Christians of England and America? (Cheers.) You say that we have retorted upon you, and said bitter things. Do you recollect that wonderful passage in Scott's "Antiquary," where a certain hero had lost his son and was next morning found by the Antiquary engaged in a work on which, having met with insuperable difficulties, he vented his grief and rage, although it, of course, was in no respect to blame ? ("Hear," and laughter.) How natural a thing it is to vent our impatience and grief upon our own property or upon our own friend. And when we had seen our children slaughtered—oh ! what noble children have fallen in this war—what tears have fallen from us day and night,—and when we found treachery in the Government and on every side, we did hope to have received some sympathy ; but instead of that, the wind that came from England was as cold as Greenland ; and if, when we were disappointed, we said bitter things of England, because we loved her and expected her to support freedom, may God forgive us. (Cheers.) You will ask me what can be done. Well, in the first place, let me say, dear Christian brethren, that I thank you very much for the kind things you have said and done for me. But I certainly would feel it to be a thousand times better, if every Christian minister and Christian brother would consent, as the result of my importunity, to open this matter on his knees before God. I have great faith in the guiding spirit of God. I do not believe he will allow his dear people of England to go wrong on this question. Well, next I ask you to remember us in your prayers. I do not mean in those circuitous ubiquities that take in everybody and everything. But I ask you to pray for the North as for those that you believe to be doing a great work for God. Pray for the North as you would have prayed for the Covenanters, for the old Nonconformists, for the old Puritans, for Christians in any age whose duty it became to resist unrighteousness, corruption, and wrong. Pray for them as for men in that dark trouble in which God frequently leaves His people before the daylight comes and the glory of victory is showered down upon them. (Cheers.) But when the trumpet sounds for peace, and what are left of us are gathered together, and there are to be congratulations, and, as it were, divisions of God's spoils, I do not want that you should be left out. I desire that **whatever may have been the misinformation regarding this conflict 3,000** miles off, for the future there may be no possible mistake—that there will be eye to eye, heart to heart, and hand to hand. We of the North represent your civilization. In the South, now seeking to become independent, there is not a point of sympathy that can attach her to England. (Hear, hear.) If the North prevail in this conflict, and the Union be restored, there is not one single point of religion and civilization in the whole cyclopædia of English attainments honourable, noteworthy, and world-renowned which would not find something corresponding thereto among us. This train of remark might be indefinitely continued, but it is unnecessary. I shall go home certainly with a much lighter heart than if I had not spoken in England, and had not through my labour here—too brief for my own comfort—been permitted to see so much of the interior and better feeling of so many Christians in England. Before I sit down let me say that I would name all those honourable names—John Stuart Mill, Professors Cairnes, Goldwin Smith and Newman, Baptist Noel, Newman Hall, and other well-known and honoured names—I would name them all but that there are so many whom I would wish to thank, whose names I either do not know or have forgotten, that if I were to try and enumerate those who have done us good and Christian service, I should do injustice to many. And for the same reason I will not mention the papers and magazines that have been towers of strength to us. Yet we *will* remember them; and the day will arrive, I trust, when those who have laboured for us in adversity will come to our shores, and we will treat them so well that you never shall see them back again. (Loud and prolonged applause.)

The Rev. JOHN CURWEN said that he wished to take that opportunity of drawing attention to the London auxiliary of the Freeman's Aid Society, which had done and was doing excellent service in ministering to the necessities of escaped slaves, and which was worthy of wider support than it received.

Mr. BEECHER said that the kind of work done by the society referred to was one in which Englishmen of all political creeds could join. If a man could not go with the Northern States he could at any rate agree with the principle of helping escaped slaves. He knew the men engaged in the work in America, and could testify to their zeal, prudence, and devotion to the cause of freedom.

The Rev. C. STOVEL said he felt that Mr. Beecher and his friends in the United States had just grounds for complaint respecting the coldness of the sympathy which they had received from this country. He was quite certain, however, that since 1833 there had been a very decided feeling in England in reference to the advancement of emancipation in America. There was ample proof that the moral influence of the British churches upon American Christians, in consequence of their repeated addresses on the subject of slavery, had been by no means small. There was no lesson arising out of this struggle so important as that which taught the moral power of the followers of Christ over the affairs of the earth. The important question to be studied was how the moral power of England and America could be best united, and he would suggest to Mr. Beecher the possibility of from time to time communicating to church organisations in England the best mode of making their words and actions take effect in the United States. (Hear.) A confiding and free communication between the churches in England of all classes and of America through some distinct organisation would, he was sure, lead to results of great importance. If the Christian Church would but act with all its energies concentrated on one point it would be strong enough to carry any great moral question. He thanked Mr. Beecher from the bottom of his heart for his labours in the cause of freedom. (Cheers.)

Mr. BEECHER said that a question in writing had been handed up to him from a highly esteemed minister to this effect—" What is to be the end of this—is it to be a war of extermination ?" Now (said Mr. Beecher), I am glad of this question. So long as there is a fraction of hope on the part of the South that the core cannot be reached, it will form a centre of cohesion; but as soon as the conviction enters their mind that slavery *must* come to an end, they will dissolve in that very hour. We have to go on fighting, until this conviction is produced. You talk of extermination! Well, the South has lost 250,000 out of a population of 5,000,000 of white men. You might as well say that a father is killing his son when he strikes him one or two blows as a punishment. The North is not trying to carry moral conviction by force, but it is trying to uphold the Government and to put down a wild attempt to destroy it. We are trying by legitimate warfare to produce an impression that the struggle on behalf of slavery is hopeless; and let me say, that when men here cry "Stop the war," when such cry reaches America, it means " Let the South have its own way." (Hear, hear.) Another written question, the purport of which was whether the tariff was no ground of Secession, was handed to Mr. Beecher, who replied—"Certainly not; if any man in America were to say that the tariff had anything to do with this Secession we should put him in a lunatic asylum." (Cheers and laughter.)

Mr. WASHINGTON WILKS said that he had listened with great emotion to the speech they had heard from their honoured guest. He wished Mr. Beecher to understand how deeply those who were present felt the rebuke he had administered to this country for her coldness in the hour of America's trial, and how bitter it was to them to have it supposed that they were so indifferent as they had been represented. He had had opportunities of hearing and reading as much about English feeling in reference to the American question as most men, and he declared his solemn conviction that with all England's faults and shortcomings it was not true that as a nation she had been indifferent. (Cheers.) He knew well that many men had been misinformed and had gone wrong on the subject. He knew well that many churches, even churches that were descended from the Puritans, had gone wrong from the same cause, and that many pastors, who would have been faithful, had had their mouths stopped by rich men. (Hear, hear.) But he had turned for consolation from the churches to the people, and had found it. (Loud applause.) He complained also that the American newspapers had been quick at taking hold of information calculated to produce bitter feelings, and had given very little heed to those who were the just exponents of English sentiment. The leaders of the English people—our Cobdens, Brights, and all the chiefs in every liberal movement—were all on the side of the North and of freedom. He could not recall the name of one person with any pretensions to be called a leader of the people who was on the other side. (A Voice: "Brougham.") Lord Brougham had ceased for twenty years to be a public leader. (Loud cheers.) When the negroes in the West Indies were emancipated Brougham's glory culminated; and happy would it have been for him if he had known then how to gather his garments of greatness about him, and sink down into dignified repose. Since when, in 1848, he raised his voice against the struggling liberties in Europe, he had been no mouthpiece of liberal principles, but simply the echo of his old renown. The nation had spoken out strongly in public meetings, not simply in the last month or two, but through the whole course of the struggle; and he was sorry that the New York papers, instead of giving prominence to such meetings, had preferred to reprint little paltry expressions of opinion against America, which were not entitled to a grain of weight. (Hear, hear.) He wished Mr. Beecher to understand that the feeling expressed towards him in this country was not only genuine, but permanent. (Hear, hear.) He had called it forth, but not created it. (Loud cheers.) He would have found it if he had come a year ago. He would have found it if he had come in the stormy days of the *Trent* business; for even then the heart of Old England beat soundly for peace, friendship, and freedom. (Applause.) He would say further, that had the question of slavery nothing to do with this contest—if it had been possible for civil war to have broken out in America on any other issue, the English people would have been found on the side of the American Union, as a great embodiment of free institutions, and a great instrument of human progress. (Hear, hear.) Mr. Beecher would go back, he hoped, to America, all the happier for knowing that while he had greatly aided them in their great work of calling forth an expression of public opinion, and bringing it to bear upon the Government and the press, he had also good reason to know that England had always been right, and would continue to be right, on the great question at issue in America. (Hear, hear.) He would only add that he rejoiced at the opportunity thus afforded to Mr. Beecher of addressing so large a number of representative Christian men. He deplored above all things the partial defection of Nonconformist ministers in this matter, for if they had been but as faithful as the poor weavers of Lancashire—(hear, hear)—no statesman, no journalist would have dared to slander England by saying that she was not faithful to America in her hour of conflict and agony. (Loud applause.)

The Rev. WILLIAM BLOOD, rector of Temple Grafton, expressed his warm sympathy with Mr. Beecher as a brother Christian and as a patriot, and assured him that it would be a great mistake to suppose that any one newspaper represented the unanimous feeling of England. If the different organs of public opinion were perused, it would be found that, with all the influence brought to bear upon a portion of the press, there was a great deal of healthy feeling in the ranks of journalism. The course taken by the *Morning Star* and the *Daily News* among the London papers was honourable to the conductors of these papers. (Cheers.)

Mr. GEORGE THOMPSON moved the following resolution:— "That this meeting of Christian ministers and Christian laymen, assembled to testify their respect, admiration, and esteem for the character and anti-slavery labour of the Rev. Henry Ward Beecher, having listened with the deepest interest to his important statements, and wise and weighty counsel, desire to tender to him their warmest thanks for the faithfulness, affection, and fervour with which he has addressed them. They would testify to the importance and timeliness of his recent public speeches, and while regretting that he cannot remain to render additional service to the cause of truth and freedom in this country, would wish him God-speed on his return to his native land, and would assure him that they in future will cherish an affectionate remembrance of his short but truly friendly and most useful visit." He felt peculiar pleasure in submitting that resolution. He had been permitted on three occasions to listen to their guest, and he had each time learned something with regard to the merits of the question which he did not know before. He was, perhaps more than any living Englishman, an American; and though he had had, in years past, to say some faithful things there, and had suffered personally in consequence, when the hour of her trial came he felt towards her only as a faithful friend. He regretted that those whose duty it was to lead public opinion in this country did not in all respects do their duty, but he could confirm the statements of his friend Mr. Wilks, that every Englishman who really understood America had given a sound and true utterance upon this great question. The only exception was Lord Brougham, who had indeed blotted his fair escutcheon by the inexplicable course which he had taken on the subject. There was a goodly array of public men who had spoken out on the side of the North, and if some to whom they were accustomed to look as leaders had not done so they had at least had the discretion to keep silent. (Hear, hear.) He had attended hundreds of public meetings on this question, and had invariably carried the people with him. With regard to once slave-trading Liverpool, it must be remembered that it had strong commercial interests which tended to identify it with the Southern side, but he still believed that at heart the feeling of the people even there was in favour of the North. (Hear, hear.) With regard to America, it must gladden the hearts of all to notice the wonderful change that had come over the country on the slavery question during the last three years. For one thing especially he begged to thank Mr. Beecher,—that, whether in his own pulpit or on an English platform, he had always generously, nobly, justly laboured in the field so bravely occupied by his father before him, bearing his testimony on behalf of truth and liberty. (Loud applause.)

The Rev. J. GRAHAM seconded the motion, which was carried by acclamation, the company standing.

On the motion of Dr. WADDINGTON, a vote of thanks was also passed to the Chairman.

The CHAIRMAN, in responding, said that he could not altogether acquit large numbers of his countrymen from the charge of coldness. He hoped, however, that those who felt differently, whether they were a majority or a large minority, would continue to refrain from anything that might be construed into asperity. Their work was to labour to promote a sound and healthy state of public opinion. (Cheers.)

Mr. BEECHER begged to specially acknowledge the address to him through his church at Brooklyn. That church had sent him abroad, and had generously supplied his pulpit in his absence; and he had no doubt they would appreciate that mark of courtesy and kindly feeling. (Cheers.)

The CHAIRMAN then offered prayer, and the proceedings were brought to a close.

MANCHESTER.—OCTOBER 24, 1863.

FAREWELL TO THE REV. H. W. BEECHER.

The Union and Emancipation Society entertained the Rev. Henry Ward Beecher at a public breakfast, on Saturday the 24th October, 1863, and, notwithstanding the early hour, and the importance of the limited time for business on that day, there was a very large attendance. In the absence of the President, Mr. George L. Ashworth, the Mayor of Rochdale, occupied the chair. The company included Professor Newman, London; Messrs. Francis Taylor, Rev. Dr. Parker; John Patterson, Liverpool; Samuel Watts, jun., J. C. Dyer, Jas. Galloway, J. H. Estcourt; T. B. Whitehead, Rawtenstall; Alderman Kell, Bradford; J. F. Wilkinson, J. C. Edwards, E. O. Greening; Robt. Trimble, A. Leighton, and J. Whitty, Liverpool; T. C. Ryley, Wigan; Alderman Harvey, Salford; Ernest Jones, Barrister-at-Law; Max. Kyllman, T. H. Barker, J. J. Raper, J. R. Cooper; Peter Sinclair, Jas. Crossley, Dr. Pankhurst, T. Johnson, Joseph Spencer, J. Hacking; J. Simpson, Sheffield; Councillors Butterworth, Hampson, Warburton, Clegg, Manchester; and Barber, Stockport; and a great number of gentlemen from all parts of the kingdom.

After the initiatory services had been fulfilled by the Rev. Dr. Parker, and the Rev. T. G. Lee, Mr. Edwards, one of the hon. secretaries, read the following extracts from letters of apology for non-attendance:—

The President, T. B. Potter, Esq.

I deeply regret my inability to be present at the Breakfast. Pray present my kind regard to Mr. Beecher, and tell him how sorry I am not to have met him again.

John Bright, Esq., M.P., Birmingham.

I cannot be in Manchester on Saturday next, and therefore cannot have the pleasure of meeting Mr. Beecher.

I am sorry for this, but you will have a good meeting, I do not doubt, and Mr. Beecher will warm the zeal and strengthen the faith of those who are on the right side in this great American conflict.

W. E. Forster, M.P., Bradford.

I am sorry that I am so engaged on Saturday next that it will be quite impossible for me to accept your invitation to meet Mr. Beecher at breakfast that morning.

Will you be good enough to express to him my regret that I am unable to take leave of him, and to wish him well in his voyage and in his earnest struggles for his country and for liberty.

P. A. Taylor, Esq., M.P., Leicester.

It will be impossible for me to be at Manchester on Saturday, but I need not say you have my best wishes and heartiest sympathies.

THOMAS BARNES, ESQ., M.P., BOLTON.

I have read Mr. Beecher's addresses with much interest and pleasure, and hope that his visit will conduce to a better mutual understanding between our own country and the Northern States. We have been like offended lovers, between whom there has been some shy cold looks, that has led both parties to be suspicious and resentful, until something like a breach has been made.

I do hope Mr. Beecher may be the healer of the breach, and the restorer of a good understanding between us. We are brethren, and nothing should divide us but the waters of the Atlantic.

SAMUEL POPE, ESQ., BARRISTER-AT-LAW.

I am much disappointed that I am unable personally to express my appreciation of Mr. Beecher's life-long efforts in favour of human liberty.

I cannot but think that he will be able to impart to his friends on the other side of the Atlantic, that the heart of the British people responds to the call he has made, and that no British Government will venture to bring our country into friendly relations with a slaveholder's confederacy.

PROFESSOR ALFRED NEWTH, LANCASHIRE INDEPENDENT COLLEGE.

I am much obliged to you for the invitation to the breakfast to the Rev. H. W. Beecher, but regret that my engagements will not allow me to be present. I regret this the more as I was away when he unexpectedly honoured the college with a visit.

PROFESSOR HENRY D. ROGERS, GLASGOW UNIVERSITY.

It stirs my heart with emotions of profound joy and gratitude to see the awakened earnestness of the more enlightened true men of England in supporting the North in its struggle to maintain the Union and to resist all recognition of the slaveholding confederacy.

CHARLES ROBERTSON, ESQ., LIVERPOOL.

I hope that Mr. Beecher's visit among us, as well as his frank and noble addresses, will form an additional link in the chain that ought to bind Englishmen and Americans, and that the manner of his reception, notwithstanding the hostile opposition awakened in some quarters (and I refer especially to this town), has satisfied him that that the sympathies and good wishes of a large and I trust a growing portion of the English people are enlisted on the side of the Federal Government, identifying it, as they do with the establishment of free institutions, free speech, and free manhood.

DUNCAN MCLAREN, ESQ., EDINBURGH.

A warm friend to the cause, I am sorry I am not able to go to Manchester at present.

Letters expressing regret at their inability to be present were received from W. Coningham, Esq., M.P., Brighton ; E. A. Leatham, Esq., M.P. ; The Mayor of Oswestry ; Jacob Bright, Esq., Rochdale ; Joseph Barratt, Esq., Southport ; Charles Wilson, Esq., Liverpool ; Robert Ferguson, Esq., Carlisle ; Isaac Ironside, Esq., Sheffield ; William Slater, Esq., Carlisle ; C. Wright, Esq., Tydesley ; George Crossfield, Esq., Warrington ; J. B. Baines, Esq., Leeds ; Oliver Ormerod, Esq., Rochdale ; Edwin Cox, Esq., Preston ; William C. Levy, Esq., Dundee ; Joseph Sturge Gilpin, Esq., Nottingham ; James Cropper, Esq., Kendal ; E. Rawlins, Junr., Liverpool ; George Wilson, Esq., Manchester, and others.

The CHAIRMAN said they were met together not so much to make speeches as to show by their presence their sympathy for the distinguished gentleman who had honoured them with his company. They were met together to give the lie to that which had for some time been current in the country, namely, that the people of England had no sympathy with the principles and cause which their guest had so long and so manfully espoused, and which they were now met to show they were prepared to defend and maintain. (Applause.) He deemed it a matter of the deepest humiliation that there was in this country even a small section of our countrymen who were prepared publicly to avow the slightest amount of sympathy with that atrocious and wicked system of slavery; and whatever faults we might have to find with the Government of this country—and I am one who thinks it is far from perfection—still on the question of maintaining a strict neutrality with America, on the whole it deserved our warmest support and sympathy. (Cheers.) It would have been impossible for Mr. Beecher to have selected a time more appropriate and opportune for visiting this country than the present juncture, in order to render, throughout the length and breadth of the land, an opportunity to Englishmen—at least a vast majority of them—of expressing their honest sympathy with the cause of the North. The speeches which Mr. Beecher had delivered in the more important cities of this great country, had gone a long way towards enlightening us on many points on which great ignorance prevailed. These speeches had dispelled much that had deceived and misled us, and he (the mayor) believed, in the language of one of the letters just read, that there would be a rapidly increasing number of people in England who would rally round the standard of liberty, and show to the Northern portion of the States that they have our sympathies, and that slavery to-day was with us just what it had been in times past, a thing we viewed with the utmost abhorrence. (Loud cheers.) We could not look upon that struggle now going on in America with feelings other than those of the strongest sorrow. We could not contemplate the vast sacrifices of life and blood without feeling the deepest commiseration. But if, in this mighty and gigantic struggle the result was what he hoped and believed it would be—the entire and permanent abolition of slavery, then terrible and vast as the sacrifices had been, that result would compensate for all. (Cheers.) Let there be no mistake on this subject. Let us render all the moral support we can to the Federal Government, and show them by our prayers, sympathies, and kindly expressions of affection that we feel for them in their present fearful conflict, and let us uphold the hands of our Government in maintaining a strict and impartial neutrality. (Loud cheers.)

Mr. FRANCIS TAYLOR said he had been requested to move a resolution which was a speech in itself, and which would render it quite unnecessary that he should detain them with any lengthened remarks. The resolution was :—"That we tender our thanks to the Rev. Henry Ward Beecher, for the able, eloquent, and manly addresses he has delivered to thousands of our fellow-countrymen, on the present national crisis in the United States of America; and express our belief that the majority of the intelligent men in this kingdom unmistakeably sympathize with the friends of freedom in America, and approve of every effort made to maintain free and constitutional government. We further express our desire that he may be spared to reach his native land in health and strength; and we assure him he will take with him the friendship of many on this side the Atlantic, who will honour his name and remember him with affection." (Cheers.) This resolution certainly required no words of his to recommend it to the hearty approval of the company, and he was equally sure that Mr. Beecher, the gentleman referred to in the resolution, needed no compliment either from the mover of the resolution or from any other person. Certainly had not Mr. Beecher established for himself a reputation which would endure for all time, before he visited our shores, the addresses he had delivered to crowded audiences since his arrival would have secured for him our most hearty approval, and have entitled him to every expression which the resolution contained. There was one point in the resolution to which for a moment he (Mr. Taylor) wished to refer. It stated that "the majority of the intelligent people of this country unmistakably sympathized with the friends of freedom in America, and approved of every effort made to maintain free and constitutional government." (Cheers.) Since Mr. Beecher addressed the audience in our Free-trade Hall, and in various other places in the kingdom, comments had been made on these meetings by various newspapers throughout the country. It was asserted by the *Times*, and by its humble follower in Manchester—(laughter)—that notwithstanding all the enthusiasm expressed at these meetings, they really meant nothing at all; that Mr. Beecher would make a great mistake if he assumed that in consequence of large attendances at these meetings, public opinion in this country sympathized with his friends on the other side of the Atlantic. All he (Mr. Taylor) had to say was this:—Let Mr. James Spence, in the advocacy of the Southern cause in England, try the experiment; let him go round to the large cities in this country and call public meetings, at which all who chose might attend; and let him thus test public opinion and see whether it went with the South. (Loud cheers, and a Voice: "Let him take Liverpool first.") When he (Mr. Taylor) presided at the meeting in the Free-trade Hall, he stated before Mr. Beecher addressed the assembly that if any person wished to ask Mr. Beecher any questions after the proceedings had terminated that person would be at perfect liberty to do so, and Mr. Beecher would be ready to answer the questions so put to him. Mr. Beecher himself made a similar offer in the course of his speech but not one person presented himself to ask any question. (Cheers.) It appeared however that some gentleman calling himself "a traveller"—whether he was at the meeting or not was not known—if he were, probably he was one of the bellowing bulls that disturbed the back settlements of the hall. (Loud cheers.) Well, this person instead of availing himself of the opportunity of putting his questions in person, sneaked off to the columns of a sympathizing newspaper in Manchester and said "it was impossible to get a straightforward answer from Mr. Beecher respecting the treatment of coloured people in the North." Now, if this gentleman had appeared on the platform at the Free-trade Hall to put these questions, he would have found no difficulty in getting a straightforward answer, and no doubt Mr. Beecher would so far notice this question as to give during the remarks he was about to make an answer that would satisfy every one. (Loud cheers.) He had much pleasure in moving the resolution he had read.

Mr. JOHN PATTERSON, of Liverpool, said that man must be very ill informed indeed upon an important subject, if he had not heard of the life labours as well as "Life Thoughts" of Mr. Henry Ward Beecher. (Applause.) Among the glorious chapters which adorned the page of humanity was a chapter which recorded the life and labours of the "fanatical abolitionists" of America. He for one gladly embraced the opportunity now afforded to him in this assembly of "fanatical abolitionists"—(laughter)—to tender his thanks to Mr. Beecher not only for what that gentleman had done in England, but for what he and his friends had done in America during the past twenty-five years. During the few weeks of the past summer which he spent in America he had the pleasure of being introduced to Mr. Beecher at his own church, and of telling him that the people in England believed that America was much indebted to him and men like him for having the courage to stand up before the world and rebuke the intentions and presumptions of one of the basest and foulest Confederacies that ever disgraced humanity. (Loud cheers.) It was important that we in England should speak out unmistakeably, as well as be spoken to by the eloquent mouthpiece of American abolitionists. There was a great mistake existing as regarded the subject of anti-slavery in this country which sometimes men fell into. He himself was but a child when the abolition of slavery was carried. It was just at that stage that it had hardly passed enough into history to be familiarized as a historical question, and when we were likely to lose accurate statements in the mist of tradition. What was the position of England with regard to this slavery question? He maintained that there was an excitement and contest like our own free-trade agitation; like that which abolished "Tests and Corporation Acts;" like that which gave to our Roman Catholic countrymen their civil privileges. When men stood up to say in England, "We are all anti-slavery, and always were;" it was either an intentional falsehood, or an ignorant mis-statement. For England was never entirely anti-slavery. When he met men on the Liverpool Exchange who said to him, "You are a great fool to talk about slavery; we are as much opposed to slavery as you, and we want to put an end to it." He asked — Why? And the answer was, "It deprives us of cotton." He had the misfortune to differ from many as to cotton grown by slaves. The cheapest way in which a man could get things was to steal them, if no one would give them to him. And on that principle the cotton grower could grow cotton cheaper with the stolen labour of the slave. Men in this age were wiser in their generation than the children of light as they always were, and hence they found that cotton could be grown cheaper by slave labour than by free. But the Ruler of this Universe was a moral governor, who ordained that terrible retribution should follow evil-doing, and it had now fallen upon the United States in the devastation which had overtaken them and which would have the effect of bringing up the price of slave-grown to **free-grown** cotton. In England we were now pretty much as we always were—the minority only possessed of power and privilege. But education was being now more generally diffused, although many men had it forced down their throats. Some only desired that the people should be so much educated as to make them subservient to selfish purposes, while the men who represented the really educated intelligence of the country desired that the people of England should not be merely what Beresford Hope wished, a "well-fed, well-clothed church peasantry"—(loud laughter)—but rather a free, intelligent, industrious, and self-elevating people. (Cheers.) We owed great thanks and obligations to the men who came to us with not only "40-parson" but 500-parson power across the Atlantic and who spoke words of truth, soberness, and logical demonstration, although opposed by the *Times, Telegraph,* and *Manchester Guardian.* (Laughter and hisses.) Many persons would say that the opposition given to Mr. Ward Beecher demonstrated the futility of his endeavouring to speak to the men of England. It showed rather the force with which he has spoken to them, and he (Mr. Patterson) stood there, a Liverpool man, to say that the reception Mr. Beecher met with in Liverpool, exhibiting as it did all the vileness that still clung around them—all the miserable tradition of an intolerant Toryism that pervaded a portion of the community; yet it showed still further how high the intelligence of Liverpool had risen—how amazingly its middle class had risen, and how, if Liverpool men were true to themselves, they could trample under foot that ancient and rotten tradition. (Loud cheers.) That meeting in Liverpool was open as the day. It had been stated that it was packed. It was untrue. Every opportunity was given to any man to attend; and pains were taken by their opponents to enlist men to come there for the purpose of opposition. But a lamentable failure the opposition was. (Cheers.) Not one-seventh of that audience held up their hands in opposition to the vote. Whilst he thoroughly sympathised with Mr. Beecher, and felt annoyed that a gentleman in his position and from such a distance should be obliged to contend with the wild beasts at Ephesus. (Loud laughter.) Yet he rejoiced for the sake of liberty that the meeting was held. (Cheers.) Many meetings had been held, but the people of Liverpool had pronounced by tremendous majorities in favour of the North. (Loud cheers.) There was another reason why he desired they should very unmistakeably pronounce their thanks to Mr. Beecher, and that was that the opposition to him had not only come from our hereditary enemies, but also from some of our false friends. He was not unmindful of past services rendered to the causes of liberty by one illustrious man before he became a lord. He had read with great enjoyment words which that man had spoken for all time, and which would never die; but he read them now as he read the words of Balaam. And deeply did he regret that Henry Brougham, once the man who claimed to be the very prince of abolitionists, should recently have stood up to pronounce words of unparalleled baseness on this question. (Loud cheers.) The justification Lord Brougham gave of this truculence was that he himself was the great leader of the anti-slavery party, and that he himself did more in this question, not only than any other man—for to say that might be excuse to him—but that he did more twice over than all the other advocates of emancipation put together. Was Lord Brougham forgetful of all the Clarksons, Wilberforces, Fowell Buxtons, Macaulays, and Jefferys—(cheers)—and was it not enough to rob the sepulchres of the dead, but he must endeavour to deprive the living of the glory that belong to them? (Loud applause.) Was Lord Derby such an unconsidered trifle that he could lay claim to no part in negro emancipation—(cheers)—and Lord Russell such a unit that he could be appropriately snuffed out by Lord Brougham at an Edinburgh banquet? (Cheers.) It was a shame to see such a hecatomb offered to the vanity of one poor, spoiled old man. (Cheers.) He cordially seconded the resolution.

The resolution was supported by Mr. W. B. Whitehead, Mr. Alderman Kell (Bradford), Mr. Alderman Harvey (Salford), and passed with acclamation.

The Rev. HENRY WARD BEECHER rose to return thanks, and was enthusiastically cheered. He said: Mr. Chairman and gentlemen— I wish I could say ladies and gentlemen. But I begin again—Mr. Chairman and gentlemen [A Voice: The ladies are represented by the gentlemen] No man can ever represent a woman. (Boisterous laughter and cheers.) It gives me great pleasure this morning to avow myself in some sense a convert. While I have seen and still see in England, even more perhaps than you will admit, of prejudice and misconception, I have been made aware of some prejudices and much misconception in myself, and in other honest men whom I may fairly be said to represent; and it is not the smallest triumph of this short course of two weeks during which I have been permitted to remain in England, that I have gained the victory over my own past impressions and am prepared to admit some things that I have stoutly denied to Englishmen of my own congregation, who used to say to me, grieved but not angered at the things I said about England, "You do not know Old England." I used as sturdily to say, "I do." But now I shall say to them, very humbly, "I did not." (Cheers.) I have been called to speak on a question which is very broad, very intricate, and multitudinous in its contents, because the question of America is simply the total question of human society. It begins at the top and goes to the bottom, and back again from the bottom to the top; from the circumference to the centre, and from the centre to the circumference; for there is nothing in political economy, philosophy, human right, or whatever can spring out of this wonderful being—man—in society, that is not involved directly or indirectly in this great American struggle. And in speaking upon a question so broad, it was quite impossible to speak exhaustively: the only thing that I have exhausted has been myself. (Laughter.) It has been quite impossible under the circumstances, a stranger in a strange community, not altogether cognisant of the prejudice or the wants or shades of thought in a community, to speak upon this large question so as always to meet the requisitions of my audience. I shall not dwell upon the interruption which I have taken very kindly—which even in its worst form at Liverpool, I do them the justice to say, was rather an exhibition of party feeling than of personal malignity—(cheers);—and although it made my work very hard, God is my witness it did not excite in my mind the slightest animosity towards them, still less towards that very noble community which they misrepresented on that occasion. There is another matter I wished to speak of; and that is, that the reports of my speeches are not authoritative, nor can they be so, until they have passed under my revision. And I wish to say that no man here is so much indebted to a class of men much abused and very little understood, but to whom I owe lasting obligations—I mean reporters for newspapers. They are young men who are generally sent out into meetings of all kinds, where men are divided, and where questions are discussed with warmth and excitement at untimely hours; and when usually crammed into the most inconvenient situations, are obliged to take down either the whole or a part of what is spoken upon arguments upon which they have not been thoroughly read, exercising at the same time an immediate judgment as to what should be omitted, or what the wants of every newspaper oblige them to produce. Then they are hurried back in the midnight hour to write out that which is so lately taken, and often because it is not presented next morning as some would wish, men blame them, and impute ill motives. (Loud laughter and cheers.) Now, I am a newspaper man myself, and have been made familiar with the life and difficulties which beset the corps of reporters. I have followed the reports of my speeches in England, but have never in a single speech seen that which led me to believe that any reporter had intentionally misrepresented what I had said. I have, however, seen the editorial column, where I know the editor, thinking he was supporting a certain party, misrepresented both my facts and principles. (Cheers.) And, if there are reporters present, I desire to express through them my sense of the obligation under which I lie to their kindness and fidelity in this visit. (Cheers.) Yet, for reasons I have stated, my speeches generally occupying more than two hours, and passing generally very rapidly over many great topics, and all having naturally to appear next morning, when the paper could not afford to put in a verbatim report, the reports, while presenting the general tenor of my speeches, have had such inevitable imperfections as to make them not exactly the things upon which to base an attack upon me. (Cheers.) I wish now, in the opening remarks which I shall make, to explain to you precisely the thing which I have attempted to do in England. I have attempted—it is the keynote—the inward keynote of my whole progress here—I have attempted to use my information, and the position which you have been kind enough to secure for me, to promote a better understanding and a lasting peace between these two great nations. (Loud cheers.) There have been therefore a great many things I *might* have said, and feelings I *might* have expressed, which I *have* not. But I have endeavoured to bring all things to the bar of a manly judgment, and to say those things which would draw closer the bonds of amity. (Cheers.) Even in the cases where I have brought up matters on which your judgment and mine have differed, and still differ, it was not so much to go back and argue them upon the merits of the question as it was to put you in possession of the American stand-point, that you might see, if we did err, what was the reason of our erring. (Cheers.) I wish, for instance, to illustrate it by one single case, and that was the *Trent* difficulty. I think it was in Manchester I mentioned the strong feeling that existed in America upon this point. And the London *Daily News*—a paper to which I should be glad to express the great obligations of American citizens—(cheers)—if I were not afraid it might be employed against it to diminish its influence with Britons— ("No, no")—I say that paper in a friendly spirit criticized my utterances, and said that it would damage my testimony with English people to be so far wrong and mistaken in facts about that question; and that it would damage my testimony amongst English people on questions with which I was better informed. They did not specify however, what was my mistake. Now, I want just to specify to you how we Americans looked at that transaction, not for the purpose of putting ourselves right and you wrong, but to ask you as I shall, when I have made my statement, if you had been in our situation, and things looked to you as they did to us, would you not have felt as we did? Is not that fair? (Cheers.) You will recollect, then, that an American naval vessel by accident— if there be such things as accidents—overhauled an English mail steamer, and took from it two men who represented themselves as ambassadors from the so-called Confederate Government to the courts of England and France respectively. I remember very well, when the ship came from Europe,—and the tidings spread across America as quick as lightning could flash,—that for a day or two the universal feeling was, "Here's a stupendous joke." Everybody laughed. It struck the comical feeling of the nation that these two men should have started off to represent the Confederates at St. James's, and in Paris, and instead, had found themselves in Fort Lafayette. (Laughter.) And there was a feeling of immense good nature, and even jollity. Then, after two or three days, some lawyer-men began to inquire in the papers, "What is the law on this subject? It may be a very good joke, but what says the law?" We began to draw down our faces and say, "Sure enough there is an England, and she will have a word to say. What then is the law?" Then began to be quoted what the English doctrine was ; our papers began to be filled with English precedents and English conduct, and there was a universal feeling that we had acted according to *English* precedent. (Cheers.) *That conviction is yet unchanged, and never will be changed, because it was the fact.* (Cheers.) But I had the opportunity of knowing from my position, both as preacher, lecturer, and editor, that the feeling of the people was, "We are going to do what is right now, whatever it is. If we are in the wrong, we shall concede this matter; but if we are in the right, we will not budge an inch, neither by bullying nor intimidation." And the moment the information came to our shores of these facts, Mr. Seward addressed a confidential communication to

Mr. Adams, instructing him to read the same to Earl Russell, the purport of which was, that this had been done without the privity or assent of the American Government, who were prepared, on the statement of England's wishes, to settle this matter amicably. Mr. Adams read that to Earl Russell, and it lay nine or ten days quiet. The letter being confidential, Mr. Adams scrupulously avoided speaking of it: but it leaked out nevertheless that there had been a communication from the American Government to the English, and everybody was asking what was its nature. This communication having been read, I think, on the 19th of December, it would be about the 29th that your *Morning Post*—which is supposed to be a semi-official organ—declared that there had been a communication from the American Government, but that it had nothing to do with the *Trent* affair. And, whereas it was a communication expressly on that and nothing else, to this hour that paper has never explained nor retracted that malicious and deliberate falsehood. From that point, I believe, complication began. But there was something before that. (Cheers.) Even before that message came from Washington, and before the British Government had heard what we had to say, orders had issued that British troops should repair to Canada, and the navy and dockyards were put on double labour. England has never shown want of promptness and spirit; but I believe you can find no other case in English history in which a misunderstanding between ships of two nations has been treated with similar precipitancy, not waiting to hear explanations, but preparing war, or threatening war, before you could possibly have the real facts. As to what took place on the other side, I am alleged to have been all wrong when I said the American Government showed instant disposition to make reparation; because, on the other hand we heaped honours on Captain Wilkes all through the nation. When we thought we were right, we did; but after we found out by the declaration of our own Government that we were wrong, point me to one instance, in which even the slightest popular assembly undertook to traverse the decision of our Government, by showing attention to Capt. Wilkes? As to whether we did not use all possible speed, let us see what were the facts. Mr. Seward wrote to the English Government saying, we were prepared to settle the matter satisfactorily to them, and awaited their demands. Many say: we ought *not* to have waited their demands, but given up the men instantly. But there were conflicting doctrines as to the rights of Governments over contraband of war in neutral vessels. There was the British doctrine and there was the American doctrine. From 1807 certainly to 1813, and I know not how much longer, the British doctrine was that you had a right to condemn a neutral vessel without bringing her into a prize court. That was the British doctrine and practice down to within a few years. I think the last recognized case—I won't undertake to say it is the last case—is that in which England acted upon the American doctrine, when they took a Bremen vessel and condemned her in an English court because she was bringing the crew of a wrecked Russian vessel from Japan home. She was condemned by a prize court, and that is the first instance I know of the American doctrine being acted on by the English Government or navy. Now, when Mr. Seward wrote to Mr. Adams he said thus:—Here is the old British doctrine, which they have never given up technically, and here is the American. Which of the two is the British Government going to take with respect to Mr. Mason and Mr. Slidell? If their own, we have committed no offence, and there is nothing more to be said. If our doctrine, evidently we must wait for them to make their own election—I ask you then, was that not a courteous and just reason for waiting till the overture should come from the English Government instead of from ours, as to what should be done in the case of these men? (Cheers.) Now, all these facts are perfectly known to our people, and I ask you not to renew this old subject. It is past for good, I hope, and it rests in peace. But then, I want you so far to review these facts as when men say " the Americans have shown an arrogant and intemperate spirit towards Great Britain, and without reason in that *Trent* affair,"—I want you then to say, " Every man, and I for one if I had been an American, should have felt just as they felt." (Cheers.) And I want to say one thing more, and it is this, that we were all very much surprised when Mr. Seward issued his decision. But so it was and so it stands. I make these explanations in the furtherance of a better understanding between us, so that there may be no unpleasant memory, and no coal that has not gone out in the embers and ashes of this old question. (Loud cheers.) Also I wish to revert to a certain topic, because I am informed that I have been destroyed by several papers, body and soul, honour and reputation, because of gross and intentional misstatements made in Edinburgh. I cannot tell the paper that has originated it, nor would I if I could. I am informed that my statements made respecting the circulation of money were totally at variance with the fact. Now all I can say is, if these statements were not correct, I certainly should be guilty of ignorance, though not intentionally. Let me then state to you, availing myself of this opportunity, what I understand about the condition of the North fiscally, and of material prosperity in this time of war. My venerable and excellent friend, Dr. Massie, is present—(cheers)— and I speak as before one who knows the truth, and although I have never till this morning seen him—may I see him a thousand times hereafter—though I, of course, know nothing of his opinions, yet I know he is an honest man, and know what an honest man must say in respect of certain points in our American affairs. I say he will not rebuke me for saying there never was a time of such material or moral prosperity as in the North at this time. Burdened as we are with war, there never was a time when husbandry was carried on with more alacrity or success, when every conceivable form of productive industry, and of manufacturing through its whole range, was more pressed by demand. It is not as it was in Manchester just before this war, when you had manufactured far beyond the consumption of your customers. It is not speculative. There never was a time when monetary affairs were so easy, and I think so healthy, notwithstanding the contrary opinion of the editor of the *Times*' money articles. You say, we shall come to a crash. It may be we shall, though we are going to it by a very pleasant way. (Laughter.) But are we doing this upon an inflated paper currency, without a proper basis and proper security? Paper must represent convertible property. Is there more paper in circulation in the North than there is actual and available property in the North which it represents? On that subject I declare it makes no difference whether paper is issued by State banks, or individual brokers, or the National Government; if there is never more paper than is needed, all then is safe, for there is no more paper than they have means to convert. Again, you may always issue more paper than you can convert in any one day. Three bills to one pound of bullion is a safe measure. The exact state of affairs in the North was, that this uprising so deranged business that it compelled a universal settlement. I don't know how it is in England; but in America we need a financial judgment day once in ten years, and we get it. These crashes, although in one way of looking at them they are unfavourable, in another are always beneficial. A new country must have credit. As countries grow old and rich, they can contract it more and more, but a new country, that has its resources to develop, requires credit, and with it you must have the attendant evils of intense stimulation of hopeful and sanguine natures. Once in ten years you work out, so that the thing comes clear round. There is a kind of miscellaneous crash, in which every man picks up his own. The bubble is broken—the paper is gone; and the property remains. The man that yesterday said: this is my house, does not say so to-morrow, but the community is not hurt; the property is there—the difference is that the owners have shifted. (Laughter.) Now, what of these commercial reverses? It is said they are unhealthy, but it is not of that kind of unhealthiness that many political economists have believed; and these periodical settlements are always salutary. We had a settlement in 1857, and there was the less at the beginning of this war to be settled. But what there was, we swept out of the way. And since the day when the infant colony of Plymouth Bay had to pay 50 per cent for money loaned to her in England, I do not believe there has ever been so sound a state of business in the North as to-day. And your business men in Manchester will see that these reasons work that way. One thing more: the thing does not stop there. As there is more or less of uncertainty in the commercial world, men will no longer go on the credit system as before. They are buying for cash; then going home and selling for cash. Some of you in Manchester can say, whether it is not the case here to an extent never before known, that American merchants are buying for cash. The business is taking that direction; certainly it is in America. Not that there may not be facts the other way, but this is in the main true. Suppose there come bye and bye further financial difficulties, how are you going to bankrupt a nation which has no foreign debts? You recollect the story of the Frenchman in Boston. He had got money enough and goods enough, but thought a man ought to fail when he could not collect his debts. We may fail so, but I don't see any other form of bankruptcy awaiting us. Our Government are issuing bonds largely that are becoming the basis of the whole banking system in the North. The Government bonds become the securities of our State banks. They issue Government notes as their circulation, and although there is an immense amount of Government notes in circulation they are taking the place of the individual State bank notes we have been driving in. I do not profess to be fully informed, but my impression is, there is no more paper money in circulation now than there has been at many periods in American history, only, it is not a circulation of individual banks, nor of States; it is a circulation of the total United States; and whereas before these bills had the security of what was in the vault of the individual bank or of the State, now the guarantee of these bills with the same circulation is the guarantee of the credit and total property of the United States. (Hear.) Neither can I state (as I should have done if I had supposed I was to be called on for these facts) exactly how much has been invested; but probably four or five hundred millions of the capital of the North, not invested already in business, has been invested in what are called Government securities, which are just your Consols over again. Our people feel two things—first, that our Government must stand; and, secondly, that it will stand, and it is safe to invest in it. (Cheers.) Our savings banks, insurance companies, trust-fund commissioners, and men who have in charge the money of widows and orphans—old men who wish to secure themselves against contingencies and bankruptcies, men who have sums in hand and are looking about for investment, are showing that of all securities none seems to them so sound as the faith and credit of the Government of the United States. (Loud cheers.) And hundreds of millions of dollars have been invested in that way; so that I may say the Government of the United States has a lien upon all the inoperative capital of the North and West, and it has become the interest of every business man and every monied man in the whole Northern States, to maintain the Government as the way to maintain himself. Now then if it be said that I have stated that the Government paper had been issued as only three to one of bullion, I never made any statement on that question at all; but that since the Central Government issued this paper—since it represents not only what has been paid in for these bonds as invested, but represents also the total available property of the Federation itself, it is a better circulation than that of Local banks, which issue three papers to one pound of bullion—that is what I meant to say at Edinburgh, whether I said it or not. And it is what I say in this great capital of business in England. I cannot, of course, speak authoritatively in this matter. I am not a financier, I am not a banker, but a clergyman and a patriot only. If you were to get hold of a man who knew a great deal more, he would state the matter still more strongly. (Applause.) If there is anything I have inadvertently omitted to notice on this fiscal question, I shall be ready to attend to any question that may be put to me now. (Mr. Beecher paused, and then resumed.) I may presume, then, that you are satisfied. (Applause.) Now there is some art in speaking so as to relieve one subject against another, and, having given you a few words upon currency, and a sound state of business in the North, I will turn to that letter in one of your local papers, to which my friend Mr. Taylor referred, containing those three questions, which the writer says have never received straight-forward answers. I will endeavour to show you what a straight-forward answer is. The first question is, "Do coloured persons ever attend your church in Brooklyn?" Yes, by scores and hundreds. (Cheers.) Second, "If so, where do they sit?" Wherever they can get a seat. (Cheers and laughter) Allow me to say our church will hold but 3,000, and it is extremely difficult for anyone to get a seat. I have said humorously, in expostulating with our people, that they are sometimes impatient of having so little use of their own pews, for which they pay an inordinate rent, "Gentlemen, you know very well when you rent pews here what it means; you pay 300 dollars for a pew for the sake of sitting in the aisle, and you knew it when you bought your pew." It is expressly stipulated that if a man is not in his pew to defend it within a certain number of minutes after the service begins, he forfeits his right to sit there. It is in his article of sale. We have from 16 to 25 active and enterprising men whose sole business is to seat people in our church; and sometimes, when there is a public question involving great interests, the entrances to the church are thronged for hours before the doors are open. Well; when our own pewholders have to bustle for their own seats, because strangers may come an hour beforehand; when this has been going on for sixteen continuous years—if you ask me whether we take coloured people by platoons, and walk them up and seat them on a platform—why, we don't treat them any better than white folks. (Loud laughter, and cheers.) We treat them just as we do white folks. (Cheers.) Now, let me say this, I have never exerted any direct influence on this subject; it has only been the Christian feeling and good sense of my own parishioners that have led them to determine their line of action towards coloured people within the body of the church. And what does it mean? I have never yet known an instance in which a coloured man was refused a seat, if he were properly dressed, well behaved, and modestly asked for a seat. I have myself invited Frederick Douglass and other men to sit in my own pew. Sometimes a man says to me,—"I would come, but I am afraid." But I give him a note to one of my friends and then he finds no trouble. To make so much of it, would seem as if I was boasting of the liberality of our people. It is just a matter of course, of Christian common sense. If my answer is not *straight*forward, it is because I had to go *round* to get all this. (Cheers and laughter.) Third, "Have you ever seen any (that is, coloured people) amongst your congregation; and would they be allowed to sit in any pew of your church, or intermingle with your white hearers?" If my people were like the man who wrote this letter, they would not be permitted to sit a moment there. (Cheers.) That is not a mere jibe. I will tell you why I make that remark in a moment. But I have seen them, not once or twice, or fifty, but hundreds of times. I tell you the truth, gentlemen, though we are not better than hundreds of other churches. We have been led by acquiescence in those great truths preached in Plymouth church; that man is not what he is on account of title, education, or wealth, but because God made him and loves him, and God will redeem him to immortality and glory. (Cheers.) And that broad ground has led us to feel insensibly, more and more, that a man in the house of God is to be treated as we would treat that man on the threshold of the judgment day. And now, these words will go back to America, and I shall have them set down to me there, and shall stand to every word I have said on America. The close of the letter, containing these queries, is as follows:—" I could multiply instances to almost any extent of brutality towards the coloured people in the North, and of kindness and indulgence towards them in the South, which I witnessed during a long and protracted tour through the States. Though my original antipathy to slavery was never eradicated, I came to this conclusion,—that a Slave in the South was a far gayer and happier creature than a free black in the North." There you have it. Ah! there never was a serpent yet that was taught to speak in human language that first or last the sibilation did not come out. Whenever I find a man undertake to tell me, that any human creature, considered in the totality that makes up a man, in his body and soul—in his loves, independence, and purities—in his relations to time and eternity—is a better man in slavery than he is out of it, I say, "Thou son of the devil, get thee behind me." (Loud cheering.) On the other side, let me say pointedly, that the treatment in the North of the blacks was bad—that we imbibed prejudice from the South—that the poison of slavery in every fibre of our body, wrought out bad laws and usages;—*nevertheless, the party now predominant throughout the North, though once a small minority, has fought up against that prejudice and wrong, until at last it is in ascendancy: and Englishmen are asked now to strike us, who have been martyrs for freedom, because of the prejudices which came from the men who are now in rebellion.* (Great cheering.) And I avow, there is a good deal of work yet to be done. We do not appear before you as a saintlike people; we are, just like you, in the midst of struggles where all sorts of influences are in combination. We have fought so far with complete success—thanks to God; but it is not done yet. There are many things we need to change, and are trying to change. All we ask is, that when our faces are as it were turned towards Jerusalem, you will not stop us. (Loud cheers.) And I say still further, that in respect to that riot which took place in New York, and so much used adversely to us, I here, and accountable for what I say, declare my conviction that that riot was nothing in the world but the sore made by a foreign blister put on our body. The rioters were as a body unquestionably Irishmen. (Cheers.) Now, you must not think I am saying this in any ill-will to them. These

Irish labourers come to us poor and uneducated creatures, easily led by more intelligent men, men who work through their passions. By corrupt Americans, I am ashamed to say, they have been assiduously taught that the emancipation of the slave would take away from them the market of labour, and that emancipation would bring the whole South Northward; which is just the opposite to the truth, that it is likely to take the whole coloured North Southward. But they have been stuffed with falsehood in the most offensive forms, for the purpose of making them mischievous; hence with the sting of the draft just about to be put on them, there was a wild furious uprising of the Irish immigrants. It was very cruel and wicked, but so cruel and wicked a thing was never done with so much excuse for the wicked actors as this. They were blind, ignorant, misled creatures, who thought they were fighting not so much against the blacks as for themselves. I make these excuses for them therefore, and I say this riot was an Irish riot, just as much as if it had occurred in Dublin or Cork, instead of New York. (Hear, hear.) When Archbishop Hughes was called upon to address them and stop it, the street before the Archiepiscopal residence was alive with the crowded thousands; his speech was reported, and he never intimated that he thought anybody else was engaged but Irishmen. He took it for granted it was they; he never excused them in any way by the oppression that they had suffered in Old Ireland. From beginning to end it is taken for granted it was the work of Catholic Irish, and he was blaming them in his very maternal and gentle way for doing such naughty things. (Laughter.) But what was the conduct of the city of New York? Between 40,000 and 50,000 dollars were subscribed to relieve the wants of these people in a few days. A large committee was appointed from the most respectable merchants, men of the highest business integrity, and of the utmost honour and purity in private life. I marked every one of them as the men who have been my opponents from the beginning of this agitation for sixteen years—men who are intensely conservative, or as we call them, "Old Hunkerish." (Laughter and cheers.) But these men had their eyes so opened by this riot, that they followed their noble and generous instincts, so as not only to give their money, but to avow as plainly as words can say:—"It has come to this. If the coloured people are thus violently treated, we will put ourselves between them and their assailants, and they shall, as long as we live, have the right to labour in freedom. (Loud cheers.) "A body of lawyers volunteered to receive and put into legal form the complaints of every coloured man who had lost property:—according to our law, the municipality is responsible for every cent of property damaged in the riot;—and there have been 145,000 to 150,000 dollars involved in the complaints already made, or making; and legal proceedings have cost the coloured people not a cent. (Cheers.) The letter they wrote of thanks, which I believe will appear in the papers, is a composition of the most poetical English, and consummate Christian kindness, showing what the grace of God can make appear in the hearts of outcast men. (Cheers.) Read that letter in the report of the Committee which has just reached this country, and the reply of Mr. Mc.Kenzie, and see how an Old Hunker can speak. When I get back, I mean, the first thing, to go to Mr. Mc.Kenzie's store and ask him to honour me by shaking hands. Are there any other questions about these blacks? [Mr. Haughton, of Dublin: "Are we to understand that the practice in your own church is the universal practice in America; that the black man is as respected in other churches as in yours?"] No, sir. Many of our churches are filled with men who are the first merchants of New York, or are politicians. The position of the black man is regulated mainly by the fact that he is the football bandied between side and side; to treat him with public attention has been to abandon your political party, and seem to show confidence in the other side. In many churches of New York—I cannot speak positively, but my impression is—they would not be received except in a particular pew, but a tendency has now been established, and is every week increasing, to receive them when they come in the churches. It is a process begun. Dr. Massie confirms my statement. I do not want to make out our case any better than it is. We do not move in perfection as the saints in glory do; all we can ask of men is, Are they in the right direction and making progress? (Cheers.) I want now to add a word or two with respect to some questions proposed to me last week. A Mr. David M'Crae, I think, of Glasgow, proposed a question as to the Constitution which I did not then quite understand. The gist of it, as far as I remember, is this:—Speaking of the fugitive slave clause of the Constitution—his question was, Are you fighting for the Constitution with that clause in it? If you are, how do you pretend that you are fighting for liberty? Secondly, if you are fighting for Emancipation, you are fighting against that Constitution, and how do you condemn the seceded states?" I will answer by a statement of facts, and leave you to settle the logic. In the first place, what is the relation of our Constitution to slavery:— First it contains the fugitive slave clause; the other is the three-fifths representation clause. I will take the last first. That clause does not legalize slavery. It merely says, (as if the founders of the Constitution recognised it as a fact, but not a doctrine or principle), "five men other than free whites shall count for three votes." Now what is the origin of that? When we first formed our present Constitution, having had ten years trial of what was called Articles of Confederation, the difficulty that struck the Government, as it strikes every Government, first was, "How can you raise funds to carry on the Government?" First, taxes were laid on the lands in all the country. But it was found impossible to obtain the statistics which were requisite for levying the tax justly, and therefore they must change their system. It was then proposed they should tax the people *per capita*. Then came the question; as the vast majority are white and free in the North, and as an immense proportion in the South are slaves, if you should tax according to the free whites, the North would pay nineteen-twentieths of the taxes, and the

South only one-twentieth part, having the monopoly of wealth. Therefore the North said, in assessing the taxes you must call every able bodied black, as well as white man, one. The South said, "No, we are willing to count four as one." That is the extreme on that side, and you see just how it was. It was on a question of raising money, whether the tax should be raised on the whole black population or not, or whether it should be raised on a white voting population, excluding Indians and slaves. And it was Mr. Madison who proposed a middle term as the compromise. He said, "Five shall count three instead of one counting one, or four counting one." So it was settled that in laying taxes on the South, there shall be three men taxed where there are five black men in the South. But in settling the basis for taxation, they settled at the same time the basis for representation. A few years afterwards we ceased to raise our revenue by taxation at all, and the very thing on which this compromise had been made ceased to exist. Then came in the unexpected operation of this clause on representation, which was *a shadowy sequence* scarcely understood to be of much importance, but had *become of prime importance* when the North was represented in Congress by a representation of men alone, while the South was represented both in the number of men and the amount of property. The South is represented both in property and in men; the North simply in men, and not in property. This clause became, by an unforeseen accident, of strength to the South. To-morrow, if slavery totally ceased, that Constitution would not have to be changed in a single letter in that regard. There is nothing that guarantees or perpetuates it, or carries the consequence along with it as inevitable. The other clause in the Constitution, concerning rendition of fugitives, appeared in our history first when New England, which was just as much slave-owning as the South, formed the first rudimental Union. So jealous were the States of their individual sovereignty, that nothing but external wars and difficulties drove them together, and they passed the substance of this fugitive slave clause. It did not appear in the Articles of Confederation in 1777, but in 1787 the present Constitution took away from each State the right to pass laws in contravention of laws existing in other States; that is to say, no man held to service in one State shall be discharged therefrom by another State into which he may go. It is a law for the peace of the whole Union, taking away the power of one *State* to nullify the laws of another *State*. Congress and the Federal Power are not even alluded to in the clause. Then it went on to provide that such persons shall, upon proper proof, be rendered up again to their claimants, on whom the proof was purposely left. But that is the fugitive slave clause. In the convention where it was adopted, it was attempted to include this clause in the one that in our present Constitution precedes it, namely, in Section 2 of Article 4:—"A person charged in any State with treason, felony, or other crime, who shall flee from justice and be found in another State, shall, on demand of the executive authority of the State from which he fled, be

K

delivered up to be removed to the State having jurisdiction of the crime." The executive can only have conference with the executive of another State, so where there were crimes and felonies, the Article requires that the executive of one State shall demand of the executive of another to deliver the criminal up. And it was attempted to introduce into this the words, "and persons held to servitude;" but it was unanimously voted down, on the ground that there was no more reason to constrain the Government to return any slave, than to ask them to return any ox or ass, and they would not push the States to that indignity. Then the next clause is the following:—" No person held to service or labour in one State under the laws thereof, escaping into another, shall in consequence of any law or regulation therein be discharged from such service or labour, but shall be delivered up on claim of the party to whom such service or labour may be due." When it was first introduced, the terms were "any person held to servitude, or in servitude." The first attempt was to reject that. Why? Because it was declared the Constitution of the United States should *not* recognize slavery. Mr. Madison has left his impartial and unquestionable authority on the subject, that the day was anticipated when slavery should cease; and the builders of the Constitution so framed it, that while it knew how to steer round slavery while it existed, it should be whole and perfect when slavery ceased. (Cheers.) The Northern view, in reference to the operation of this, was, that if a slave escaped from Maryland into Pennsylvania, and the master found his slave there, and brought proof before magistrate and jury that it was his beast of burden, he should take it back if he could. Thus it left the man to manage his own property without being hindered or obstructed. What, then is the objection we take to the fugitive slave law of 1850? *That to please the South it was laid down to be a duty of the whole United States to hunt the slave down* WITHOUT PROOF, *and at the mere summons of the claimant, to deliver up the person claimed and saddle the costs on the population of the United States.* I answer then, in respect to this whole subject, that if to-morrow slavery should cease by the force of arms, the Constitution is not touched, nor is a right that is guaranteed by this Constitution impaired; for as long as slavery exists there is an Article which gives a man the right to go and find his slave and take him back without molestation, and that is bad enough; but if to-morrow slavery ceases to exist, what change is there to be made? For our courts have construed that the term "persons held to service," includes all apprentices under indenture, and that a slave is included in that, not as a slave, but by virtue of the fact that he is held to service. Are we then, by maintaining the Constitution, maintaining slavery? No, not at all—slavery does not exist in the Constitution, nor by virtue of it. It has been settled a hundred times by the lawyers of every slave State that slavery is a *local* institution, and can exist only by special *local* statutes. Nay, the very conflict between the South, under Mr. Douglas, and the nascent republican party, was whether slavery should be local and municipal, or national. They tried to make it national; that is the last form of the political conflict between North and South—they seeking to show that the Constitution did endorse slavery, and we saying the Constitution never did, and never shall. I don't know whether Mr. M'Crae will think I have answered his question, but I am sure I have tried to give you grounds and facts on which every man can answer it for himself. (Cheers.)—[Mr. Haughton asked—"Is it not the case that William Lloyd Garrison and his party have invariably maintained that the Constitution is in favour of slavery; have not the judges of your land so interpreted the Constitution, and has not your Supreme Court decided, that the black man has no rights which the white man is bound to respect."]—No questions could be more pertinent. We all admit that slavery existed as a fact when the present Constitution was adopted; that two clauses were introduced to meet certain practical difficulties arising out of local slavery in its relation to general government. The framers of the Constitution undertook to recognize the bare political fact of slave property then existing in some States. They undertook to form a Constitution which should in the widest scope represent liberty, yet should not abruptly destroy slavery, but should neither encourage nor help it. Now, in every slave State that has given a definition of slavery, it is declared to be the condition in which a man ceases to be a man and becomes a chattel—a thing, not a being—a person. With this definition before them, when the Constitution was in formation, they after debate and full explanation of what they meant, declared they would not put into the Constitution a description or allusion to slavery that should characterize it by its technical term, but only by terms that brought it out of "chattelhood" into mere "subordination." Therefore in our Constitution slaves are called "persons," always. This was no accident—no indiscriminate use of words. (Cheers.) It was done by men who said among themselves "Not many years can pass before slavery will cease;" and what they tried to do was to have a Constitution that could hold together and keep us afloat for the moment, but yet should not give countenance to slave doctrines. When a man undertakes to steer a ship he does not necessarily include in his ideas of successful shipbuilding all the shoals and sandbanks that may impede its voyage; and when the Constitution of the United States was formed, the formers merely made two provisions in order that local State rights might be divested of their power of mischief. Now, as to public sentiment. There has been recently a small body of men who held that our Constitution did not recognize slavery as doctrine or fact. I differ with them—it does recognize it as fact but not as doctrine. Other people say, "No matter whether the Constitution does or does not; courts that bind us have declared that it does; therefore let us break the Union in two to clear ourselves." That is the party of Mr. Garrison, and Mr. Wendell Phillips. The great middle-class have said this :—"Slavery is dying, bound to die; free men made a Constitution for liberty, and made it so that while slavery was dying, the Constitution need not be wrecked by running on it." As to the decision of the judges, allow me to say that our

Federal courts have been packed by Southerners; while the North has had either to accomplish this change by revolutionary process, or to do it by peaceable methods, such as are organized in the Constitution itself. We knew perfectly well it was part of the plan of the South, by packing the courts, and by process of construction to transmute liberty into slavery in our laws, and in the fundamental law of the land. That was what we believed and prophesied. We warned the nation, and they would not be warned. That declaration was construed into slander of the courts and of men in authority, when I made it up and down through the land, and said, "The South are taking away your Constitution by dry-rot—(cheers)—but give us time, and we will by popular *discussions* reverse this policy, and fill Congress and the courts with different men, and then we will reconstrue it back again, and we will find yet the voice of liberty that shall stand by the Constitution, and say unto the bondsman, "Come forth, and he shall come forth, and stand among living men, a man again." (Cheers.) This was my doctrine as distinguished from that of Mr. Phillips and Mr. Garrison. I have said, "Give us time, there are in our Constitution and in our nation those elements which will bring back to us liberty in the Constitution itself." The South knew it just as well as the North. (Cheers.) But they lay in wait and watched, and the moment that *discussion* had produced a majority for us and Mr. Lincoln was elected, they rebelled. Whatever you may say about Southern men, it must be said that they are as sagacious as children of darkness. (Cheers.) And we said—so long as our courts are corrupted and construe the Constitution adverse to liberty, we cannot help ourselves. Wherever they do wrong to us, we will bear the wrong; but when they command us to do wrong to others, we will not; we will take a remedy; it is only a question of time when we put this thing right. We said, "Wait—there is liberty in patience;" they said, "There is safety only in rebellion;" so they rebelled. (Applause.)—[In reply to another inquiry addressed to Mr. Beecher as to the Dred Scott decision.]— He said, the friends of the judge have thought it convenient to deny that he ever used the words imputed to him, that the black man has no rights which whites are bound to respect; but whether he did or not, it is universally conceded by our lawyers that it was not the point before the court, but an extra-judicial opinion. He was a Maryland slaveholding judge: the very instrument by which the South meant to transmute our institutions. But what he said was his own opinion, not a legal decision.—[Another questioner asked if the Fugitive Slave Law of 1850 was still part of the Constitution.]— It never was part of the Constitution. In England your Constitution is what your Parliament determines to be law; in America our Constitution is what was originally written. There is a marked distinction between law founded on written principles, and those written principles that we call the Constitution; so that if your Parliament had passed a Fugitive Slave Law, it would have become part and parcel of the British Constitution, but with us the State Constitution and the National Constitution stand unchanged by legislation. If the Constitution is contravened by laws based on other than the principles it enunciates, the courts set them aside. The Fugitive Slave Law is simply a law, not a part of the Constitution, which we hold to be an outrage, yet inoperative, as having no power beyond the year in which it was passed. It is just as dead now, and has been the last eight or nine years, as the snake's skin that was sloughed ten years ago. It is said we ought to have abolished it. When Congress came together they passed so many reformatory laws that it was thought seriously they should abolish this; but they said—we are charged with coming together for revolutionary purposes, and to destroy the local municipal power of the States, and we must not do anything in our national legislation that shall countenance the doctrine that we are revolutionizing State sovereignty. [A gentleman asked how the great religious associations in America regarded the anti-slavery question?] There are two parties—one is very small and able, and is called Abolitionist; the other comprises all the rest of the North, and is called Anti-slavery. The distinction is not one of doctrine, but of method. Mr. Garrison and Mr. Phillips said the North must save itself by disunion; the great body of those who hated slavery said, we cannot consent to that. I was one among the latter, from first to last, and that paragraph in the newspapers which says I once said "there could be no getting rid of slavery under the Constitution" is a total and absolute falsehood. (Cheers.) I would not burn a barn in order to get rid of the rats. (Great laughter.) We have always said, the thing is bad enough, but not so bad but we can cure it by moral means. I have avowed over and over again to Southern slaveholders :—" You shall not go off. We will hold you in the bosom of liberty until your slavery is dead." (Cheers.) This is the point which you English are liable to misunderstand. A great many good men seem to you to have paltered and connived, but you should recollect it belongs to the nature of free discussion and moral suasion to take time and patience. You cannot convert a whole nation as you may one man, by sitting down and talking to him. Prejudices melt slowly, but we have always had such faith in the ultimate victory of Liberty over Slavery that we have said, "With God on our side we can fight and shall win." (Cheers.) Those men who were opposed to any decisive and summary remedy as too dangerous, were called Anti-slavery men; those who were in favour of immediate disruption, as the summary and necessary remedy, were called Abolitionists, that was the distinction. But now there is no distinction at all. Mr. Garrison and Mr. Phillips are both of them my personal friends. I would not for all the world, say a word in England that should carry back pain to their hearts: and although I have differed from them all my life long, I have never failed to see that men more heroic in asserting a great principle, never existed in the world. Mr. Garrison has said at a public meeting, that when he declared that the Constitution involved slavery, he never expected to see the Emancipation-proclamation of the President of the United States. (Cheers.) I can tell you there is no more welcome speaker in any part of the United States, than that man of genuine senatorial nature, of polished scholarship, of exquisite gentlemanly manners, of most truly Christian feelings and sentiments, even if sometimes over excited,—Mr. Wendell Phillips. But we are all one to day. There are now but two parties in the North. An overwhelming majority say: "Since they have taken the sword, let slavery perish by the sword." (Cheers.) True! there is a small party that lives in crevices and cracks,—a small malignant party called "Peace Democrats," with that thrice-rotten Catiline Wood at the head of it, whom the *Times* newspaper is accustomed to hold up as the exponent of American peace doctrine. Him I have heard praised by the lips of Christian men, who, if they could know his crimes, vices, and Satanic wickedness, would blow him from their parlours, as you do Sepoys from the mouths of your cannon. (Great cheering.) [Mr. Robertson asked Mr. Beecher's attention to two clauses in the Constitution, frequently quoted to demonstrate that it was pro-slavery,—the clause where Congress legalized the slave trade until 1808, and the clause requiring the executive to lend assistance to any State Government in case of domestic insurrection. A third argument was the New England States repealing the Personal Liberty Bill, and recognizing the Fugitive Slave Law.]—If you ask me whether I think what was then done was ineffably wicked, I say yes, but that it has no force now, everybody admits. When this Constitution was made, the question was, how much each separate State would give up, in order to endue the central Federal Government with authority— *how much the Federal Government should receive of sovereignty from the States that had thus far held the whole sovereignty.* They proposed to give the Government in Congress the power to abolish the slave trade, but they would not let them have that power till 1808. It was then not a question of the Constitution at all, but of the convention of these sovereign States, and *they refused to put into the hands of the Federal Government* until such a date *the power* which after that date the Government was to have. In all these stages, it was the opinion of every man who founded the Constitution, that slavery was dying, and they did not feel as you and I would have felt, but said: "Ease it off in every way," Slavery was like some brigand brought into an Alpine convent, where he was given a room and a place to prepare to die in decently. On the contrary, the old brigand did not die, but called in his confederates, and domineered over the very hospital where he was being nursed for Christian burial. As to the prevention of rebellion in any State, the National Government is of course bound to exert its whole power to save any State from the intestine mischiefs of insurrection. If this covers slavery as much as liberty, yet because it is a principle born of liberty, slavery gets the benefit of it. Every nation must undertake this duty; the hand to which you give the national sword, must defend every part of the nation from internal disorder. The repealing of the Liberty Bill only took place in one or two States. I wish to say that I feel convinced, when Dr. Massie issues his report of his visit, he will be able to say he found the educated, intelligent, and religious-minded people of the North, wherever he went, settled down to the conclusion as final and irremovable, that this war must be supported till rebellion shall be crushed, and that rebellion can not be crushed till slavery has been destroyed. I do not mean merely what you mean here by the "intelligent classes." The phrase with us includes farmers, mechanics, the very bulk of our people. For it is the legitimate effect of democratic instruction, that no line can be drawn between the college-educated man at the top, and the common-school educated man at the bottom. A thoroughly educated common people, with collegiate men to be their leaders and mouthpieces, in sympathy with them—all moving together—is better than any society where the bottom is ignorant, and the top is educated. (Cheers.) With some further remarks Mr. Beecher concluded, having spoken nearly two hours.

The Rev. Dr. MASSIE said that from what he himself had heard while in America, he was convinced the people in that country would place the greatest confidence and faith in the honesty of Mr. Beecher's reports. He could fully confirm that gentleman's reference to the opinion of the intelligent classes of America, who were resolved to maintain the Government in its war against rebellion, and that the rebellion, with its twin sister slavery, should be buried in one tomb. (Loud applause.)

Mr. J. C. Dyer having taken the chair,

Mr. ESTCOURT moved, "That the thanks of the meeting be accorded to the Mayor of Rochdale for presiding in so able and courteous a manner;" and expressed a hope that the Queen of England would ever be found by the side of the President of a free and intelligent Republic, and never have her pure and womanly feelings outraged by the residence at her court of the representative of any empire whose "corner stone" was that of human bondage.

The motion was seconded by Mr. Greening, and passed unanimously.

With a kind and complimentary message to Mrs. Beecher Stowe, the talented sister of the honoured guest, three cheers for the Queen, President Lincoln, and Mr. Beecher, the morning's proceedings terminated.

LIVERPOOL.—OCTOBER 30, 1863.

FAREWELL TO THE REV. HENRY WARD BEECHER.

YESTERDAY morning the Rev. Henry Ward Beecher was entertained by the members of the Liverpool Emancipation Society at a public breakfast in the St. James's Hall, Lime-street, prior to his return to America to-day. A party of about 200 ladies and gentlemen sat down at ten o'clock to the repast, which was provided with much taste by Mr. Lynn, of the Waterloo Hotel. The chair was occupied by Mr. Charles Wilson; and among those present we observed the Rev. Dr. Graham, Rev. Professor Griffiths, Rev. J. S. Jones, Rev. W. Rees, Rev. W. Graham, Rev. Philip Hains, Rev. J. Jones, Rev. H. W. Thomas, Birkenhead; Rev. Dr. Sanders, Birkenhead; Rev. J. Hughes, Birkenhead; Rev. Noah Stephens, Rev. S. H. Booth, Rev. H. Rees, Calvinistic Methodist; Lieut.-Colonel M'Corquodale, Liverpool Press Guard; Messrs. Thomas Bold, jun., James Alsop, Charles Robertson, E. K. Muspratt, John Patterson, David Stuart, Peter Stuart, A. Leighton, W. Crosfield, jun., J. Turner, Maurice Williams, W. H. Whittemore, J. H. Estcourt, Manchester; Dr. Scott, F. Thorpe and J. Crook, Preston; C. Macqueen, J. Bickles, Bradford; T. R. Arnott, R. Trimble, J. Innes, S. Pearce, jun., Alex. Eccles, C. E. Rawlins, jun., C. R. Hall, H. J. Cook, Rev. John Thomas, Rev. W. Roberts, Rev. F. Skinner, Blackburn; W. W. Fennell, E. Bevan, T. S. Bickersteth, H. Young, G. Golding, Dr. Henry, John Mure.

The Rev. J. B. Robberds said grace before breakfast. After the repast the Rev. Dr. Graham offered up a prayer.

The CHAIRMAN (Mr. C. Wilson, president of the Liverpool Emancipation Society) said: It gives me great pleasure to preside, as I have no doubt it also gives you great pleasure to be present on this, which may be the last, occasion on which Mr. Beecher will ever address an English audience; and I feel that I may thank him in your name, in my own, and in the name of the friends of Emancipation and of Union generally, for the ability, the power, the kindly goodwill with which he has advocated the cause of liberty during his stay in England. (Hear, hear.) He has stated publicly that his desire is to draw closer the bonds of amity and good fellowship between his country and ours—(cheers)—and if I have one wish above another it is to do what little I can to promote kind and generous feeling "between the two great nations which speak the English language, and which are alike entitled to the English name." (Cheers.) I have lived in both countries, and I can never forget the kindness and the hospitality which I and my family experienced when in America ; and I bear this testimony that there is more kindly feeling in the Americans towards England and the English than there is here towards America and the Americans. (Hear, hear, and applause.) It is not unnatural that it should be so. They have ties and affections towards the land of their forefathers which we cannot have towards any new country. This island contains the ashes of their ancestors. She is the place from whence they sprung. To them she is ever their mother country—their dear Old England. They claim her as well as we. Every American who comes to England makes, as it were, a pilgrimage to the old home of his family. I remember a connection of my own who visited this country some years ago. He was so blind he could not see across the street ; but he related with the rapture of a school boy a visit he had paid to some remote part of Yorkshire where his family once lived ; how he had met with an old lady who had taken him to the leaded roof of her house to show him the country round ; the joy, the delight with which he stood there, looking in every direction, and in imagination seeing the same fields, breathing the same Yorkshire air—in fact, living again the life so familiar to generations of his family. He is now a chaplain in the Federal army ; but wherever he may go, there is fastened in that spot a cord, invisible, reaching to his heart, which neither time nor space shall sever. Some months ago I had a letter from a loved relative of mine, a lady residing in Philadelphia, whose husband lies buried in the town of Warwick, in the very centre of England. Think you there are no heartstrings there ! She mourns in plaintive accents the more than want of sympathy of dear Old England, and thinks it strange that in their hour of trial a mother should so forget her child. But she concludes with this line, uttered from the very depths of her heart. "England, with all thy faults, I love thee still." (Hear, hear.) Not long ago I met with Mr. Whiting, the eminent lawyer, who has lately been over from the American Government. He also spoke with pride of his English ancestry, and related with the freshness of yesterday a former visit to the home of his family in Lincolnshire —how he found the old escutcheon hanging on the wall—how he had examined the family registers, in the old Church, and the tombstone beneath which his people lay in the quiet grave yard. No spot on earth seemed fraught to him with such dear recollections. These are the heartstrings which bind Americans to England. As Earl Russell said the other day, they have our language, our literature, our laws, our early history is also theirs. These appeal to the understanding and the intellect ; but those quiet spots, the homes and the graves of their kindred, bind their very hearts to England. O, let us cherish, and seek to return the love that ever flows towards us with the Atlantic wave. Now, let me congratulate you, Mr. Beecher, on the success which has attended your recent efforts. (Cheers.) In the capital of Scotland you had the opportunity of addressing perhaps the most learned, the most scientific, the most critical—(hear, hear)—and, at that particular juncture, the most philanthropic assembly which could be got together in this kingdom. I understand that there was not one dissentient voice. (Cheers.) In the capital of England no room could be found large enough to contain one-half of those who flocked to hear and support you. (Hear, hear.) You have had large and influential meetings in other great towns and cities; and, sir, you have fought with beasts at Ephesus—(hear, hear)—but, even here, the closing scenes must have convinced you how impotent were the bellowings and howlings, the occasional bleatings and cacklings of the Southern hirelings to stifle the voice of Liverpool for freedom. (Applause.) You will relate these things when you go home. You may also tell them of the great meetings of the Confederate cause—how they are held in caves and holes of the earth —(hear, hear)—and the first thing publicly known of them is from the newspaper report next morning, when you learn that they have had the same thing over again—a few dozen people to partake of some cock-a-doodle-doo for the chief dish, and the correspondent "S." for garnish. (Laughter and cheers.) You may also tell your people that it is not from any want of employing the most subtle and devoted agents, and conducting their cause with the most consummate skill, that the whole British nation has not been prostituted to the Southern cause. Mr. James Spence was their agent here. He is an elegant writer, a fascinating speaker, a man so skilled in rhetoric and sophistry that he can hide the protruding hoof, and represent the devil of the South as an angel of light. His courage is equal to his accomplishments, for I have heard him, in effect, say, before an audience of Englishmen, that if anyone wanted to know who had the "courage" to defend slavery from the Bible, he was the man. I never heard a man so hissed in the whole course of my life. They have had Mr. Laird for their shipbuilder—they might have sought England through and not found such another; not only has he built them ships which cannot be surpassed, but he has sacrificed for them his Parliamentary reputation, making unverified statements which have been repudiated with scorn. If Mr. Laird had any hankerings after a Northern contract, he certainly did not seek the front door. The next time he makes a pretended statement of facts in Parliament he will be reminded of these anonymous letters, and will not find it so easy to ride off on a piece of empty clap-trap about Mr. Bright setting class against class. (Cheers.) These shores do not contain a nobler or purer patriot than John Bright. Mr. Laird may say that he would rather be known as the builder of the *Alabama* than as he; but I venture to predict that the name of John Bright will be honoured, and cherished, and loved by the English nation when the name of the builder of the Alabama, if remembered at all, will be as that of a man who, to fill his own pockets with gold, not only violated the proclamation of his Sovereign, but did his utmost to bring two kindred nations into collision, to cover sea and land with fire and blood, and to involve the whole British race in all the horrors and calamities of war. The Chairman concluded by briefly congratulating Mr. Beecher on the success which had atttended his labours in this country.

Mr. C. E. RAWLINS, jun., said: Mr. Chairman, and ladies and gentlemen,—I shall content myself on this occasion, by simply reading the address presented to the Rev. Henry Ward Beecher, and ask for your approval of it. He then read the following address :—

To the Rev. Henry Ward Beecher, of New York, U.S.

After a brief sojourn in Europe—a short respite from ceaseless labours of philanthropy—you are returning to your country to resume those labours with renewed health and strength, and we trust a yet firmer faith in their ultimate success.

Standing, as it were, on the very shores of the "old country," and in a town which is the last—and, perhaps, through its commerce, the strongest—link in that chain which individually unites the interests of England and the United States, let us regard you as the representative of your countrymen, and take counsel together ere we bid you farewell.

There is no feeling more common on both sides of the Atlantic than pride in our common descent. Hardly a century has elapsed since you had no separate history from our own. Until then we were fellow-countrymen—united under the same crown, and claiming protection from the same Constitution. The same page recorded for us both all the glorious associations of the past—the same battles for national independence, and the same national struggles for civil and religious liberty. To this day we are sharing the inheritance of political freedom purchased by the blood of our ancestors. Better than all, we worship at the same altar, and reverence the same heroes of art, literature, and science.

With such recollections crowding upon us, let us this day pledge each other not only by the memories of the past, but our still more glorious hopes of the future, that, so far as in us lies, there shall be perpetual peace between England and the United States.

Now, there are common principles which mark the genius—nay, which must be essential to the life and civilisation of both nations·alike, and which are not materially affected by our differing forms of Government. The latter are, in fact, but mere accidents of our national existence. On the one side we have an hereditary monarchy and an hereditary House of Lords, around which entwines a loyalty to the crown of centuries. On the other hand, in a country where no feudal aristocracy had ever existed and no King ever reigned, you were obliged to make both your President and higher chamber elective. All our other political and municipal institutions are the same.

What, then, so closely assimilates the two nations in the hopes and fears, the present condition and future prospects of their civilisation ? What but the love of freedom—freedom personal and national—which has always distinguished the Anglo-Saxon race above all others ? Subject to this higher law, both Englishmen and Americans hold all their institutions.

We do not this morning trace the origin and progress of the institution which has been so sad an exception to the history of both nations. England some years ago wiped out the foul blot from her own constitution, and it is now her proud boast that the foot of a slave can never press her soil.

The peculiarites which distinguish a Federal Union of States previously independent have presented the same course with you. Slavery was found to be a State, not a national institution. All action thereon by the Federal power was excluded. But when the slaveholding States claimed to extend this institution not only to the territories but throughout the Union, the free spirit of the North was aroused, and in the Senate, in the House of Representatives, in the courts of justice, in the still higher courts of public opinion, but everywhere and on all occasions in a constitutional manner, they resisted the claim. They fought the battle of freedom against slavery in Missouri, in Texas, and in the Supreme Court of the United States, and at length they succeeded in placing in the Presidential chair a man who was equally pledged to the constitutional obligation not to interfere with slavery within the States themselves, and to his personal obligation to prevent its further extension.

We clearly recognise the fact that the Secession of the Southern slaveholding States was declared by themselves to be because they had lost this power of extension; that it was to maintain this unconstitutional Secession that the national flag was violated at Fort Sumter; that the war which has resulted has been carried on by the Federal Government for the suppression of a rebellion and the maintenance of the national interests. But while deeply regretting the miseries thus occasioned, we rejoice with you that treason placed within the power of that Government what peace and order had denied to it; and it is with reverential acknowledgment of that great Providence which still educes good from evil that we sympathise with you in those acts of the Legislature upon which is founded the glorious proclamation of freedom to slaves of rebellious States. We trust you may not fail in the self-sacrifice which may yet be needful ere that proclamation is realised.

There is yet one other point on which we could speak with a candour which no one can appreciate better than yourself.

If the friendly relations of the two countries are to be maintained unbroken in the future, it must be on the basis of mutual interests. A free interchange of commodities between them will soon annihilate the prejudices which still unworthily linger on both sides of the Atlantic. (Hear, hear, and cheers.) As in the past we have noticed that the gradual relaxation of your protective tariff was breaking down the barriers between the two nations, so we attribute no small portion of the bitterness of our Southern sympathisers to those disturbances in our commerce which have resulted from your return to vicious principles of taxation. That this is a violation of the rights of the consumer, and opposed to the established laws of political economy, you have yourself acknowledged.

Freedom of commerce with other nations is but an extension of freedom of production and interchange within our own. To prohibit it by high duties for the sake of protecting particular manufactures by high prices is a robbery of the consumer. England has set a noble example of universal free-trade. She offers no exclusive privileges; she asks no previous conditions. You have but to follow in her footsteps. You have not shrunk from the mighty task of organising the industry of 4,000,000 coloured labourers and 5,000,000 of whites. With equal courage, attempt the far easier task of reorganising your system of taxation on the same basis of freedom. (Hear, hear.) Your immediate and primary duty is the suppression of a foul rebellion and the emancipation of the slave; but we are convinced that no single act could be more effective in securing and maintaining friendly relations between our two nations than a thorough revision of your fiscal policy. Hundreds of thousands of our surplus population are every year emigrating to the United States. In future they will feel that every State, from Maine to Texas, and every rood of soil between the Atlantic and Pacific Oceans, may be a home for the free. When the electric chain shall again, as once it did, unite us, the first message that shall flash with lightning speed along its wires will be "Glory to God in the highest, peace and freedom to man on earth, without distinction of creed, or class, or colour, to the end of time."

(Immense cheering.)

The Rev. Mr. JONES seconded the adoption of the address, and the motion was unanimously adopted with a display of enthusiastic feeling.

The Rev. H. W. BEECHER, on rising to respond to the addresses, was received with enthusiastic cheers, which continued for some minutes. He said:—Mr. Chairman, ladies and gentlemen—Although this is a festive scene, it is rather with feelings of sadness and solemnity that I stand in your midst; for the hours are numbered that I am to be with you, and the ship is now waiting that I trust will bear me safely to my native land. If already I have to the full those sentiments of reverence and even romantic attachment to the memories, to the names, to the truths, and to the very legends of Old England which have been so beautifully alluded to by the Chairman on this occasion—if I had already that preparation, how much, working on that predisposition, do you suppose has been the kindness, the good cheer, the helpfulness which I have received from more noble English hands and hearts than I can name or even now remember. I have to thank them for almost everything, and I have almost nothing to regret in my personal intercourse with the English people ; for I am too old a navigator to think it a misfortune to have steered my bark in a floe or even a storm, and what few waves have dashed over the bows and wetted the deck did not send me below whining and crying. (Hear, hear, and laughter.) It was a matter of course. I accepted it with good nature at the time. I look back on it, on the whole, with pleasure now ; for storms, when they are past give us on their back the rainbow, and now even in those discordant notes I find some music. (Applause.) I had a thousand times rather that England should be so sensitive as to quarrel with me than that she should have been so torpid and dead as not to have responded at a stroke. (Cheers.) I go back to my native land ; but be sure, sir, and be sure, ladies and gentlemen that have kindly presented to me this address, that though I needed no such spur I shall accept the incitement of it to labour there for a better understanding and for an abiding peace between these two great nations. (Hear, and cheers.) I do not know that my hardest labour is accomplished on this side. (Hear, hear.) I know not what is before me—what criticisms may be made upon my course. I think it likely that many papers that never have been ardent admirers of mine will find great fault with my statements, will controvert my facts, will traverse my reasonings. I do not know but that men will say that I have conceded too much ; and that, melting under the influence of England, I have not been as sturdy here in my blows as I was in my own land. (Laughter.) One thing is very certain that, while, before I came here, I always attempted to speak the words of truth, even if they were not of soberness—(laughter)—so here I have endeavoured to know only that which made for truth first—love and peace next. (Cheers.) Of course I have not said everything that I knew. So to do, would have been to jabber in season and out of season, and fail to promote the sublimest ends that a Christian man or a patriot can contemplate—the welfare of two great allied nations. (Cheers.) I should have been foolish if I had left the things which made for peace and dug up the things that would have made offence. (Renewed cheers.) Yet, that course was not inconsistent with frankness, with fidelity, and with a due statement of that blame which we have felt attached to the course of England in this conflict. (Hear, hear.) I shall go back to represent to my own countrymen on fitting occasions what I have discovered of the reasons for the recent antagonism of England to America. And I shall have to say primarily that the mouth and the tongue of England have been to a very great extent as were the mouth and the tongue of old of those poor wretches that were possessed of the devil,—not in their own control. (Laughter and applause.) The institutions of England—for England is pre-eminently a nation of institutions—the institutions of England have been very largely controlled by a limited class of men ; and, as a general thing, the organs of expression have gone with the dominant institutions of the land. Now, it takes time for a great unorganised, and to a certain extent unvoting, public opinion, underneath institutions, to create that grand swell that lifts the whole ark up—(hear, hear, and cheers); and so it will be my province to interpret to them that there may have been abundant, and various, and wide-spread utterances antagonistic to us, and yet that they might not have been the voices that represented, after all, the great heart of England. (Hear, hear, and applause.) But there is more than that. Rising higher than party feeling, endeavouring to stand upon some ground where men may be both Christians and philosophers, and looking upon the two nations from this higher point of view, one may see that it must needs have been as it has been, for it so happens that England herself, or Great Britain I should say—I mean Great Britain when I say England always—(loud cheers)—Great Britain is herself undergoing a process of gradual internal change. (Hear, hear.) All living nations are undergoing such changes. No nation abides fixed in policy and fixed in institutions until it abides in death—(hear, hear); for death only is immovable in this life, and life is a perpetual process of supply. Assimilation, excretion, change, and sensitiveness to the causes of change, are the marks of life. (Applause.) And England is undergoing a change, and must do so so long as she is vital; and when you shall have put that round about England which prevents further change, you will have put her shroud around her. (Hear, hear, and cheering.) Now, changes cannot be brought to pass amongst a free, thinking people, as you can bring about changes in agriculture or in mechanics, or upon dead matter by the operation of natural laws. Changes that are wrought by the will of consenting men imply hesitation, doubt, difference, debate, antagonisms; and change is the final stage before which always has been the great conflict, which conflict itself, with all its mischiefs, is also a great benefit, since it is a quickener and a life-giver; for there is nothing so hateful in life as death; and among a people nothing so terrible as dead men that walk about and do not know they are dead. (Laughter and cheers.) It therefore comes to pass that in the normal process of a change such as is taking place in England, there will be parties, there will be divided circles, and cliques, and all those aspects and phenomena which belong to healthy national progress and change for progress. Now, it so came to pass that America too was undergoing a change more pronounced; and since, contrary to our hope and expectation, it was a change that went on under the form of revolution, and war in its latter period, it at first addressed England only by her senses; for when the rebellion broke out and the tidings rolled across the ocean, everybody has said "England was for you" at first. (Hear, hear.) I believe so : because before men had time to weigh in the balances the causes that were at work on our side; before the patrician had had time to study: "What might be the influence of this upon my class?"—and the churchman, "What will be the influence of these principles on my position?"—and the various parties in Great Britain—"What will be the influence of these American ideas, if they are in the ascendancy, on my side and on my position?"—before men had time to analyse and to ponder;—they were for the North and against the South ; because, although your anti-slavery feeling is hereditary and legendary, there was enough vitality in it, however feeble, to bring you on to the side of the North in the first instance. Much more would it have done, had it been a really living and quickening principle. It is said that up to the time of the trouble of the *Trent*, England was with us, but from that time she went rapidly over the other way. Now that was merely the occasion, but not the cause. I understand it to have been this—that there were a great many men and classes of men in England that feared the reactionary influences of American ideas upon the internal conflicts of England herself—(hear, hear);—and a great deal of the offence has arisen, not so much from any direct antagonism between Englishmen and Americans, as from the feeling of Englishmen that the way to defend themselves at home was to fight their battle in America—(hear, hear)—and that therefore there has been this strange, this anomalous and ordinarily unexplained cause of the offence and of the difficulties. Let us look a little at it. I will not omit to state, in passing, that there has been a great deal of ignorance and a great deal of misconception. (Hear, hear.) But that was to be expected. We are not to suppose—it would be supreme egotism for an American to suppose—that the great mass of the English people should study American institutions and American policy and American history as they do their own ; and when to that natural unknowingness by one nation of the affairs of another are added the unscrupulous and wonderfully active exertions of Southern emissaries here, who found men ready to be inoculated, and who compassed sea and land to make proselytes and then made them ten-fold more the children of the devil than themselves —(applause)—when these men began to propagate one-sided facts, suppressing—and suppression has been as vast a lie in England as falsification—(hear, hear)—perpetually presenting every rumour, every telegram, and every despatch from the wrong point of view, *and forgetting to correct it when the rest came*—(hear, hear)—finding, I say, these emissaries and these easy converts, the South has propagated an immense amount of false information throughout England, we are to take this into account. But, next consider the antagonisms which there are supposed to be between the commercial interests of North America and of England. We are two great rivals. Rivalry, gentlemen, is simply in the nature of a pair of scissors or shears ; you cannot cut with one blade, but if you are going to cut well you must have one rubbing against the other. (Hear, hear, and laughter.) One bookstore cannot do as much business in a town as two, because the rivalry creates demand. (Hear, hear.) Everywhere, the great want of men is people to buy, and the end of all commerce should be to raise up people enough to take the supplies of commerce. (Hear, hear.) Now, where in any street you collect one, five, ten, twenty booksellers or dry goods dealers, you attract customers to that point, and so far from being adverse to each other's welfare, men clustering together in rivalry, in the long run and comprehensively considered they are beneficial to each other. There are many men who always reason from their lower faculties, and refuse to see any questions except selfishly, enviously, jealously. It is so on both sides the sea. (Hear, hear.) Such men will attempt always to foster rivalry and make it rancorous. They need to be rebuked by the honourable men of the commercial world on both sides of the ocean, and put in their right place—under foot. (Applause.) Against all mean jealousies, I say, there is to be a commerce yet on this globe, compared with which all we have ever had will be but as the size of the hand compared with the cloud that belts the hemisphere. (Applause.) There is to be a resurrection of nations; there is to be a civilization that shall bring up even that vast populous continent of Asia into new forms of life, with new demands. There is to be a time when liberty shall bless the nations of the earth and expand their minds in their own homes; when men shall want more and shall buy more. There is to be a supply required, that may tax every loom and every spindle and every ship that England has or shall have when they are multiplied fourfold. (Applause.) Instead therefore of wasting energy, peace, and manhood in miserable petty jealousies, trans-Atlantic or cis-Atlantic, the business of England, as of America, should be, to strike those keynotes of liberty, to sound those deep chords of human rights, that shall raise the nations of the earth and make them better customers because they are broader men. (Great cheering.) It has also been supposed that American ideas reacting will have a powerful tendency to dissatisfy men with their form of government in Great Britain. This is the sincere conviction of many. Ladies and gentlemen, England is not perfect. England has not yet the best political instruments any more than we have; but of one thing you may be certain, that in a nation which is so conservative, which does not trust itself to the natural conservatism of self-governing men, but even fortifies itself with conservatism by the most potent institutions, and gives those institutions mainly into the hands of a conservative class, ordained to hold back the impetuosity of the people—do you think that any change can ever take place in England until it has gone through such a controversy, such a living fight, as that it shall have proved itself worthy to be received? And will any man tell me, that when a principle or a truth has been proved worthy, England will refuse to receive it, to give it house room, and to make any changes that may be required for it? (Hear, hear.) If voting *vivâ voce* is best, fifty years hence you will be found voting in that manner. If voting by the ballot is best, fifty years hence you will have here what we have in America, the silent fall of those flakes of paper which come as snow comes, soundless, but which gather, as snow gathers on the tops of the mountains, to roll with the thunder of the avalanche, and crush all beneath it. (Loud applause.) But it is supposed that it may extend still further. It is supposed that the spectacle of a great nation that governs itself so cheaply will re-act in favour of those men in Europe, who demand that monarchical government shall be conducted cheaply. (Hear, hear.) For men say, look at the civil list—look at the millions of pounds sterling required to conduct our Government, and see 30,000,000 of men governed on that vast Continent at not one-tenth part of the expense. (Hear, hear.) Well, I must say, that if this report comes across the sea, and is true, and these facts do excite such thoughts, I do not see how it can be helped. (Hear, hear, and laughter.) I do not say that our American example will re-act to the essential re-construction of any principles in your edifice. I have not in my own mind the belief that it will do more than re-adapt your economy to a greater facility and to more beneficence in its application; but that it will ever take the crown from the king's head, or change the organisation of your aristocracy, I have not a thought. (Cheers.) It is no matter what my own private opinion on the subject is. Did I live or had I been born and bred in England, I have no question that I should feel just as you feel, for this I will say that in no other land that I know of under the sun are a monarchy and an aristocracy holding power under it, standing around as the bulwark of the throne—in not another land are there so many popular benefits accruing under the Government; and if you must have an aristocracy, where in any other land can you point to so many men noble politically, but more noble by disposition, by culture, by manliness, and true Christian piety? (Loud and reiterated cheering.) I say this neither as the advocate nor as the adversary of this particular form of Government, but I say it simply because there is a latent feeling that American ideas are in natural antagonism with aristocracy. They are not. American ideas are merely these—that the end of government is the benefit of the governed. (Hear, hear, and cheers.) If that idea is inconsistent with your form of Government, how can that form expect to stand? And if it only requires some slight re-adjustment from generation to generation, and if that idea is consistent with monarchy and aristocracy, why should you fear any change? (Cheers.) I believe that monarchy and aristocracy, as they are practically developed in England, are abundantly consistent with the great doctrine, that Government is for the benefit of the governed. (Hear, hear.) There has also been a feeling that the free church of America, while it might perhaps do in a rough-and-tumble enterprize in the wilderness, is not the proper form of church for Great Britain. Well, you are the judges, gentlemen, about that, not we; and if it is not the proper form for Great Britain, you need not fear that Great Britain will take it. If it is, then it is only a question of time; you will have to take it. (Cheers.) For I hold, sturdy as you are, strong as your will is, persistent as you may be for whatever seems to you to be truth, you will have, first or last, to submit to God's truth. (Applause.) When I look into the interior of English thoughts, and feelings, and society, and see how in the first stage of our conflict with your old anti-slavery sympathies you went for the North; how there came a second stage, when you began to fear, lest this American struggle should re-act upon your own parties. I think I see my way to the third stage, in which you will say— "This American struggle will not affect our interior interests and economy more than we choose to allow; and our duty is to follow our own real original opinions and manly sentiments. (Cheers.) I know of but one or two things that are necessary to expedite this final judgment of England, and that is, one or two conclusive Federal victories. (Applause.) If I am not greatly mistaken, the convictions and opinions

L

of England are like iron wedges; but success is the sledge hammer which drives in the wedge and splits the log. (Hear, hear, and cheers.) Nowhere in the world are people so apt to succeed in what they put their hand to as in England, and therefore nowhere in the world more than in England is success honoured: and the crowning thing for the North, in order to complete that returning sympathy and cordial good will is to obtain a thorough victory over the South. (Cheers.) There is nothing in the way of that but the thing itself. (Laughter and cheers.) Allow me to say, therefore, just at this point and in that regard, that, whilst looking at it commercially, and whilst looking at it sentimentally, the prolongation of this war seems mischievous, it is more in seeming than reality, for the North was itself being educated by this war. This North was like men sent to sea on a ship that was but half built as yet; just enough built to keep the water out of the hull: but they had both to sail on their voyage and to build up their ship as they went. We were precipitated at a civil crisis in which there were all manner of complications at all stages of progress in the right direction of this war, and the process of education has had to go on in battle-fields, in the drill camps, and at home amongst the people, while they were discussing, and taxing their energies for the maintenance of the war. And there never was so good a schoolmaster as war has been in America. Terrible was the light of his eye, fearful the stroke of his hand; but he is turning out as good a set of pupils as ever came from any school in this world. Now, every single month from this time forward that this struggle is delayed unitises the North—brings the North on to that ground which so many have struggled to avoid:—"Union and peace require the utter destruction of slavery." (Loud cheering.) There is an old proverb, "There's luck in leisure." Let me transmute the proverb, and say, "There is emancipation in delay." (Loud cheers.) And every humane heart, yea every commercial man that takes any comprehensive and long-sighted instead of a narrow view of the question—will say, "Let the war thus linger until it has burnt slavery to the very root." (Renewed cheers.) While it is, however, a great evil and a terrible one—I will not disguise it,—for war is dreadful to every Christian heart,—yet, blessed be God, we are not called to an unmixed evil. There are many collateral advantages. While war is as great, or even a greater evil than many of you have been taught to think, it is wrong to suppose that it is evil only, and that God can not, even by such servants as war, work out a great moral result. The spirit of patriotism diffused throughout the North has been almost like the resurrection of manhood. (Cheers.) You never can understand what emasculation has been caused by the indirect influence of slavery. (Hear, hear.) I have mourned all my mature life to see men growing up who were obliged to suppress all true conviction and sentiment, because it was necessary to compromise between the great antagonisms of North and South. There were the few pronounced anti-slavery men of the North, and the few pronounced slavery men of the South, and the Union lovers (as they were called during the latter period) attempting to hold the two together, not by a mild and consistent adherence to truth plainly spoken, but by suppressing truth and conviction, and saying "Everything for the Union." Now during this period I took this ground, that if "Union" meant nothing but this—a resignation of the national power to be made a tool for the maintenance of slavery—Union was a lie and a degradation. (Great cheering.) All over New England, and all over the State of New York, and through Pennsylvania, to the very banks of the Ohio, I, in the presence of hisses and execrations, held this doctrine from 1850 to 1860—namely, "Union is good if it is Union for justice and liberty; but if it is Union for slavery, then it is thrice accursed." (Loud cheering.) For they were attempting to lasso anti-slavery men by this word "Union," and to draw them over to pro-slavery sympathies and the party of the South, by saying, "Slavery may be wrong and all that, but we must not give up the Union," and it became necessary for the friends of liberty to say, "Union for the sake of liberty, not Union for the sake of slavery." (Cheers.) Now we have passed out of that period, and it is astonishing to see how men have come to their tongues in the North—(hear, hear, and laughter)—and how men of the hightest accomplishments now say they do not believe in slavery. If Mr. Everett could have pronounced in 1850 the oration which he pronounced in 1860, then might miracles have flourished again. (Hear, hear.) Not until the sirocco came, not until that great convulsion that threw men as with a backward movement of the arm of Omnipotence from the clutches of the South and from her sorcerer's breath—not until then was it, that with their hundreds and thousands the men of the North stood on their feet and were men again. (Great cheering.) More than warehouses, more than ships, more than all harvests and every material form of wealth is the treasure of a nation in the manhood of her men. (Great applause.) We could have afforded to have had our stores of wheat burnt—there is wheat to plant again. We could have afforded to have had our farms burnt—our farms can spring again from beneath the ashes. If we had sunk our ships—there is timber to build new ones. Had we burnt every house—there is stone and brick left for skill again to construct them. Perish every material element of wealth, but give me the citizen intact : give me the man that fears God and therefore loves men, and the destruction of the mere outside fabric is nothing—nothing ;—(cheers)—but give me apartments of gold, and build me palaces along the streets as thick as the shops of London ; give me rich harvests and ships and all the elements of wealth, but corrupt the citizen, and I am poor. (Immense cheering, during which the audience rose and enthusiastically reiterated the applause.) I will not insist upon the other elements. I will not dwell upon the moral power stored in the 'names of those young heroes that have fallen in this struggle. [Here the speaker manifested considerable emotion.] I cannot think of it, but my eyes run over. They were dear to me, many of them, as if they had carried in their veins my own blood. How many families do I know, in which once was the voice of gladness, in which now father and mother sit childless ! How many heirs of wealth, how many noble scions of old families, well cultured, the heirs to every apparent prosperity in time to come, flung themselves into their country's cause, and died bravely fighting for it. (Cheers.) And every such name has become a name of power, and whoever hears it hereafter shall feel a thrill in his heart—self-devotion, heroic patriotism, love of his kind, love of liberty, love of God. (Renewed applause.) I cannot stop to speak of these things; I will turn myself from the past of England and of America to the future. It is not a cunningly-devised trick of oratory, that has led me to pray God and his people that the future of England and America shall be an undivided future, and a cordially united one. (Hear, and cheers.) I know my friend *Punch* thinks, I have been serving out "soothing syrup" to the British Lion. (Laughter.) Very properly the picture represents me as putting a spoon into the lion's *ear* instead of his *mouth*; and I don't wonder that the great brute turns away so sternly from that plan of feeding. (Laughter.) If it be an offence to have sought to enter your mind by your nobler sentiments and nobler faculties, then I am guilty. (Hear, hear, and cheers.) I *have* sought to appeal to your reason and to your moral convictions. I have, of course, sought to come in on that side in which you were most good-natured. I knew it, and so did you, and I knew that you knew it; and I think that any man with common sense would have attempted the same thing. I have sacrificed nothing, however, for the sake of your favour—(cheers)—and if you have permitted me to have any influence with you, it was because I stood apparently a man of strong convictions, but with generous impulses as well. It was because you believed that I was honest in my belief, and because I was kind in my feelings towards you. (Applause.) And now when I go back home I shall be just as faithful with our "young folks" as I have been with the "old folks" in England—(hear, hear, and cheers)—I shall tell them the same things that I have said to their ancestors on this side. I shall plead for union, for confidence. (Cheers.) For the sake of civilization; for the sake of those glories of the Christian Church on earth which are dearer to me than all that I know; for the sake of Him whose blood I bear about, a perpetual cleansing, a perpetual wine of strength and stimulation; for the sake of time and for the glories of eternity, I shall plead that mother and daughter—England and America—be found one in heart and one in purpose, following the bright banner of salvation, as streaming abroad in the light of the morning, it goes round and round the earth, carrying the prophecy and the fulfilment together, that "The earth shall be the Lord's, and that his glory shall fill it as the waters fill the sea." (Loud and prolonged cheering.) And now my hours are moments, but I linger because it is pleasant. You have made yourselves so kind to me that my heart clings to you. I leave not strangers any longer—I leave friends behind. (Loud cheers.) I shall probably never at my time of life—I am now fifty years of age, and at that time men seldom make great changes—I shall probably see England no more; but I shall never cease to see her. I shall never speak any more here, but I shall never cease to be heard in England as long as I live. (Cheers.) Three thousand miles is not as wide now as your hand. The air is one great sounding gallery. What you whisper in your closet, is heard in the infinite depths of heaven. God has given to the moral power of his church something like his own power. What you do in your pulpits in England, we hear in America; and what we do in our pulpits, you hear and feel here; and so it shall be more and more. Across the sea, that is, as it were, but a rivulet, we shall stretch out hands of greeting to you, and speak words of peace and fraternal love. Let us not fail to hear "Amen," and the responsive greeting, whenever we call to you in fraternal love for liberty—for religion—for the Church of God. Farewell!—(The rev. gentleman resumed his seat amidst enthusiastic applause.)

The Rev. H. REES rose and read an address from Welsh ministers. The original is in Welsh, and is accompanied by the translation appended.

To the Rev. H. Ward Beecher.

REVEREND SIR,

We, the undersigned ministers of the Welsh Congregational Churches in the town of Liverpool and Birkenhead, desire to embrace the opportunity on your departure from this country to express our high esteem of your fame and character as a Christian minister and an enlightened philanthropist.

More especially would we express our profound admiration of your uncompromising self-sacrificing labours on behalf of the oppressed African race, and your efforts to wipe out the foul blot of slavery from the otherwise fair escutcheon of your great and noble country: efforts which in common with those of others of your family have made the name of Beecher dear to the broken hearts of downtrodden slaves, and illustrious in the eyes of all the true friends of justice, freedom, and humanity throughout the world.

We beg to assure you, and through you our countrymen in America, that we deeply sympathise with your Executive in its endeavours to put down the rebellion in the Southern States, and to establish the Federal Union on a basis of equality of rights between the white and black races.

A rebellion whose declared object was the extension and perpetuation of negro slavery must, we think, be regarded by every enlightened and sober mind as the grossest insult, alike to God in heaven and to man on earth. The infamous avowal of a determination to found a government whose "corner-stone" was to be the irredeemable subjugation of the black man—the assumption that such a theory is in accordance with the will of God as revealed in nature and in His word, we believe to be the climax of human presumption and effrontery, which must ever remain a black scandal in the annals of the 19th century, and consign the memory of its abettors to the just execration of mankind to the last ages of the world.

We rejoice to have it to say that we believe there is not a solitary minister of our denomination in the Principality who would not have gladly subscribed to these sentiments had an opportunity of doing so been afforded; and to the best of our knowledge the entire body of Nonconformists in Wales, of every denomination, entertain similar opinions; indeed, our whole nation, with comparatively but very few exceptions, are wholly of the same mind.

The warm and hearty demonstrations of welcome with which you have been received in the great cities and towns of our kingdom will have sufficiently proved to you that after all the heart of Old England is in its right place.

Honoured sir, we congratulate you on the results of your visit. You will leave our shores with the pleasing conviction that your labours among us have not been in vain. Many minds have been interested in and enlightened on the issues now pending in America—waverers have been confirmed—misapprehensions have been corrected—personal prejudices against yourself have been removed—and the amount of moral sympathy with your Government has been greatly augmented through your instrumentality. The scurrilous attacks upon you in a portion of the daily and weekly press are the highest tribute which could have been paid to the influence of your name and the power of your eloquence.

Dear sir, tens of thousands of the best men in England will long cherish fond recollections of your visit ; and their best wishes will accompany you to your home. We doubt not similar recollections will be cherished on your own part ; and when you shall have proclaimed to your countrymen what you have witnessed and experienced during your visit to this country, it cannot fail to prove the means of strengthening and cementing peace and love between our two powerful nations. May the amiable relations between England and America be never interrupted. May it please God to put a speedy termination to the lamentable strife now raging in your beloved country, and to overrule the issues of the struggle to the relief of the oppressed, and the hastening on of that Kingdom in which there is no difference between Jew or Gentile, bond or free. And if it pleases Him, may it terminate in the restoration of the Federal Union and the speedy liberation of the slave.

To your country we say again—" Peace be within thy walls, and prosperity within thy palaces. For our brethren and companions' sakes, we will now say, peace be within thee. Because of the house of the Lord our God, we will seek thy good." And to you, sir, we say, Go in peace. May the good hand of your God be upon you to lead you back safely to the bosom of your family and friends ; and may your valuable life be yet spared many years to "serve your generation according to the will of God."

WILLIAM REES,
JOHN THOMAS,
NOEL STEPHENS,
WILLIAM ROBERTS,
H. C. THOMAS.

The Rev. Professor GRIFFITH, seconded the adoption of the address, and the motion was cordially carried.

The Rev. H. W. BEECHER, in receiving the address, remarked that he could not recognise one single word in the original except his own name, which stood in English. Although this was the case, he was more than pleased to say that he owed no inconsiderable part of himself to the Welsh blood which he had in his veins. Mary Roberts was his great great grandmother, and she was as fully blooded a Welsh woman as ever lived. (Cheers.)

Mr. J. H. ESTCOURT, Chairman of the Executive Committee of the Union and Emancipation Society, Manchester, was received with cheering. He said he appeared there in an official and in a private capacity : in the latter as a participator, with the friends present, in the last farewell to their friend, the Reverend Henry Ward Beecher; in the former, as one of a deputation appointed to present to the reverend gentleman an album, duly inscribed, containing about 200 carte de visite portraits of the President, Vice-Presidents, Executive, and General Council of the Union and Emancipation Society, of Manchester (each carté de visite being inscribed with the autograph of the person represented) as a token of the esteem and affection entertained towards Mr. Beecher personally ; and also of their admiration of his manly and eloquent advocacy of the claims of the bondsmen in his own country, to freedom and to manhood. (Applause.) These portraits comprised the leading Liberal members of the House of Commons, ministers of the Gospel, eminent men in literature and scholastic position, and honest-hearted intelligent representative men of the nation. Many of the best citizens of the kingdom were represented in that album— those whose sympathies were true to liberty under all circumstances, and whose moral support was ever given to maintain constitutional Government. (Applause.) He trusted that to Mr. Beecher might be vouchsafed physical and mental vigour, so that his future may be as nobly used as had been his past. He believed that the time would come, and at no distant day, when the "sum of all villanies" would no more infest the earth with its presence, when it would have gone into the great past; and the oppressed would be free. When from the Saxon language would be banished all words derivable from or appertaining to slavery, and our noblest song should be, "All men are free." (Cheers.) He anticipated that time with much joy and hope. If the friends, who now are gathered around their guest, a man honoured with success and the blessing of God as well as with the love of his fellowmen; if they with him should be living then, and see the grand triumph of freedom over bondage, of goodwill over hatred, of peace and right over crimson war and chronic wrong,—what a jubilate would be sung by them in company with all the great and good men of all the nations of the earth. May we all do our duty in our own time, earnestly and with courage, and the fruits would certainly be seen, though perchance after many days or even years. (Applause.) In concluding he expressed his belief that the memorial he had the honour to present to Mr. Beecher, would be the medium of "sunny memories," and that some of the pleasant hours which he had spent in Old England with some warm-hearted and loving friends, would be revived on the other side of the Atlantic, across which he prayed for the reverend gentleman a safe voyage. (Applause.)

The Rev. Mr. BEECHER, in acknowledgment of the gift, said on his voyage home he should feel that multitudes accompanied him, and as he lay alone in his berth he should feel himself to be a noun of multitude. The friends of Emancipation should remember that there was room enough on his side of the Atlantic for them. As this country had sent hundreds and thousands of men who had hindered Emancipation— the ignorant emigrants, suborned to the pro-slavery cause—so he thought it only right and fair that we should send them a few from the other extreme to help the great cause of human liberty; and if so, he would accept this volume, literally, as the shadow of great things to come.

The CHAIRMAN announced that letters regretting inability to attend had been received from the Mayor of Manchester, the Rev. Enoch Mellor, Mr. W. C. Forster, M.P. for Bradford, and one by Mr. Beecher from Mr. John Bright, M.P., couched in the most cordial language, and regretting exceedingly that an engagement which he could not possibly leave in London prevented him coming to meet their guest here, or he would most certainly have done so. The Chairman having announced this fact to the meeting, said they were now called upon to part.

This announcement was received in silence, and for a few moments the pause was not broken, many of the audience being apparently disposed to take a silent sorrowful farewell of the reverend gentleman. At length it was proposed by a gentleman that they should bid Mr. Beecher good-by in the good old English style, with three cheers. This suggestion was immediately adopted, and three ringing hurrahs were given. Many of the reverend gentleman's admirers afterwards flocked round him and shook him by the hands.

APPENDIX.

THE REV. MR. BEECHER AT LANCASHIRE INDEPENDENT COLLEGE.

On Saturday afternoon, October 10th, 1863, the students of the Lancashire Independent College, Withington, seized the opportunity of the Rev. Henry Ward Beecher's short visit to this neighbourhood to invite him to the College, to receive from them an address. The presentation took place in the library. Mr. Beecher, who was accompanied by Mr. J. H. Estcourt, met with an enthusiastic reception.

The following is a copy of the address, which was read and presented by Mr. Atkinson, the senior student:—

REVEREND AND DEAR SIR,
We, the students of the Lancashire Independent College, heartily welcome you amongst us to-day. We rejoice to see you in our college. Though we have not had the opportunity of becoming personally acquainted with you till now, we have long known you through your writings, and through the fame you have acquired in your own country and the world as a Christian minister and a philanthropist. We have heard much of your public career. And it is with a special admiration that we call to mind the firm and persistent opposition which you presented to the compromise which issued in the Fugitive Slave Law—the protection which, in defiance of that law, you have undauntedly afforded to the negro runaway—the manly stand you have taken in society in opposition to an unworthy and unchristian prejudice against men of colour—and the efforts you have made against overwhelming odds to obtain liberty and free speech for black men and white men alike. But while we hail you as the friend of the negro and the champion of the oppressed, we, as students for the Christian ministry, are still more deeply interested in your career as a minister of the gospel; and we take this opportunity of assuring you that the noble example you have set us, in earnest, self-denying, and practical work for Christ, has inspired us with the warmest sympathy and regard. We wish you, reverend and dear sir, health and long life; and our prayer shall be that you may be enabled, by God's blessing, still further to promote the interests of pure religion in your country, and to place the top-stone on that edifice of social and religious freedom which you have so nobly laboured to raise.

The Lancashire Independent College, 10th October, 1863.

Mr. BEECHER, on rising to reply, was loudly applauded. He said: Although I am pressed for time, I could not deprive myself of the pleasure of meeting you, for I feel a most lively interest in all young men who are preparing themselves for that which I esteem to be the most honourable and by far the happiest work in life—the Christian ministry. My father, you know, was a clergyman before me, and it pleased God to give him eight sons. Every one of them is a minister of the gospel, and their children are—not all, but in numbers, also becoming clergymen. I can say that I am a Hebrew of the Hebrews.

(Laughter and applause.) My own ministration has extended over a period of from twenty-five to thirty years. Having been born and educated in New England, I was called, immediately after my graduation at college, to leave for the West, where I laboured for fifteen years as a settled pastor in the Presbyterian Church. In our country, Presbyterians take Congregational Churches, and Congregationalists Presbyterian, indifferently; and I was called to minister in the Presbyterian Church in the West, studying and preaching in the midst of communities where, from recent settlement and spareness of population, there was much missionary work to be done. My study was my saddle, for years of my life. After that I was removed to the great metropolis of our country—Brooklyn being really part of the city of New York, separated only by a river. There I have pursued my ministry from that day to this, in a time of agitation unparalleled in the history of our country. I have stated these facts because I wish to bear witness that after this experience, and with the knowledge that I now have, if any office of state, or any office in society of any description whatever were proffered me as an honour, or as a place of joy and comfort, I should, without any hesitation, reject them each and all, as being less than the gospel ministry. (Applause.) To a young man who looks out with some proper diffidence of his own powers; who is uncertain whether he shall succeed or not; who has, if he be a cautious man by nature, some provident fears as to support and as to relative position in society, it ought to be something encouraging to hear one as old as I am, and after so many years of ministration, say that there is nowhere else in the world where the promise of the Saviour is so sure to be fulfilled, "Seek ye first the kingdom of God and his righteousness, and all these things shall be added unto you." Young gentlemen,—if you seek a settlement for the purpose of forestalling God's providence and making your own arrangements; if it is an ambitious settlement, if it is a profitable settlement, you put that promise away from you. You make men your almoners and treasurers, not God. But I had rather settle in poverty with God for my treasurer than take the most ambitious position in life with only man to lean upon. He never betrays his promises, and although I have seen days of poverty, days also of abundance, under both circumstances I have the most simple, unfeigned, and child-like faith in this, that if a man will without reserve give himself to the work of God, God will put about him the everlasting arms of his support, and he never, not for an hour, not for a moment, whatever the seeming may be, will be betrayed or forsaken. You may trust God, and you may give yourselves, without a thought for external matters, to the work of the ministration of the Lord Jesus Christ. But this leads me to say that for this work you must love Christ. There are a great many religious people in the world, but I am afraid not many Christians. There are many whose religion is duty; whose religion is worship, or submission, or holy fear and reverence; which are all indispensable auxiliaries. But no man is a Christian who does not love. And it is love, as a very torrid zone in the heart, and love to Christ as distinguished from the Father or the Spirit that makes a man a Christian.

And where one has that heroic inspiration; where more than father, more than mother, more than wife, more than child, more than friends, more than self, he, loving the Lord Jesus Christ, has the witness of it day by day in his own soul, so that all these other relationships derive their odour, their flavour, their light, and their beauty from the reflection of the higher love in him to the Lord Jesus Christ; where it is his life, so that he can say with the apostle, "The life which I live in the flesh I live by faith in the Son of God"—then it will become easy to do it; otherwise hard. I beseech of you never to neglect a duty; never to cease to cultivate conscience; but I beseech of you do not go into the ministry to be merely duty-performing ministers. Let me say, without offensive personality, that I do not preach because it is my duty, I do not work because it is my duty. I both preach and I labour, because I don't know anything on earth that is so pleasant to me. I love it. Every year it pleases my people to give me some four Sabbaths of rest, and the weeks on either side make it a rest of about six secular weeks. I am always glad to go away and rest, for I am very tired when the hot month of August comes; but I can bear witness that I go back a great deal more glad to my work than ever I went away from it. (Applause and laughter.) I have to say again and again, "After all, vacation is the heaviest month in the year to me." And yet that season is happy, it is floral, it is full of God in nature; but to stand among my people,—to look among those faces that I shall see yet glorified,—to know that I bear my Master's heart in my hand, and that I am labouring for Christ, and am to present spotless before the throne of eternal glory those whom He has committed to my charge; to see the evolutions of God's grace in the hearts of men; to trace, to follow, to aid—I know of nothing under the sun that is such fruition and such joy, and such continual peace as that. If you consulted but selfish joy, if that were a possible thing, you had better be a minister of Christ's gospel—not a fearing minister, not an anxious minister, not a minister that is always talking and thinking about his "awful responsibilities." (Laughter.) That is the way a slave should talk, but that is not the way, as a son of God, you should talk. You are children!—not servants—who have been taken into the bosom and confidence of the Lord Jesus Christ, and what have you to talk about "awful responsibilities." Love and trust are the victorious mottoes of every Christian minister. No evil can befal you; nothing can harm you, if ye be followers of Christ. To go cheerfully, and hoping, and loving, and courageous, and undaunted, always sure that there is a Providence in which you are moving—this is, indeed, to be a free man. And there is nothing that takes away the fear of man and the fear of human society, and nothing which takes away that fear which is the most troublesome of all, the fear that works through conscience, so much as love. "Love casts out fear," and it is not perfected till it does. And is there no fear in Christian experience? Yes. Just like the sub-bass in the organ; while both hands are carrying the full harmony and the melodies above, there is, far down, but as a mere lower foundation, the rolling sub-bass. Down there let conscience and fear thunder, but high above let all the harmonies and melodies of heaven sound out more full, clear, and more cutting, and lead the rest. (Applause.) I do not know how it is with you in England—I am not competent to speak to you of your duties in parishes here—things are different. I shall not venture a single word in that regard. In our country ministers are more free. I take, and we take, a larger scope than you do here. Everything of that kind must depend on your own good sense, which must judge of the institutions, manners, customs, and opinions that are round about you, and that will take on a different form in different periods and different nations. With us, because all public questions are settled by the common people's vote, we are obliged, wherever that public question carries moral influence with it, to regard the moral side of all public questions. And that gives a latitude to the minister of the gospel. I don't know but you take it here; but I have an impression that you do not to any such extent as we do. Just now, the ministry of our own country are called, in a signal and extraordinary manner, into public affairs. I shall not trouble you with any general remarks in respect to the struggle in America, but only to say this, that never before or since the founding of the colonies, were all the churches of America so nearly unified as they are to-day. I have with me elsewhere the resolutions of Lutherans, Baptists, Methodists, Presbyterians; of every shade of Congregationalists; of Episcopalians, and all and every denomination save the Catholic, running through three years, from North, South, Middle States, East and West—the most Conservative hitherto—all of them with one testimony and one feeling, in respect to the condition of things in our country. It is sometimes said that the North deserves no sympathy, because there is no sincerity, no heartiness in its movements in this subject. The man that says that in England is but ignorant; the man that says that in America is a knave. No sincerity! There is nothing else in the Christian community—ministers and people—that is so inwrought into the very feeling and fulness of their life as never was any external and secular aspect of affairs before since America was discovered. (Hear.) Why, it is a portion of their religion, just as much as the emancipation of the Israelites was a part of Moses' religion. We feel called in the matter of God by a Providence which speaks as loud to our ears, as ever the top of Sinai spoke to Moses', or to the Hebrews' ears. And it is the business of the Gospel to produce the manhood of four millions of the human race, denuded of manhood—we feel that it is the peculiar work of the Gospel in America in this age. The whole air is full of sincerity and of religious conviction, and there is almost no division of opinion on that subject. There never was a more sublime moral spectacle than that singular and unsought unison which it has pleased God, by the pressure of external circumstances, to bring to pass in the American Church at this time. And now I ask—not that you should commit yourselves one way or another, but you are men of prayer, or why are you here preparing for sacred avocations?—I ask that you will not forget to pray for America. And I ask that you will pray such prayers that angels can with self-respect carry them up to God, for I have heard prayers that I did not believe an angel would touch. (Laughter.) Not, then, those prayers so cautiously circuitous as to touch everything without touching anything—(laughter)—not prayers that shall give you an appearance of doing your duty, without committing yourself one way or another; not prayers, so far South as not to commit you with the North, and so far North as not to commit you with the South. (Applause.) Pray for something, and mean it. (Hear.) And if you believe that liberty is a part of the Gospel work; if you believe that God is preparing the way for the emancipation of four million men: and I know it, I feel it in my soul as if it were an inspiration and a revelation—then pray that the hand of those men in the North—the whole Christian brotherhood—that are now being lifted up to support the hands of our President may be strengthened. For while his hands are up Israel prevails, and when they fall, Amalek prevails. Pray that his hands may be held up, and that the church of Christ may not in America backslide from her witness, and her fidelity to this great cause of God among men. Should any of you come to our shores—it is not improbable—come early. After men are forty years old it is not wise to emigrate as a rule; men should emigrate while yet young, if they are ever to do it. Then, they change circumstances easily. Their roots are not grown into the soil; they are adaptable to new times, new circumstances, new relations. I suppose you are wanted in England. I do not know how much; but I do know that there never were fairer fields, nobler opportunities for usefulness for men that in the ministry sought not themselves but the Lord Jesus Christ than in the ample and ever new opening states of our Western country. I have laboured there. I know the privations; but I know the joys. It is a supreme gladness to labour at the foundation. Other men shall come and build finer structures, but the tears that missionaries shed, the prayers that men offer under the trees where they labour in the woods; the sacrifices men make, and are glad that they make them, and quite laugh at them; there is nothing more precious in human experience, than the joys of Christ's missionary, with hope and faith very far surpassing the joys from secular sources. The nearer you live to God, the more you give yourselves up to him, the higher and happier you will be, and the stronger. And while I would not ask you to dismiss the gifts of understanding, or to seek less than the most perfect education your time and means allow, for you will have need of all of it; yet the foundation of all education, the very prime motive power by which it should be all directed, is love—love to God, and love to man. (Applause.) May that God, by whom we both live and hope, bless you; and may our respective spheres of labour bring us to meet together in the unchanging clime of Heaven. (Applause.)

On the proposition of Mr. Handley, seconded by Mr. Robinson, a vote of thanks was given to Mr. Beecher for his visit and address.

Mr. Beecher was then conducted over the college, and departed, the students cheering him from the steps till the cab in which he rode away was out of sight.

MR. BEECHER AND THE NONCONFORMIST COLLEGE STUDENTS.

On Thursday evening, October 22nd, 1863, the Rev. Henry Ward Beecher was entertained at a *soirée*, and presented with an address by the students of five of the Nonconformist Colleges in and about London—namely, the Independent Colleges of St. John's Wood and Hackney, the Countess of Huntingdon's College at Cheshunt, the Baptist College, Regent's Park, and the Presbyterian Theological Hall, Queen's Square. The place of meeting was the Institution, at St. John's Wood, and the number of students that assembled was about 250. When tea and coffee had been served, the company repaired to the spacious library, and on Mr. Beecher's entrance accompanied by Dr. Halley, Dr. Spence, Dr. Tomkins, Rev. T. Binney, Rev. A. Raleigh, Rev. James Stratten, Professors Newth and Nenner, the Rev. Kilsby Jones, and some other gentlemen, he was greeted with loud and prolonged applause.

The Rev. ROBERT HALLEY, D.D., president of the college, took the chair, and a hymn having been first sung, he said he was sure he might say that it afforded all present the highest gratification and delight to receive in their midst from the other side of the Atlantic such a man as the Rev. Henry Ward Beecher—(loud cheers)—not only as the son of Dr. Beecher, whose writings were well known in this country and greatly valued, or as the brother of Mrs. Stowe, the talented author of that remarkable book, "Uncle Tom's Cabin," but also, and chiefly as a man who was himself both well known and esteemed in Great Britain as a writer, a preacher, and a platform orator, and one who had rendered most important service to the cause of human freedom in America long before the existing war broke out. (Cheers.) They could not have such a gentleman among them without feelings of pleasure, and would rejoice to receive any of those honoured men whose names Mr. Beecher had mentioned on Tuesday evening, who had done and suffered so much for what they believed, and what the Christian people of England believed, to be the cause of liberty, of truth, and of Christianity in America. (Cheers.) This being a students' meeting, he would say no more, but call upon Mr. Jones, the senior student of New College, to read the address.

Mr. JONES accordingly stood forward and read the following document :—

REV. AND DEAR SIR,

We, the students of the Independent, Baptist, and Presbyterian Colleges are glad to welcome you among us this evening. We do this in no spirit of cold formality, but in the sincerity of our hearts, assured that you are a man called of God to a great and good work. We esteem it an honour, knowing that your time is so limited and so fully occupied, to receive a visit from so distinguished a stranger and so eminent a minister. We recognise in you one who has devoted his best energies and the rare abilities with which God has endowed you to the cause of civil and religious freedom, and the moral and social elevation of the degraded and oppressed. During the whole course of your public life you have ever indignantly condemned the monstrous sin and curse of slavery, and maintained with all your eloquence and at much cost the common rights and heritage of humanity. And our earnest hope is that you may soon see the reward of your labour in the abolition of the social distinctions of colour, and in the renewed prosperity of the American Republic. Not only do we honour you as a social reformer, and one to whom the best interests of your country are dear, but we especially welcome you to this college as a Christian minister. While thankful that in the past God has so eminently blessed you as a preacher of the Gospel, we pray that He will graciously bestow upon you health, strength, and long life, that you may be still more useful in your important labours in the Christian ministry, and that you may be increasingly able by your advocacy in the pulpit, on the platform, and through the press to hasten the time when God's will shall be done on earth as it is in heaven." (Loud cheers.)

The address was signed representatively by the senior students of each college.

Mr. BEECHER on rising to respond was again warmly cheered. He felt deeply grateful, he said, for the kindly greeting that had been given him. It was much pleasanter to his mind and heart than the tumultuous welcome of larger and more promiscuous assemblies ; and he was particularly pleased with that part of the address in which he was recognised as a Christian minister. Love towards Christ was a bond which united them so closely as to make them blood relations, and caused them to be dear to each other on earth, and filled them with the hope of sweeter friendship and nobler joys. He disclaimed the idea of having suffered losses on account of his exertions in the cause of human freedom, because he had never looked for the rewards of position and public favour on account of anything he had done, and because he had always felt it to be an unspeakable honour and reward to be permitted to engage in the work of Christ, and to do anything for Him. Even sufferings for the Master's sake was a blessed thing. In accepting the invitation to meet the brethren now present he had no thought of speaking to them on American affairs, and would confine his remarks to matters relating to Christian work. Accordingly, he proceeded to advise the young men regarding their studies while at college, and touched upon various points appertaining to the propagation of the Gospel in their after days. He set out by strongly urging due attention to the laws of bodily health, as often fundamental to success. Morbid ideas of religion, and many of the heresies of the Church had sprung from bad digestions—(laughter and cheers)—for depend upon it a very close connection subsisted between the brain and the stomach. The New Testament commanded men to consecrate their bodies as much as their souls to God. He earnestly exhorted the students to acquire as much knowledge as possible before the time came for them to enter upon the active duties of their profession, assured that they would find their work vastly easier by so doing; and cautioned them against supposing that any sort of degree of mental attainments would make up for the want of personal piety. By this, he said, he did not mean merely the ecclesiastical idea of piety, the relation of the soul towards God, but its relations also towards man—the Divine awakening of the entire faculties, powers, and affections, and their employment for the good of humanity as well as for the glory of the Most High. Religion did not consist only in prayer and meditation, but in genial sympathy and brotherly love, showing itself in acts of benevolence. As ministers, they were not to seek their own ease, or for high social position, but to forget themselves in their work, endeavouring only to be useful, and then a blessed reward would never fail to be obtained. Mr. Beecher discoursed at some length, and in eloquent words, upon the necessity of fervency of feeling in order to rouse the indifferent and to be generally successful in the preaching of the Gospel. Good sense was also an indispensable qualification, and this would regulate the warmth and zeal which should never be allowed to run wild ; let them be disciplined, but never lost. (Cheers.) The minister of the Gospel, moreover, must have a firm faith in the truths he taught, believe in them as undoubtingly as men did in material things, and resolve to stand by his convictions at all costs, ever keeping before the mind the shortness of time and the eternity that is to follow. Mr. Beecher concluded by offering prayer.

A vote of thanks for the address, moved and seconded by the senior students of Regent's Park and Cheshunt Colleges, was carried unanimously, and with the utmost enthusiasm.

In response to the wish of the meeting, Mr. Binney, Dr. Spence, Mr. Raleigh, and Mr. Stratten each made a few remarks expressive of the pleasure they had derived from Mr. Beecher's address, and wishing for him all manner of happiness and success.

Dr. HALLEY spoke with much earnestness and feeling upon the essential unity subsisting between the peoples of England and of America, and uttered a fervent hope that before a great while, by the intervention of Divine Providence, the horrors of war might cease, and liberty for all ranks and races prevail over the broad and glorious continent of America, and, united in sympathy and in effort with England, set an example to the world, and diffuse Christian civilisation over every region of the earth. (Loud cheers.)

The benediction having been pronounced, the proceedings terminated.

www.ingramcontent.com/pod-product-compliance
Lightning Source LLC
Chambersburg PA
CBHW020252170426
43202CB00008B/341